What People Are Saying About
Wild Earth, Wild Soul

Bill Pfeiffer has followed his own wild heart in growing ways to build an Earth-honoring culture. His passion to heal our alienation from the natural world led him to deep ecology and then on to aboriginal elders of Siberia and the Americas. Knowing that a shift in consciousness at the personal level is essential, he has developed workshops to bring us back to our true nature as conscious members of the sacred living body of Earth. It is good news for us all that Bill has chosen to share his approach and his methods in this manual. I've known Bill for twenty years and would trust him with my life.
Joanna Macy

Bill Pfeiffer is a pioneer in bringing the technologies of Reunion to our wounded Western culture. This book was a blessing for me, both for its clear, vibrant articulation of basic principles of shamanic and ecological healing, and for its practical transmission of how to create powerful experiences for others.
Charles Eisenstein

Pfeiffer's *Wild Earth, Wild Soul* is a recipe for realizing our greatest longing: to live in a culture rooted in the Earth where each of us is treated with love and respect. Filled with indigenous wisdom; this rich, practical offering provides a way for small groups to experience that now as well as hope for the well being of future generations.
Thom Hartmann

A bridge is being built between indigenous beliefs that have been environmentally successful for millennia and the wise probing recently of intelligent non-Indians. Pfeiffer is an excellent bridge builder. *Wild Earth, Wild Soul* is a must read.
Ed Eagleman McGaa

Pfeiffer offers a valuable step forward in advancing our lives and the lives of our children—a life not only of compassion but also of ecstasy.
Manitonquat (Medicine Story)

Bill Pfeiffer's book is a generous and deeply felt articulation of how we can approach sustainable habitation of this planet that is our home. And, most uniquely, it supports people in feeling, rather than suppressing, the deep emotions they have about the damage to our planet. And from those deep feelings, to trust the crafting of a genuine individual response to that damage.
Stephen Harrod Buhner, author of *The Secret Teachings of Plants, The Lost Language of Plants*, and *Ensouling Language*

Wild Earth, Wild Soul: A Manual for an Ecstatic Culture is a major contribution to indigenous wisdom at a time when it is much needed by an ailing modernity. It provides an insightful entry into life giving changes much craved for and must be read with deep reverence.
Malidoma Some

Wild Earth, Wild Soul

(2nd Edition)

A Manual for an Ecstatic Culture

Wild Earth, Wild Soul

(2nd Edition)

A Manual for an Ecstatic Culture

Sky Otter (Bill Pfeiffer)

**MOON
BOOKS**

London, UK
Washington, DC, USA

CollectiveInk

First published by Moon Books, 2025
Moon Books is an imprint of Collective Ink Ltd.,
Unit 11, Shepperton House, 89 Shepperton Road, London, N1 3DF
office@collectiveinkbooks.com
www.collectiveinkbooks.com
www.moon-books.net

For distributor details and how to order please visit the 'Ordering' section on our website.

Text copyright: Sky Otter (Bill Pfeiffer) 2024

ISBN: 978 1 80341 832 2
978 1 80341 868 1 (ebook)
Library of Congress Control Number: 2024937550

A CIP catalogue record for this book is available from the British Library.

Design: Lapiz Digital Services

UK: Printed and bound by CPI Group (UK) Ltd, Croydon, CR0 4YY
Printed in North America by CPI GPS partners

We operate a distinctive and ethical publishing philosophy in
all areas of our business, from our global network of authors to
production and worldwide distribution.

Contents

Acknowledgments   ix

Foreword by John Perkins   x

Preface to the 2nd Edition   xii

Introduction   xv

Chapter 1 Why a Wild Earth Intensive?   1

Chapter 2 How to Use This Book   10

Chapter 3 Leadership: A Note to Guides and
          Facilitators   14

Chapter 4 A Spiritual Permaculture   20

Chapter 5 Getting Started: Guidelines and Overview   45

Chapter 6 Listening   59

Chapter 7 Feeling and Healing   78

Chapter 8 Nature Connection and Immersion   103

Chapter 9 The Power of Story   131

Chapter 10 Ceremony   150

Chapter 11 Altered States of Consciousness   171

Chapter 12 Play   188

Chapter 13 Stillness   204

Chapter 14 Elders and Mentors   213

Chapter 15 The Magic of Mentoring: Including an
           Interview with Mark Morey   231

Chapter 16 Art and Music   258

Chapter 17 Vision and Manifestation   280

Chapter 18 Final Thoughts   298

Appendix: Wild Earth Intensive Sample Schedule   301

Reference Notes   308

Selected Bibliography   324

For Ariel, Aminy, Abby, and Emily,
daughters of the Earth.
May they continue to shine like the sun.

Acknowledgments

If it were not for Larry Buell, Jeffrey Weisberg, Moses Draper, Nika Fotopulos-Voeikoff, Cathy Pedevillano, Ivan Ussach, Llyn Roberts, and my dear mother, Naomi Pfeiffer, this book would not have been written. They have provided invaluable inspiration and support. Thank you!

Chris Crotty, Jeremiah Wallack, Erjen Khamaganova, Shanti Gaia, Shen Pauley, Caryl Jesseph, Jackie Damsky, Shea McGovern, Chas DiCapua, Heart Phoenix, Una Gallagher, Mark Morey, Jim Beard, Miriam Dror, Jason Cohen, Jon McGovern, Pam McDonald, Hilary Lake, Paul Rezendes, Jari Chevalier, Susan Cutting, Dave Jacke, Kemper Carlsen, Lydia Grey, Jim Farnham, and Ann Kaplan have kept me on track, filling in key pieces at just the right moment. Thank you!

I am deeply grateful to Roberta Louis, who managed to continue superb editing through most difficult circumstances, and to Lorrie Klosterman for making sense out of the chaotic mess that I first handed her. And to the indefatigable Lynnette Struble, whose copy and line editing, and many other outstanding contributions to the book defined the term *excellence*.

Thank you to the one hundred and twenty-six people who contributed financially. I know who you are, and you are *greatly* appreciated.

My deepest thanks to my human elders and teachers: Joanna Macy, John Perkins, and the late Leon Secatero. And especially to Thomas Berry, who made his transition into the spirit world a few days before the impetus for writing this book occurred.

And most of all, praise and gratitude to our cosmic parents, Mother Earth and Father Sky, who always teach unconditional love.

Foreword

John Perkins

I've known Bill Pfeiffer since he first came to one of my workshops in the mid-nineties. The subject of the workshop was ecstasy and indigenous wisdom. I noticed that a fire was starting to burn within him to really *know* this subject—not as a temporary high but as a way of life.

During that time, I led many trips to the Amazon and the Andes where a wild and connected relationship with nature was part of the present, not a relic of the past. I shared with Bill much of what I learned. Bill, in turn, told me about his adventures in Siberia. There he experienced the ecstatic culture of several indigenous tribes embedded in a dazzling mosaic of rivers, steppe, and snowcapped mountains.

A bond formed between us, centered on this common experience and a common aspiration. How could we preserve ancient wisdom and adapt it for our own people? How could we change the modern vision that "technological progress will provide ultimate fulfillment" into an Earth-honoring dream?

A Shuar shaman deep in the Amazon once told me:

> The world is as you dream it. You in the North have dreamed of lots of cars, huge buildings, extreme materialism. Your dream came true and now threatens to destroy the Earth as we know it. But you can change that, create sustainable societies among your people. Just help your people change that dream.

Wild Earth, Wild Soul sprang from the Earth herself. It takes complex concepts and puts them together in a user-friendly way. It doesn't merely ask, "What if?" It shows the reader how to. It is a manual for creating a culture that works with, not against, nature. Bill makes it clear that to achieve this balance, we must go deep into our own souls. It's not about duplicating the customs and mores of Native cultures, but rather is about having the courage to take the amazing journey into the depths of who we are. On that journey, we can find a different way to see; reality becomes a high-definition experience that is malleable and full of possibility.

Talk is cheap. Bill invites you to see for yourself through his Wild Earth Intensive. You will soon find out what that is.

And he takes the long view. Yes, we need to do everything we can to slow and stop the Earth-destroying juggernaut of materialistic consumption, but at the same time we need to start putting in place the kind of culture our descendants will inherit with gratitude. That will require patience, discipline, and tenacity. Bill's recipe makes this sacred work a joy.

What's most original about *Wild Earth, Wild Soul* is not the parts, but the whole. Where else are you going to find the ingredients of a thriving nature-based culture all in one place along with a practical method of experiencing them?

Read it and take it to heart for our children's sake. And also take it to heart if you long to inhabit a world imbued with beauty

Preface to the 2nd Edition

It has been more than 10 years since the first edition of this book presented readers with a novel idea: why don't we modern humans practice the successful cultural skills of our indigenous ancestors? In so doing, we can experience a busting out—even for only 10 days during a Wild Earth Intensive or similar—of the restrictive confines of economic necessity, the jarring speed of both Internet and actual highways, and the malaise born of an illusory sense of separation from other humans and the natural world. Wild Earth Intensive (WEI) participants have all expressed some version of: "What a relief to know there is so much more to the human experience" and "I never realized this level of connection was possible." Thus, I believe, *Wild Earth, Wild Soul* remains more relevant than ever.

To illustrate, these 3 WEI participants are seen "outside" and then, along with 17 others, they spent the latter part of the day going "inside" to explore these places further through shamanic journeying (see Chapter 11). Why are the quotes around the words inside and outside? Because those 20 participants, and most people who do these journeys with me, report those distinctions to be only place markers in navigating a fluid, seamless, and astonishing universe. A universe teeming with intelligence that informs the rest of their lives once they learn to access it.

Although it may be tempting to evaluate these pages as a persuasive attempt to return to the Paleolithic Age that is not the case; here, we move away from the colonialist obsession of eliminating "the primitive" and, instead, receive the liberating embrace of what made us thrive in the first place.

The addition of a graphic that lists the key cultural ingredients for an ecstatic relationship with life is the template for all that follows. One may ask, "Where is love and gratitude on this medicine wheel?" and the answer is they are at the center. They are the Alpha and Omega.

Furthermore, I do not use the word ecstasy lightly. Ecstasy is not bliss but rather a full immersion in the forces of nature. Sometimes life is hard. The consciousness of ecstasy helps us meet the difficulty directly and unflinchingly. Why should we settle for less?! Why not become as strong as we are capable, together, to meet the inevitable challenges that lie ahead?

I remain excited about the overarching focus of this book: bolstering the urgent need for a foundational shift in human thinking and perception. This is especially true for leaders who are ready to meet the challenge of a denatured civilization, especially those who are young and can utilize the many tools and perspectives of this manual to bring harmony and balance to future generations. To my surprise, many college professors of ecological science have said this is the more comprehensive course they wish they were taught! They are integrating it into their curriculum because students need more than a strictly materialist and reductionist explanation of the universe.

Finally, *Wild Earth, Wild Soul* is an offering plate to the Ancestors, human and non-human. We *do* stand on their shoulders and from truly knowing that powerful vantage point, can see vistas of unparalleled, creative possibility.

—Sky Otter (Bill Pfeiffer),
Vermont, USA, Spring 2024

Introduction

All will come again into its strength:
the fields undivided, the waters undammed,
the trees towering and the walls built low.
And in the valleys, people as strong and varied as the land.

And no churches where God
is imprisoned and lamented
like a trapped and wounded animal.
The houses welcoming all who knock
and a sense of boundless offering
in all relations, and in you and me.

No yearning for an afterlife, no looking beyond,
no belittling of death,
but only longing for what belongs to us
and serving earth, lest we remain unused.
                                                    —Rainer Maria Rilke

It was the twelfth of June 1998. My friend and I had just returned from the deserts of Utah, where we had been on a vision quest that seemed rather ordinary at the time. It had been beautiful and powerful, yet in a very modest kind of way. There had been no "fireworks," no messages from on high. But, after having prayed and fasted for four days, I was not concerned about the outcome of the quest, because the beauty of the red rock was now in the marrow of my bones.

That evening, the two of us had dinner and went to sleep at the Prospector Lodge in the small town of Moab. The name of the motel would soon prove portentous. To my complete surprise, a "vein of gold" would appear just a few hours later, when I awoke from one of those vivid, Technicolor dreams that make waking life seem black and white by comparison. I immediately grabbed some paper and started to write down whatever streams of ideas I could hold on to from the torrent of information that had flooded through me during the dream. There was no premeditation or sense of control as I wrote. "I see a vision of peace" was the first line. "I see the Warriors of the Rainbow* remembering who they are" was the second. The feeling was one of both exhilaration at the possibilities for human transformation and urgency about completing certain tasks before "The Change."

The Change—a shift of gargantuan proportions for the human race that I was convinced lay just ahead, in my lifetime— reverberated through my consciousness. I had thought about it a lot as an intellectual concept, but at that moment, as I awakened from the dream, I experienced what felt like a tidal wave of revelation. The Change is not about fire and brimstone, floods, or war, as many have predicted. It's about a complete break with an environmentally unsustainable past. This vision did not promise that negative scenarios were out of the question, but that they would not have the last word. Something would outlive the death grip of industrial civilization and it would be good.

I kept writing, and writing. A dozen pages later, there were three overarching "instructions" in what had emerged on paper, all written in a metaphorical and stilted style. In essence, they were:

1. Participate in and lead "workshops" that facilitate a remembering of the true nature of humans, with an emphasis on aboriginal teachings. In this case, *aboriginal* does not mean native to Australia, but refers to the original wisdom coming forth from the Earth and flowing into alert and receptive humans.

2. Organize an ongoing exchange of spiritual and cultural knowledge between Native Americans and Native Siberians.

3. Pass on any essential knowledge revealed from the carrying out of the first two instructions, in an organized fashion, using the medium of print on paper, and protect the contents by translating it into other languages. The word *protect* is important; the sense from the dream vision was that the digital world of electronically stored materials could not be taken for granted during and after The Change.

The late Thomas Berry, ecologist and philosopher, author and lecturer, stresses the crucial importance of truly listening to our innate Earth wisdom when he states:

> One of the significant historical roles of the primal people of the world is not simply to sustain their own traditions, but to call the entire civilized world back to a more authentic mode of being. *Our only hope* [my italics] is in a renewal of those primordial experiences out of which the shaping of our more sublime human qualities could take place.[1]

I had been fulfilling those first two instructions, in various ways, for many years, but I was unsure how to interpret the third one. It did not feel directed at me specifically. The written recording of any acquired wisdom needed to be done by someone, or several someones. Maintaining a sacred covenant between human beings and the Earth was at stake.

Now it seems clear—and I am hopeful I've got this right— that this book is a fulfillment of the third instruction.

But this volume did not emerge immediately following that dream in Moab. Like so many things, even those that seem most important can get lost in the rush of modern life. It would take a provocative and ambitious question five years later, in 2003, from my long-time friend Larry Buell (Professor Emeritus, Human Ecology, Greenfield Community College), to inspire me to begin acting on instruction three.

"Okay," he said, "so many of us understand the severe limitations of the dominant paradigm. If you were given ten days minimum — to allow for more than a temporary 'workshop' feel — in a beautiful outdoor setting with fifteen to twenty-five people gathered together, how would you reconstruct a culture that works for all beings?"

Larry posed that audacious question in the middle of a long New England winter, and, after our conversation, I immediately went to my computer and started writing. That was unusual; writing is usually one of the hardest tasks for me (except when I am awakened in the middle of the night in Moab, Utah!). Ten pages later, I sensed I was on to something. But I knew that without more research and development, I could not find the answer I was working toward.

What became clear almost immediately was that the reconstruction of human culture that Larry was asking me to envision would start on a small scale and grow from there. Although it might have been tempting to put lots of energy into a grandiose panacea, that was not on my mind or his when he posed the question. And whatever "model" I could muster up needed to be based on both personal and proven experience, and not an abstract "thought experiment." That group of fifteen or twenty-five people would not be creating another think tank! I wanted to direct my efforts toward developing a model of experiential education that would be rooted in people's *hearts and souls* — one that could help each of us see through eyes of connection and oneness.

As the years passed, I co-created, facilitated, and refined several "Wild Earth Intensives" — ten-day workshops designed to stimulate the crucial remembering mentioned earlier: a remembering of the attitudes, values, perceptions, and practices that served our ancestors successfully for a hundred-thousand years. And amazingly, by uncovering the best of the past, I became particularly open to a new, powerful, and creative aspect of human consciousness that appeared to be gathering strength in the present. Together, these formed the backbone of my approach.

The more I led those Intensives, the more I noticed there was something of lasting value in them—something that would give people a collection of tools that would persist beyond the typical post-workshop euphoria and settle into their awareness more deeply than a strictly intellectual university course does. In fact, the Wild Earth Intensive (WEI) was the answer to a calling of the heart—the one that had been pulling at my shirttails since that night in Moab.

I also realized that a final and conclusive answer to Larry Buell's question about reconstructing human culture had not yet emerged—not from me nor from anyone. Any attempts at living in a sustainable way would be tainted by the psychological conditioning and existing conditions of the dominant culture. They would be relative solutions. Yet, try we must! Those of us who are called to serve the quest for a viable human presence on planet Earth have a passion for "giving it our best shot."

And here is my best shot. The Wild Earth Intensive that has meant so much to me is both a blueprint and a microcosm of how an ordinary group of people can embody the *essence* of sustainable living. The dream I have for this work is that you will try it and grow through it; that you will spread it far and wide as a way of life, not *the* way of life. It is offered as a tool, among many others being contributed around the world at this time, that can guide us through The Change—not just to a sustainable life but to a deeply joyful and grateful one.

Although The Change may turn out to be less dramatic than in my vision, the industrialized world's sense of invincibility is likely to be humbled by the events of the next hundred years. We need a way into the future that is both practical and inspirational. Various aspects of sustainable living—such as healthy childrearing practices and lasting ways of providing energy, food, shelter, and clothing—are covered quite well in numerous books by many brilliant people. What the following pages of this book address is the central question of how humans can sail forth into an unknown but potentially beautiful future, with a nature-based spiritual rudder—an "Earthdharma"—that satisfies the age-old hunger for meaning and healing.

Note: Concerning any "spiritual" language used in this book, feel free to substitute your own synonyms for Spirit, God, Source, Intelligence, Love, Creator, etc. For me, they are all interchangeable, and I have no attachment to any particular word. In essence, the Great Mystery is far beyond words and concepts. Martin Luther King, Jr., spoke to this well when he said: "Whether we call it an unconscious process, an impersonal Brahman, or a Personal Being of matchless power and infinite love, there is a creative force in this universe that works to bring the disconnected aspects of reality into a harmonious whole."[2]

* From a Cree tribe prophecy, as told to Lelanie Stone by Grandmother Eyes of Fire, that "there would come a time when the 'keepers of the legend, stories, culture rituals, and myths, and all the Ancient Tribal Customs' would be needed to restore [the Earth and her inhabitants] to health ... They were the 'Warriors of the Rainbow.'"[3]

Chapter 1

Why a Wild Earth Intensive?

*This was quite possibly the most profound ten days
I have ever experienced. If this is what a small group
of people can create in ten days, I know that we can
transform this world. We were doing it every second of
every day—we were living it.*

—Wild Earth Intensive participant

What if a culture embedded in nature was not a relic of the past but a living reality? What if you did not have to travel thousands of miles to experience indigenous wisdom but felt it in your heart? What if you knew in your bones the "rightness" of learning sustainability from the inside out? This is the promise of a Wild Earth Intensive (WEI), "a time out of time" where a small group of people can create the kind of world they want to live in. Although that world is temporary, the participants come away with a much "higher bar" for what is possible in the wider world.

A WEI is the culmination of twenty-plus years of experimenting with a variety of "deep ecology" workshops, blended with what I have learned during numerous trips to visit the aboriginal peoples of America and Siberia. Those workshops and journeys were created under the umbrella of Sacred Earth Network (SEN), a small not-for-profit environmental organization that I founded in 1988.

The workshops were a response to the unanimous sentiment of SEN board and staff members that the environmental movement was, unfortunately, solely focused on what Joanna Macy, the remarkable Buddhist scholar and systems theorist, termed "holding actions." When Julia Butterfly lived atop a huge,

1

threatened redwood tree for two years and when Greenpeace helped stop nuclear testing, they galvanized tremendous sympathy for their causes, but, by themselves, those actions and the thousands of lesser-known ones were insufficient to reverse the tremendous momentum of worldwide environmental degradation underway. Hopefully, these actions bought time for a wiser understanding to kick in.

To achieve that, Macy and others began to recognize something longer term and more effective was called for; something that rocked people to their core and made them look at the world differently. These innovators wanted to help create a living culture where ecosystems would be honored and kept intact. Then, as now, we needed a shift in consciousness to spur a different way of living—and, simultaneously, a different way of living to spur a shift in consciousness!

The growing desire to create a new, living culture—one that is (dare we say) ecstatic—is a response to the tremendous environmental and social pressure we are all experiencing. That pressure makes the vision of a life lived in balance with the rest of nature ever more compelling. Anyone who has really investigated the monumental trends that are shaping our world knows that changing how we live is imperative. But the re-creation of a living culture is considered by many to be the thorniest of problems. The critics' balk: "It's impossible, idealistic, and utopian. Don't waste your time." They are voicing a pervasive sense of hopelessness that can paralyze one's best intentions to work to change things for the better. However, the brilliant work of Joanna Macy, John Seed, John Perkins, and other Western eco-spiritual activists showed me that the feeling of hopelessness was just that—a feeling—and not an immutable truth. Furthermore, the track record of thousands of indigenous tribes who have lived lightly all over the planet is evidence that a dynamic balance between humans and nature is not some weird anomaly but a living reality.

This was the main reason SEN sponsored Sacred Travel journeys over the course of ten years (1999–2009), taking small groups of North Americans and Europeans to meet indigenous people in Siberia and the Four Corners area of the United States. The dominant intention of these journeys was to listen to and learn from these indigenous groups, especially with regard to their relationships with the land and one another. We came to them to learn what aspects of their cultures allow them to remain connected to the land in a way that honors future generations, both human and nonhuman. We were able to visit sacred sites (with the blessing and guidance of local indigenous leaders) and witness how the people draw spiritual nourishment from Earth and Sky. We found in them an eagerness to share with us not just their information and wisdom but their hearts.

A different but complementary kind of journey was also birthed by SEN; we facilitated cultural exchanges between some of the indigenous peoples we had met, in which Native Siberians traveled here to meet Native Americans, and vice versa. These two majestic peoples, separated by half a planet, have much in common. Their wisdom, rituals, and enduring celebration of all life are woven into many of the WEI activities described in this book.

Rekindling Wildness

While organizing and co-facilitating these journeys and cultural exchanges, I was able to observe cultural survival skills that had stood the test of time against seemingly impossible odds. Whether in the steppes of Siberia's Altai Mountains or in the deserts of New Mexico and Arizona, I noticed that the wildness of the land penetrates the core of its Native people who, despite centuries of outside rule, exhibit a stubborn refusal to be domesticated.

Leon Secatero, a well-respected Navajo elder who participated in these programs and became a SEN advisor, spent the last twenty years of his life gently yet powerfully encouraging non-Natives "to make a culture based on Indian ways that work."[1] He did this by immersing sincere non-Natives in the Navajos' and Pueblos' land, their ceremonies, and the indigenous rock art of their ancestors. He would say, "You non-Natives outnumber us ten to one, and you are not going anywhere, so you better figure this out."[2]

A WEI—and a growing number of other alternative educational models—invites wildness back into our souls by helping us remove the imagined separation between "out there" and "in here." This is what Secatero kept pointing toward. And contrary to the modern notion that to be wild is to be dumb and brutish, it is, in fact, extremely intelligent. To re-experience the wild does not imply a return to our Paleolithic past but a return to our inherent spontaneity and natural strength, a freeing up of the playful wonder we each had as children and that still lives inside us. Simply put, it is an unselfconscious, passionate love of life!

Anthropologist Bradford Keeney, Ph.D., who has written one of the most comprehensive field studies of healing and shamanism, the Profiles of Healing series, describes what drew modern cultures away from this wildness: "The problem began when someone said that words and meanings must explain, domesticate, and cover up wild experience. Within this hegemony of words, we demystified whatever was mysterious and walked away from the wild in order to become semantically tamed. We sacrificed our link-to-the-universe-heart for a delusional body-less-head-trip that has imprisoned us far too long. Consider a re-entry into the wild."[3]

Furthermore, Keeney writes: "The greater mind of nature that holds our psyche is a small part of a more encompassing interdependent though always-changing network of relations."[4]

Reentering the wild and embracing the greater mind of nature is at odds with the dominant culture's obsession with control.

Most of us born in this culture have been conditioned to believe in its core tenets unquestioningly. For example, we have been taught that we can *think* our way out of any problem. Therefore, the prevailing educational assumptions are that a "left-brained" academic approach is the primary mode of understanding and that knowledge is bestowed upon the student by the teacher. A culture made up of wild souls certainly encourages the intellectual abilities of each individual and provides mentoring by the more experienced to the less. But, more importantly, it relies on the larger intelligence that is already within each of us—that includes but is deeper than thought—to guide the way.

A WEI is designed so that this intelligence can blossom and flourish. It honors the many equally important forms of this intelligence: feelings; intuition; awareness; body sensations; impressions gleaned from nature; wisdom perceived from our ancestors (both human and nonhuman); information gained from visioning and inner journeys; and cognitive insight. Each participant is encouraged to trust this intelligence—his or her deepest knowing—rather than simply conforming to the ideas and perspectives of the facilitators. In this way, a WEI models what our culture badly needs, direct experience with nature (in its broadest sense) as a foundation for learning.

The WEI is not a place to simply "go wild" and "hang out," although there is plenty of time for spontaneous interaction or being alone. It is a spiritual training ground for joyous, creative self-expression and community building. Logic, reasoning, science, and abstract thought have their places, both in the world and at a WEI; but ideally, they are in the service of a wild soul.

Elements of a New Culture

We long for the expansiveness of knowing and feeling that we are one with all that is. But in some ways, we are also frightened by it—and for good reason. To discover the reality of oneness threatens our narrow sense of self. It is a wonderful paradox that a WEI, while providing a nurturing container where we don't lose our individual uniqueness and emotional stability, strengthens our sense of interconnection with each other and the universe. Participants come to recognize or develop their unique gifts and see how they enrich the group and, eventually, the larger community. We experience personal empowerment through activities that make us feel safe enough to be authentic: to be ourselves and to think for ourselves.

The premise is that this place of wholeness, connectedness, and gratitude is where wise actions, healthy lifeways, and sustainable cultures grow. It is the wisdom of the Earth herself, flowing through each of us, that can provide the clearest direction for the way ahead. It is about each of us trusting our deepest experience by being open and receptive to that flow.

There is immense power in the gathering of a community of people holding this intention. What is prescribed in this book is done in community, with all of us working *together* for our individual and collective freedom. And this community is larger than just the human realm. Each of us is held in multiple relationships that nurture us: relationships with the elements of earth, air, water, and fire, as well as with the plants and animals. A WEI is a space in which to really experience this.

The many people I've come to know during WEIs do not need to be taught anything during the workshop—not in any conventional sense. They don't need another dogma or formula for living. They don't need another tight schedule where they are expected to rush to the next activity, where time is experienced more like a noose than a pillow. What they need most, I believe, is simply an environment in which to love and be loved—to be cherished, accepted, and celebrated for who they truly are.

And I cannot underscore enough that the natural world is the ideal setting for this to take place. Nature is a profoundly important companion, mentor, and advisor, because it is our

Ground of Being. If you sit under a tree and observe its textures, listen to its surroundings, rub the fallen leaves on your palms, and be still, you will gain a sense of connection, gratitude, and awe. I can't explain how it works, but it does—and not just with trees, but almost anywhere "out there" when we make the intention to connect.

Spiritual yet Practical

Most of the experiential activities in a WEI correspond to indigenous practices I have witnessed, techniques I have learned from other workshop facilitators and "dharma" teachers, or ones I have created spontaneously as a response to the needs of the moment. The ones I have learned from others are never exact duplicates. The idea here—and this is extremely important—is that the *essence* of the activity, not its precise form, has universal value and a regenerative function.

This book describes a *practical methodology* based on the experiences of many people who have participated in a WEI, including those who have been guest mentors and facilitators. It is a "how-to" manual of ecologically based spirituality, both ancient and modern, that expands our sense of self to include all life.

I emphasize the term *practical* because many people who are working toward environmental and social change are ambivalent about the term *spiritual*. Their bias is that spirituality—a vital part of the human experience—is not really effective for making positive change, or that it is something apart from daily life.

Martin Prechtel, prolific author, artist, educator, and adoptee of the Tzutujil Maya, speaks about this well:

> Spirituality is an extremely practical thing. It's not a thing that you choose to do on the weekends. Spirituality ... has to have some degree of social accountability, no matter what layer of life you're stuck in or aiming at. It's

only in everyday life that spirituality makes a difference. Otherwise, if spirituality is an entertainment or something that is removed from life itself, then it ceases to become spiritual ... I think spirituality is as essential as eating or holding hands or being warm in the winter or being together as a village. It's all in there.[5]

Mahatma Gandhi was probably the most revered luminary who combined spirituality and social change. He writes in his autography: "I should certainly like to narrate my experiments in the spiritual field which are known only to myself and from which I have derived such power as I possess for working in the political field."[6]

Fruits of a Wild Earth Intensive

Concluding a WEI, we often come to realize that we have gathered a lot of low-hanging fruits that were previously hidden by the pace of our busy lives. These fruits are both the means and ends of an integrated spiritual practice. They include:

- *Community*: learning together while supporting one another.
- *Safety*: living in an atmosphere of emotional and physical safety while exploring our "edges" and taking risks.
- *Connection*: breaking through societal and self-imposed isolation to perceive our oneness with Earth, Spirit, and one another.
- *Empowerment*: feeling the beauty and power of our true selves.
- *Feeling*: allowing all facets of our emotional palette, including grief and pain, to arise and find expression.
- *Fun/play*: expressing our innate, limitless ability to rise above the difficulties of life through spontaneous, joyful creativity.

- *Meaning*: choosing to experience a universe that is intensely alive and express our unique selves within it.

A typical WEI combines indigenous wisdom, Buddhist teachings, eco-psychology, and the central message of most religions: love! However, the philosophical underpinnings of a WEI are far less important than the open-mindedness and open heartedness that the facilitator and any helpers or guests bring to the experience. A WEI does not impose a belief system but inspires a belief in Life. This goes beyond the intellectual concept that humans cannot be separated from the rest of creation. It engenders a *felt* knowing that we *are* the consciousness, or Spirit, that interpenetrates the mountains, the rivers, the stars, and so much more.

Chapter 2

How to Use This Book

And the day came when the risk to remain tight in a bud
was more painful than the risk it took to blossom.

— Anaïs Nin

Deep down in the hidden recesses of our psyches are ancestral memories of when we lived in deep relationship with the land and each other. These memories refuse all manner of subjugation. In these pages, I want to impart the hope and enthusiasm I feel for our ability to *re*-create an Earth-honoring culture for new times.

My approach is twofold:

1. *To provide a blueprint for any small group* of people to practice and experience—through a workshop† called the Wild Earth Intensive (WEI)—the key components of that culture.* These components are based on what has been historically (and prehistorically) successful and, when adapted for the strengths and weaknesses of modern participants, are transformative in the present. Herein you will find a variety of exercises and activities that make these components deliciously real instead of abstract ideas. The exercises and activities have been highly valued by people of all ages but are particularly suitable for young adults who are disillusioned with the dominant culture and are seeking alternatives.

2. *To explain the concepts that support the various WEI activities.* I hope by doing this to increase your motivation to remember your "original instructions." Throughout

this book, you will find quotes from, and references to, a multitude of Native elders, progressive thinkers, frontier scientists, poets, and spiritual luminaries who make the case that a whole new level of consciousness is possible, based on what already lies within us.

Chapter 4, Spiritual Permaculture, is devoted to these concepts, but if you find the degree of intellectual discussion found there does not interest you, turn instead to the other chapters, where the WEI experiential activities are described in detail. I invite you to try these exercises and activities whenever you want, with whomever you wish! Adapt them to your own situations, even when not part of a WEI, but please keep in mind that there is a logic and cumulative effect to combining this set of practices as they are described, and in the order recommended (see Sample Schedule). Furthermore, do not be put off by the cultural forms that have a Native American feel to them. If they do not speak to you, instead research and remember the Earth-honoring practices of your country, ancestry, and bioregion. Substitute accordingly. Make them relevant to your indigenous soul, wherever you live!

There are many other practices of remembering and reconnection besides the ones described that, in a WEI lasting more than ten days,‡ could amplify the impact of the Intensive. Some of my personal favorites are fasting for a vision (the vision quest), the responsible use of psychoactive plant medicines, and various forms of holotropic breathwork. There is also a vast reservoir of knowledge in the healing arts, sacred sexuality, and nonviolent communication that is not only complementary but ultimately essential for the kind of radical change we are discussing. These areas are beyond the scope of this book but are recommended for exploration. The content of a WEI is certainly open to expansion, especially if more time is available.

As you explore the practices in the book, you will notice that it is written as if you are a WEI facilitator. Although you may not actually facilitate a WEI (and they are never led alone), we invite you to read from the vantage point of being a powerful agent of change.

The Intensive is designed for the whole person: physical, mental, emotional, and spiritual. It is a flexible container with two essential features:

- Nurturing the awakening process currently underway in human consciousness§
- Remembering the cultural skills embedded in nature to pass on to future generations

My dream is that as many people as possible will enjoy the fruits of what the WEI has to offer—using it among many powerful tools available today.

One of the misunderstandings that can arise in coming upon a book with such an ambitious title is that it is attempting to get all people to adopt the same cultural forms, and to do so *en masse*. This is not the case. The invitation here is to allow nature and direct experience to determine what kind of Earth-honoring culture is best suited for a particular community. There is a place for everyone in helping to sculpt a diversity of cultures where the health of the land and the people is primary. Each person is encouraged to bring their own gifts into play. Each can make a unique contribution to a vibrant, enriching atmosphere. You are one of those people.

---

* I have found that groups ranging from fifteen to twenty-five people (including facilitators) are ideal for a WEI. Other group sizes are possible, depending on the facilitators' level of experience, but I recommend that a WEI not be held with fewer than twelve participants

and that groups of over thirty participants be divided into two or more smaller groups (running parallel if space permits).

† By *workshop*, I mean an experiential educational seminar of any specified length of time.

‡ I have found that ten days is an ideal minimum time frame for a WEI. Longer periods will allow more in-depth immersion in the many activities offered, as well as the opportunity to experience new ones. Shorter periods may be effective, depending on group goals and facilitator experience, but they will lack the "full-bodied experience" of living in alignment with the principles of Earth-honoring culture. In other words, it takes time to *embody* the understanding and potential available through a WEI. Ten days includes adequate time for a cohesive group to form and go through three critical stages: (1) leaving old ways of being behind, (2) becoming deeply immersed in transformative group and individual practices, and (3) integrating and preparing for return to life outside of the WEI.

§ In his book *The Future of Man*, written in 1945, professor of geology and mystic Pierre Teilhard de Chardin explains such a process: "In the passage of time a state of collective human consciousness has been progressively evolved which is inherited by each succeeding generation of conscious individuals, and to which each generation adds something. Sustained, certainly, by the individual person, but at the same time embracing and shaping the successive multitude of individuals, a sort of generalized human super personality is visibly in the process of formation on the earth."[1]

Chapter 3

Leadership: A Note to Guides and Facilitators

I told my students that to become intimate with the outer landscape it is important to become intimate with the inner landscape. The two are not separate. The inner landscape is as vast, deep, and wild as the outer landscape.

—Paul Rezendes

This chapter is directed toward those of you who feel called to serve as guides or facilitators in a Wild Earth Intensive (WEI) and to leadership in general. The words *guides* and *facilitators* will be used interchangeably throughout this book to describe the role that you will embody. While some of your functions will involve teaching, you will not be teachers in a conventional sense. Instead, you will be agents of trust—trusting that the intelligence of the universe will more fully inform the lives of the participants as they experience a variety of consciousness-expanding WEI activities. Your role will be less to provide information and more to allow each person's true nature to come forth.

The WEI is designed to be conducted by people like you who are called to create cultural alternatives that have sustainable living at their core. Why? The world will likely change significantly in the twenty-first century, in ways we cannot foresee. Many old forms and structures will exit this world. They will die as naturally, but probably not as gracefully, as leaves fall from the trees in autumn. A cultural vacuum will be created, and a viable, comprehensive, and heart-centered understanding of reality—embodied by the new cultural forms—will be needed to fill this vacuum.

Beneath all the competing viewpoints that may arise, people will have common concerns: How can we live in a healthy and functional way? How can we live freely, breathing clean air and drinking clean water? How can our children grow up to realize their potential in a loving environment, on land that can sustain them as long as the sun shines?

In order to ensure the positive resolution of these concerns, true leadership is necessary. Contrary to the popular but superficial notion that leadership is, by nature, somehow arrogant and authoritarian—a reputation that it has acquired because it has been abused—the view presented here is that leadership is a natural and beneficial human characteristic.

Manitonquat (also known as Medicine Story), an elder of the Wampanoag nation of the eastern shores of Massachusetts, says that good leaders "are like a walking stick. They don't dictate, but help the people get where they want to go."[1]

Leadership can help you grow in ways you may never have thought possible. In your role as a WEI guide, you may feel your power—deep within yourself, not over others—in new and exciting ways. This is likely to happen as you help the participants deepen their connection with the ecstatic nature of life; you will feel good that you made a difference in their lives.

Of course, leadership can also feel scary. Leaders may be perceived as parental or other authority figures and not as equals. You could be verbally attacked for not meeting the participants' expectations or for guiding them to emotional territory where they feel insecure and uncomfortable. Or, more likely, your own fear may arise in the face of your internal challenges. "Am I up to this task? Can I remain present when someone is feeling deep emotion? Is it OK for me to be visible and powerful? What if I let others down?" These are but a few of the questions that may surface before, during, and after a WEI. It is important to remember that feelings of inadequacy and doubt are part of your humanness. When you accept these feelings, you become even more effective and "real."

Keep in mind that a participant's personal experience — whatever it may be — is not a valid judgment, positive or negative, on your natural goodness. Get your ego out of the way as best you can. You can't possibly "make it all better" for someone who is feeling down, nor can you claim direct responsibility for someone feeling joy or elation. Your main job is to serve the Earth by showing up and helping out! Recognizing this will lessen your fear and build humility.

Here are a few useful ways that you, as a facilitator, can nurture the growth and flourishing of others:

- Look for the best in everyone.
- Demonstrate open-mindedness and open heartedness.
- Notice how each person has a unique contribution to make, how each holds a "piece of the puzzle." Inclusion is a primary principle of effective group process.
- Think about each individual, but also keep a pulse on the entire group.
- Remain flexible; be willing to change an activity if you sense it would serve the group better to do so.
- Let go of any expectations that people will react a certain way to a process, or even that they will enjoy it.
- Encourage and validate authentic expression of feelings, even if someone expresses anger or sadness when others are happy.
- Don't isolate yourself in a role of ongoing solo leadership. Find two or three assistants, preferably of a different gender than you, who are eager to eventually assume full leadership after they have been mentored by you for some time. Co-leadership is also possible.

- Forgive yourself when you make "mistakes." They are part of the learning process.
- Respect people's defenses and resistance.
- Do your own inner work. This is a crucial and ongoing process that allows you to be as open, honest, and in touch with your feelings as you want others to be.

During a WEI, you can remind yourself of the fundamentals of good leadership with the following cue. Look at one hand, and let each finger represent one of these leadership qualities: (1) the courage to journey with the group into the unknown; (2) the ability to act and speak from the heart; (3) the willingness to learn from the group and the Earth; (4) the readiness to take risks; and (5) the skill of allowing the group to integrate highlights and important "teachings."

This last point, concerning integration, includes recognizing the importance of allowing sufficient time to reinforce and evaluate what has been learned. Rushing on to the next activity can diminish the power of what has come before.

While leading the group, you may come across expressions of sexism, classism, racism, homophobia, and speciesism (human chauvinism), even if veiled. These are major impediments to healthy human development and are the direct consequences of the illusion of separation. Molded by habit and society, they are results of the wounds and trauma we have all experienced.

As leaders, we are actively engaged in transforming these narrow and destructive ways of looking at the world. Those mindsets can sometimes seem intractable, yet each time we contradict them by gently but firmly insisting on the truth, we get closer to the kind of world we all want to live in, just as water passing over a stone again and again will eventually polish it to a beautiful sheen. To be crystal clear, men are not better than women; white people are not better than black, yellow, and red people; people with more money are not better than people with less money; straight people are not better than gay people; and humans are not better than the rest of creation.

By working to change this deep conditioning wherever we encounter it, whether in ourselves or in others, we are performing an invaluable service. But beware—this type of conditioning is pernicious as well as tenacious. Creating a new culture requires patience, so don't beat yourself up when you don't see permanent changes right away. Most of us involved in this type of work are healing from PITSD, post-*industrial* traumatic stress disorder. As this healing takes place, be prepared to see remarkable breakthroughs!

As you design your own WEI, keep in mind that the framework outlined in this book can be adapted to suit a variety of venues and circumstances. However, adhering to the general sequence and the content of the majority of activities is likely to have the maximum impact. Other practices can be substituted for some of those described in this book, but they should directly relate to the essential themes discussed here (ceremony, nature immersion, play, etc.). These themes are the glue that bonds the participants of a WEI because, together, they draw out of each individual deeply felt states of well-being such as:

- Gratitude
- Connection to Earth, Spirit, and one another
- Empowerment
- Joy and humor
- Meaning
- Healing

When you see these wholesome states emerge, in part because you guided well, you will be filled with a deep sense of satisfaction. You will know with assurance that humans can create wonders when they are "swimming" in their place of origin: the ocean of nature and Spirit. You will feel good knowing that you stepped aside from any need for self-aggrandizement and allowed the larger intelligence of the universe to flow through you.

And don't forget humor. People have to laugh and not take things *too* seriously. As a facilitator, you will always be looking for opportunities to balance out the depth of emotional and spiritual exploration by lightening the mood.

Finally, this book is a map, not the territory. Experiment with it. Make it work for you. Each of you has your own gifts and talents. Each has different passions that bring you to this transformative work. As you use this framework, know that it has led many through remarkable journeys. Through your own guidance from Spirit, it will become your own unique version — and your unique gift to yourself and others.

Chapter 4

A Spiritual Permaculture

*Who will prefer the jingle of jade pendants if he once has
heard stone growing in a cliff?*

— Tao Te Ching

Permaculturists have devised ingenious methods for physically
sustaining human presence on the land. There are countless
examples of their approaches: water catchment in dry climates,
edible forest gardening, construction of zero energy dwellings
that mimic their natural surroundings, cultivation of traditional
vegetables even in the coldest winter, and much more.
However, Dave Jacke, a well-known permaculture expert in
the United States and author of the landmark book *Edible Forest
Gardens*, wants to take it a step further. He described to me his
understanding that "a harmonious cosmology is at the center
of sound permaculture design."[1] Jacke realizes, as do many
others, that a time-tested worldview is central to the long-term
success or failure of human settlements. And the design of those
settlements is a product of a worldview or cosmology that either
is or is not informed by the intelligence embedded in nature.

This book is devoted to developing human cultures that are
guided by that intelligence. Its basis could be called *spiritual
permaculture. Spiritual,* in this context, signifies access to that
mysterious, invisible, intelligent energy permeating existence.
Permaculture is the science, ethics, and practice of humans living
cooperatively with nature, *as* nature. A growing number of
people are realizing these terms are two sides of the same coin.

The mindset so characteristic of industrial culture — that
the Earth's riches are at our disposal — is causing tremendous
ecological destruction. All we have to do is look around to see

that such a mindset is tragically flawed. It views the Earth as composed of "stuff" that has little value until we humans do something with it, and it holds that there is nothing wrong with using up or dramatically modifying that stuff. It assumes we can continue to grow indefinitely—in population size, in land usage, in resource extraction, and in our consumption-based economies—and pay no consequences.

The Illusion of Separation

Inextricably tied to that mindset is a deeper flaw in our perception. It is the *illusion of separation*, which is deeply engraved within the human psyche. What does that mean? It means that the rock-bottom, core sense of self that most humans carry (with differing degrees of intensity) is one that is fundamentally isolated from the rest of nature. But our perception of ourselves as separate is not based on reality. Albert Einstein called it an "optical delusion of consciousness."[2] Alan Watts called it the "skin-encapsulated ego."[3] Charles Eisenstein, whose book *The Ascent of Humanity* is about the evolution of the human sense of self, refers to the past five-thousand years, culminating in the twentieth century, as the "Age of Separation."[4] It's the air we breathe but rarely notice.

This basic error in our perceptual lens—our operating system, if you will, from which our creations emanate—leads to a culture that is at war with the Earth that sustains it. Each of us, gripped by a gnawing fear that we are separate and alone, acts in ways that are making our living womb, the Earth, a tomb. The mixture of overpopulation, a blind allegiance to technology, and an attitude of "economic necessity" that puts the Earth's ecosystems on the chopping block for financial gain is a lethal cocktail for our planet.

At first glance, the cause may seem too obscure, too theoretical, to be at the root of so much suffering and destruction. Yet on closer examination, it makes so much sense. Eckhart Tolle puts it this way: "The dysfunction of the egoic human mind, recognized already 2,500 years ago by the ancient wisdom teachers and now magnified by science and technology, is for the first time threatening the survival of the planet."[5]

By *planet*, Tolle means all the complex ecosystems that have evolved over time—and these include us. How much of this will survive if we do not wake up to another way of being, based on who we truly are: one of the Earth's many organisms living in one interdependent system?

Fortunately, many people are indeed waking up. They are seeing through the illusion of a separate self and becoming more conscious of connectedness rather than isolation. In so doing, they are addressing the problem's roots and therefore creating the possibility of a lasting solution. They are birthing a collective shift toward a transformed relationship with nature, which includes the rest of humanity.

One of the aims of this book is to motivate more people to be part of such a shift, and to do so in a spirit of joy and gratitude. And although a shift in consciousness is foundational to lasting solutions, I believe it is very important that we do not expect a specific outcome, that we not get attached to the future fruits of our actions. Why? Paying more attention to the ends rather than the means is a waste of energy and, ultimately, is self-defeating. No one truly knows how things will play out on planet Earth, and yet whatever good we create today can positively affect the world of tomorrow.

Simply put, we need a powerful, compelling, enjoyable way of being alive and fulfilled in the moment, *in connection with nature and each other*. And when we remember that we will make choices that nourish that connection. We will share that perspective and pass it on to future generations. Out of necessity, we will come to know our ecological self—at one with the living Earth.

A Bridge to the Ecological Self:
The Wild Earth Intensive

The Wild Earth Intensive (WEI) is a training ground for relearning our deep connection to the natural world in an atmosphere of healthy human relationships. One of the foundational beliefs that led to the creation of the WEI is that humanity's destructive behavior—born from a belief in a separate self—is a psycho-spiritual illness in need of healing. And that healing will only arise in an atmosphere of compassion, drawing on forms of medicine that truly heal the psyche as well as the body. One of the most exciting things about being alive at this time is that there is so much medicine available!

The WEI directly explores a variety of potent medicines, such as meditation, ceremony, nature immersion, deep listening, and play, which together, I believe, have cultural curing ability. They are a healing amalgam that removes or overrides—even if temporarily—the old mental structures that hold in place our deeply ingrained sense of isolation. Those old structures can be likened to the legs of a multi-legged stool, with the seat being our core perception of separateness from nature and each other. During an Intensive, one of our goals is to skillfully remove each of the stool's legs to topple it, and then to reseat ourselves on a cushion of gratitude, focusing on the miracle of our existence and unity with all of creation. By removing the illusion of separation, we reconnect with who we are.

The old mental structures just mentioned are constellations of thoughts—core beliefs—that have been taught to us systematically by authority figures over countless generations. They are servants of the separate self. Some examples of those core beliefs include: "The universe is not a friendly place"; "There is not enough to go around"; "Life is a struggle"; "I am bad." These convictions may be held in the subconscious and may rarely be acknowledged as foundational beliefs that influence our whole way of being. When they are unchallenged, we live with an impoverished view of reality. On an emotional level, they result in, at best, our not feeling well, and, at worst, psychoses.

The good news is that we can become aware of and transcend these old, unworkable mental constructs. The WEI is designed especially to nurture this awareness in a supportive way. During an Intensive, we begin to experience many "Aha!" moments, in which a way of life that is both very old and yet very new starts to permeate our being. Of course, our ego* tends to put up a fight, and we don't always feel on top of the world during the process, but we sense we are on the right track.

A WEI incorporates seven principles that make it a rich and often transformational experience. Those principles are:

- There is power in remembering ancestral wisdom.
- We can dream a new world into being.
- We are a tribal species.
- The Earth is alive and full of meaning.
- Humans naturally live in abundance.
- Women and men are partners in a common destiny.
- Ancient wisdom is mirrored by twenty-first century science.

The principles discussed below when applied together, are like a vital community of plants in a permaculture garden. Each plant enriches and nourishes the others, so that we have a healing and thriving community of people in a healthy, dynamic ecosystem.

There Is Power in Remembering Ancestral Wisdom

The Age of Separation could also be called the Age of Forgetting. Modern humans have severe amnesia; we have forgotten who we are in relation to everything else. Martin Prechtel, the maverick cultural historian and artist, calls it "the amnesia of modernity"[6] and says our task is a "Holy Remembrance [which has been] forced to survive homeless under bridges."[7]

In truth, each one of us is vertically connected to everything through the present moment, and horizontally connected through time to all of our ancestors (and descendants). And what a lineage that is! Not only are we a pedigree in the world of mammals but our nonhuman ancestors go back to the first blue-green algae appearing on Earth 2.5 billion years ago. Moreover, only abstract thinking makes a distinction between animate and inanimate forms. In the words of John Seed, deep ecologist and rainforest defender, "We are the rocks dancing."[8] The late Carl Sagan, author and highly successful popularizer of astronomy in the 1960s and 1970s, goes even further back in time and reminds us that "we are star stuff."[9] The rocks, and our bodies, are literally made from the stars. Nearly every atom from which we are made was once inside our star, the sun, which was, itself, synthesized from the interstellar medium of past stars. Fortunately, there have been cultures that understood this not as an exciting intellectual truth, but as a deeply felt experience — an all-encompassing reality, which the Lakota Indians express in the phrase *Mitakuye Oyasin*, or "All My Relations."

That is why a big part of forging a sustainable culture requires that we *go back, to go forward*. Why not rediscover what was at the core of successful cultures for many thousands of years and retrieve it for our time?

David Kyle, who has written extensively on this subject, says:

We must go back to reclaim a fundamental connection that we as modern individuals have lost. This means going back to Paleolithic times. In those ancient times, some 15,000 years ago, our ancestors were physically and intellectually like us today, but they were still deeply connected with the Sacred Other as it was mediated through nature. Paleolithic human experience still exists today on planet Earth in some indigenous, native, and aboriginal peoples. I am not urging that we "go native" but rather that we listen to, learn from, and understand the messages and teachings native peoples are willing to give to us.[10]

This view stands in stark contrast to the European academic tradition, where it was taught well into the twentieth century that ancient indigenous peoples were quaint savages who lived primitive, brutish lives. But just as we are composed of star stuff that has miraculously transformed into the "rocks dancing," we are also these very ancient people. They are our ancestors. Without them, we would not exist. We are all indigenous to some land if we go back far enough.

Our task, then, is to remember and reclaim our indigenous souls and learn to truly live in balance with the land once again, yet in a new and creative way. In doing so, we will remember we are good to the core, in the same way plants, animals, clouds, and stars are good to the core. This is not just a philosophical concept but a felt experience of the well-being of the universe, no matter how difficult the worldly circumstances we encounter. We can also remember that the lasting joy of life is not found in acquisition or in achievement but in *relationship* with others, human and nonhuman.

Whenever I have witnessed this remembering firsthand, I have been incredibly moved, whether it happened on an Indian reservation, in the wilds of Siberia, or in a WEI. Often, as if by grace, the remembering spontaneously manifested in the form of a long-forgotten song, chant, dance, or dream—the old medicine ways revealing themselves in new conditions. They are the healing waters from the past re-emerging into the present.

Terence McKenna, the late consciousness explorer, scholar, and ethnobotanist, termed this remembering, on a collective level, the "Archaic Revival."[11] The Archaic Revival is marked by a tremendous resurgence of ancient ways of knowing that is underway in most of the industrialized countries. It manifests in various ways, such as a keen interest in indigenous culture; a relearning of shamanism, including those traditions with roots in Europe; a renewal in the art of animal tracking and primitive wilderness-survival skills; and the exploration of herbs and ethno-pharmaceuticals. McKenna says the Archaic Revival is about "shedding the dominant cultural operating system and getting in touch with something much older and more vitalistic."[12]

Author Paul Devereux, emphasizing the need to remember the mythic way in which we once perceived nature, says in his book *Re-Visioning the Earth* that "history floats on the ocean of prehistory in the way the waking, conscious self ... floats on the vast deeps of the unconscious mind."[13]

Although the onslaught of industrialized "civilization" has fractured the continuity of many indigenous cultures into the present day, there is a resurgence of interest among these peoples in reclaiming their culture. This means that the Archaic Revival is also growing within Native communities, whose elders are teaching their ancient ways anew to the younger generations.

We Can Dream a New World into Being

Part of remembering our true nature is remembering our inherent powers. One such power is the power to dream, and not just when we are sleeping. Dreaming is the fuel for manifestation in this world. We simply do not have to settle for the attitude "This is the way it has been, so it is always going to be this way." Instead, we can draw on the vital power of dreaming to create a *conscious, directed* process toward the world we want. The Australian Aborigines call the place from which that vital power emanates the Dreamtime.

Every time we think a thought, we are activating this creative energy. And while we in Western culture tend to deny the concept of thought as energy, many cultures acknowledge it absolutely. They assert that each of our thoughts is an energetic seed holding the potential for something larger to grow. How we as individuals sow these seeds determines a lifetime. Cumulatively, they make up our waking dream. This is what the Buddha meant when he said, "All that we are is the result of what we have thought ... What we think, we become."[14]

John Perkins, the "economic hit man,"[15] turned author, environmentalist, and champion of indigenous peoples, writes about the power of dreaming in his book *The World Is As You Dream It*:

Many [cultures] equate dreams with the latent energy of the seed and embryo. Their beliefs are not unlike Carl Jung's theory that humanity's collective unconscious contains the knowledge of all past and future events and that dreams are a key for tapping into a vast library of information.[16]

Perkins quotes Robert Lawlor's remarkable book *Voices of the First Day: Awakening in the Aboriginal Dreamtime*:

The Australian Aborigines, and indeed indigenous tribal peoples all over the world, believe that the spirit of their consciousness and way of life exists like a seed buried in the earth. The waves of European colonialism that destroyed the civilizations of North America, South America, and Australia began a five-hundred-year dormancy period of the "archaic consciousness." Its potencies disappeared into the earth ... Dreams, deep collective memories, and imaginings are more potent than religious faith or scientific theories in lifting us above the catastrophic ending that confronts us all.[17]

Because thinking is happening most of the time—when we are on the phone, eating, sleeping, driving, and so forth—we are almost constantly dreaming. The question becomes, *what* are we dreaming? Can we become conscious of this process, so we can harness it for positive benefit not just for us as individuals but for our civilization?

The responsibility to consciously evolve using our dreaming power is enormous, but what other choice do we really have? Thomas Berry, the "geologian" and one of the main inspirations for this book, writes in his *The Dream of the Earth*:

> What we seem unwilling or unable to recognize is that our entire modern world is itself inspired not by any rational process, but by a distorted dream experience, perhaps by the most powerful dream that has ever taken possession of human imagination. Our sense of progress, our entire technological society, however rational in its functioning, is a pure dream vision in its origins and its objectives.[18]

When the industrial vision is understood in this way—not as some evil force outside of us that needs to be overcome or some permanent solid object blighting the landscape, but as a malleable dream formed in our minds—then we can say with some certainty that creating a different, healthier reality is possible. At a *minimum*, each of us can choose to dream an ecstatic dream where life is fully lived in balance with nature because the power to do so already lies within us.

We Are a Tribal Species

For hundreds of thousands of years, we humans succeeded in living within our means on planet Earth. We thrived without compromising the ability of the various ecosystems we inhabited to support us. We lived in small, mobile, and fluid groups within a system of mutual care that was as natural as our bones. As Daniel Quinn, author of the immensely popular *Ishmael*, says: "The people of our culture don't want to acknowledge that the tribe is for humans exactly what the pod is for whales or the troop is for baboons: the gift of millions of years of natural selection, not perfect—but damned hard to improve upon."[19]

True tribal living (as opposed to tribalism dominated by warlords and competition) can weather any storm, yet modern society has no use for it. I'm not suggesting that we return to the hunter-gatherer lifestyle of our successful ancestors but that we apply their wisdom—in this case, social organization—to today's set of circumstances. Doing so can enable another strong and creative social "shoot" to grow from the ashes of industrialism. It is not about living in isolated bands, cutting ourselves off from others, but about joining a planet made up of diverse thriving tribes.

The first woman Navajo surgeon, Lori Arviso Alvord, writes in her autobiography, *The Scalpel and the Silver Bear*:

> The outside, non-Indian world is tribeless, full of wandering singular souls, seeking connection through societies, clubs, and other groups. White people know what it is to be a family but to be a tribe is something of an altogether different sort. It provides a feeling of inclusion in something larger, of having a set place in the universe where one always belongs. It provides connectedness and a blueprint for how to live.[20]

In a Wild Earth Intensive, participants become a small tribe of sorts, and they have the added benefit of being in close contact with the natural world. Inevitably, the group starts to bond emotionally, and as it does, they begin to model exactly the kind of cooperation that has been so essential to the survival of our species. To quote biologists Lynn Margulis and Dorion Sagan, the newest findings in biology alter "our view of evolution as a chronic, bloody competition among individuals and species. Life did not take over the globe by combat but by networking."[21]

Our current Age of Forgetting will expire as we start to live in mutually supportive tribes (or clans/bands, if you prefer) that are also resuscitating the true self—the ecological self. Resuscitation of our true selves leads to an experience of love— not just love for "others" but love *with* all Life. It becomes the bottom line in all our relationships, human and nonhuman. In the process, we help each other to know that this way of life is our birthright and that we need each other to "get back to the Garden."

The importance of building tribal community, where caring and support of one another are the priority, cannot be overstated. The Buddha viewed the *sangha* (the community of people committed to freeing their hearts and minds) to be just as important as the *dharma* (natural law) and the awakened mind itself (as represented by the Buddha).

The Earth Is Alive and Full of Meaning

Most people today are aware that, about five-hundred years ago, Europeans who settled in the New World brought with them a host of disease-causing viruses that annihilated many of the indigenous tribes living on the North American continent. Less well-known is that two very peculiar core beliefs swept out of Europe at that time as well. They were foundational to the rationale for the "Age of Expansion" (a euphemism for colonialism), and later to the industrial world's myth that its form of mechanized progress was inherently best.

These core beliefs are: (1) nature works like a machine, according to mechanical principles; and (2) nature is essentially made up of dispensable material that we may use, solely to serve human needs.

These human-centered beliefs are mutually reinforcing. They are assumptions, rarely questioned, about what is real and true. Even as a growing number of people today consider themselves environmentalists, there remains a powerful momentum for human dominance at any cost. This dominance — supported by the notion that what humans want is all-important — is commonly thought of as "just the way things are." Our destruction of the natural world is derived from these beliefs.

By standing apart from nature, considering it something different from ourselves, we objectify it and become numb to our destructive actions. In short, we don't really *feel* what we are doing.

When we recognize that this mindset has been unconsciously adopted by billions of people, it is a little easier to understand how vast areas of continents have been mined, blasted, and harvested, laying waste not only to natural treasures but to everything and everybody in the way. Huge economic systems are served by this worldview.

In stark contrast, cultures whose people *knew* (as opposed to *believed*) that nature is alive and pregnant with intelligence once inhabited much of the globe. Their stories did not end up in the history books. Now referred to as indigenous peoples, most (not all) lived in a variety of ecosystems for thousands of years without destroying or overtaxing them. For them, nature encompassed not just biological life but everything, from stones to stars, and it was all permeated by Spirit. This worldview was finally popularized for mainstream audiences worldwide through the story of the fictional Na'vi people of the planet Pandora, in the tremendously popular movie *Avatar* (2010).

That film has made it possible, like never before, for us "moderns" to imagine what it might have been like to live as an aboriginal Australian, an African Bushman, or an American

Indian before their collision with the cultures that eventually overran them (today's dominator cultures). Every event in their lives was loaded with meaning. Each member of the tribe was taught how to make sense of the symbolism laden in these events and to use it for creative, empowered action (or nonaction). Each animal had a message, the stones and insects told stories of long ago, and the present moment pulsed with mysterious power. Not only the birds but *everything* had its own song.

One example of such a way of life is presented by Malcolm Margolin in his book *The Ohlone Way*, which describes what existence was like in traditional times for the Ohlone people. The Ohlone were a group of tribes who lived along the extremely fertile region of California between what is now San Francisco and Monterey for seventy-five hundred years. Margolin writes:

> The Ohlones ... lived in a world perhaps somewhat like a Van Gogh painting, shimmering and alive with movement and energy in ever-changing patterns. It was a world in which thousands of living, feeling, magical things, all operating on dream-logic, carried out their individual actions ... Power was everywhere, in everything, and therefore every act was religious. Hunting a deer, walking on a trail, making a basket, or pounding acorns were all done with continual reference to the world of power.[22]

As late as the 1960s, indigenous tribes that had never been contacted by the outside world were discovered to still be living in similar ways. The Senoi of Malaysia was such a tribe. Here is a passage from *Original Wisdom*, a book by Robert Wolff, who lived among them on and off for many years:

> The People [Senoi] I knew were quiet. They smiled rather than guffawed. They never argued. I remember all our discussions as slowly paced, thoughtful and strangely

orderly, as though people took turns. I cannot remember ever hearing two people speak at the same time. There was always that little pause when everyone looks in the middle distance, then one person will speak as if he or she were the designated speaker though nobody had said anything. I thought about this new way of talking for many years; I could not let it go. I could not imagine that they were *telepathic*, but they certainly seemed to know each other's thoughts. Of course, they lived together; they were around each other all the time. They must have known each other intimately. I thought that maybe this explained it. But it remained a baffling and confusing fact.

Gradually I came to realize that their world, their reality, was what we call a spiritual reality; it was not the tangible reality we are more familiar with. It was a reality where things were *known* outside of thinking.[23]

In 1974 and 1975, Wade Davis, the celebrated *National Geographic* explorer and anthropologist, spent time with the Ika and Kogi tribes in the rugged Sierra Nevada de Santa Marta mountains in northern Colombia. The Ika and Kogi consider themselves to be the elder brothers of humanity (people of the dominant civilization are the younger brothers). They have been living in isolation for four-hundred years, since escaping the Spanish conquest. They call their mountain home the "Heart of the World." Davis writes about them in his book *One River:*

For both the Ika and the Kogi the earth is alive. Every mountain sound is an element of a language of the spirit, every object a symbol of other possibilities. Thus a temple becomes a mountain, a cave a womb, a calabash of water the reflection of the sea. The sea is the memory of the Great Mother.

The life spun into being at the beginning of time is a fragile balance, with the equilibrium of the entire universe being completely dependent on the moral, spiritual, and ecological integrity of the Elder Brothers. The goal of life is knowledge. Everything else is secondary. Without knowledge there can be no understanding of good and evil, no appreciation of the sacred obligations that human beings have to the earth and the Great Mother. With knowledge comes wisdom and tolerance. Yet wisdom is an elusive goal, and in a world animated by solar energy, people invariably turn for guidance to the sun priests, the enlightened *mámas* who alone can control the cosmic forces through prayer and ritual, songs and incantations. Though they rule the living, the *mámas* have no evident privileges, no outward signs of prestige. They share the same simple food, live in identical stone houses, wear the same cloth, woven by their own hands. Yet their pursuit of wisdom entails an enormous burden, for the Kogi and Ika believe that the survival of the people and the entire earth depends on their labors.[24]

Davis relates this explanation by Tim Plowman, who traveled with him: "They believe that as you move from one valley to the next, you must thank the mountains' guardians for their protection. Every time they cross over a divide, they place a quid of coca on the rock cairns that mark the high passes and blow prayers into the wind."[25] Their Ika companion, Adalberto Villafañe, replied, "For everything there must be a payment."[26]

Except for the coca leaves, this last paragraph could be written almost identically to describe the behavior of the indigenous Siberians whom I have visited extensively. Picture another set of mountains on the other side of the world. Thousands of streams pour through the huge cliff outcroppings surrounded by endless stretches of pine, fir, and larch trees. Petroglyphs and sacred burial mounds hug the valley edges. And still, after a few hundred years of oppressive Russian and Soviet rule, indigenous elders and shamans lead their people by foot, horse, and car to honor thousands of natural features: caves, mountain passes, unusual trees, sacred springs, boulders, and so forth. Few of these features are on any maps. The shamans and elders make offerings to the spirits of these places in the form of poems, chants, and food. Sometimes, the people sing songs and dance. They always leave a white ribbon on a nearby tree as a gesture of gratitude. When they are done, they make their way back to their six-sided houses and pastoral lifestyle. One Altai elder told me: "Our life is not easy; we have many problems, but we keep giving thanks to the spirits because they keep us alive."[27]

Such reverence for all of creation has been similarly described in hundreds of books about numerous tribes throughout the world. Arguably, these accounts by anthropologists and laypeople who have acted as "participant-observers" of indigenous peoples are the most important gifts to modern society. Why not honor these gifts by gathering in small groups with the intent of connecting with each other and the natural world? Why not revive the Earth-honoring cultural skills these accounts point to that lead to contentment and vitality?

Humans Naturally Live in Abundance

After 4.5 billion years of evolution on planet Earth, sometime around the fifteenth century, a zenith of biological diversity graced the Earth. Over the five hundred years since then, however, that biodiversity has been erased by human activities; and in the last half-century, extinction rates have accelerated. Our species is responsible for the largest extinction spasm since the demise of the dinosaurs sixty-five million years ago.

Yet, even now, the Earth teems with life. This is truly a miracle, and it illustrates what this amazing planet can do by sheer fortitude if given some breathing room between spasms. The United Nations' 1995 Global Biodiversity Assessment estimated the total number of species to be at fourteen million, although other estimates have ranged from five million to more than a hundred million. What magnificent abundance!

This fecund matrix of life is our earthly home. How can humanity expect to go forward if not *with* Mother Earth who gave birth to us? How could we have ever imagined we were anything less than her children, embedded in the web of life? This is not romantic sentiment but the truth of our existence. Nature is our larger body: abundant, sensual, and ecstatic.

The late California poet Robinson Jeffers puts it this way:

> *I entered the life of the brown forest,*
> *And the great life of the ancient peaks, the patience of stone,*
> *I felt the changes in the veins*
> *In the throat of the mountain ... and, I was the stream*
> *Draining the mountain wood; and I the stag drinking; and I*
>   *was the stars*
> *Boiling with light, wandering alone, each one the lord of his*
>   *own summit; and I was the darkness*
> *Outside the stars, I included them, they were a part of me. I*
>   *was mankind also, a moving lichen*
> *On the cheek of the round stone ... how can I express the*
>   *excellence I have found, that has no color but clearness;*
> *No honey but ecstasy ...*[28]

We long to experience this ecstasy as a steady diet. *Ecstasy* is a synonym for oneness. It's not necessarily a state of bliss; the natural world is not always pleasant. She can be tough; but we don't have to keep resisting the basic ground rules: everything that takes form—whether it's a star, an emotion, or a person— arises and then passes away. Not resisting the way things are, actually accepting them, frees up tremendous energy. Instead of wishing for some future salvation, we start noticing that we already live in paradise.

Women and Men Are Partners in a Common Destiny

To bring about the cultural shift from a dominator/industrial society to one of cooperation with each other and nature, we need to dismantle sexism. For some five thousand years, in most cultures, men have held dominance over women, and this is still largely true. Sexism posits that one gender (in this case, men) is superior to another, and therefore deserves privilege. This concept, which permeates societies worldwide, has led to extraordinary suffering, not just for women, but also for men — though the latter outcome is often overlooked.

Although great strides were made during the twentieth century to ease sexism's stronghold in certain countries, there is still a long way to go. Even within the most "spiritual" gatherings, sexist conditioning is still prevalent. Most women have been socialized to hide their power and let men act and speak first. Feminism has loosened the grip of sexism in some societies, but it should not be taken for granted that the eventual liberation of all women is assured.

True partnership between genders is the way out of this suffering. Riane Eisler, in her groundbreaking book *The Chalice and the Blade*, tells a story of our cultural origins that differs from the patriarchal model in which most of us have been steeped. It shows that the "battle between the sexes" is dictated neither by biology nor by psychology. Eisler provides scholarly evidence that a healthier culture is possible because of what happened in our past: partnership between men and women, and, by extension, everyone.[29] She writes:

> Partnership is a commitment to a way of living, it is a way of life based on harmony with nature, nonviolence, and

gender, racial, and economic equity. It takes us beyond conventional labels to a future of flourishing untapped human potential. It is part of our human nature to be caring, sensitive, and creative ... During much of our prehistory, humanity was rooted in the partnership model. This is our lost heritage. Through a cultural shift, history became the familiar tale of violence, injustice, and domination.[30]

I wholeheartedly believe men and women can once again embrace a partnership model, but, obviously, a lot needs to change in order for this to take place. A common reaction to the violence and inequity facing us to today is to say that men need to change, that they and their egos are at the root of the problem. Yes, men do need to change, but so do women. Women have also taken on that deep sense of separation that drives the collective pathology. It isn't fair—or helpful—to blame each man as though he made the decision to create the sexist society in which we struggle today.

I have witnessed many individual men, when they recognized the full extent to which their gender has collectively perpetrated massive criminal behavior (against nature and other humans), becoming appalled and ashamed. Often their remorse turns to guilt, and they feel personally responsible for the abuses of patriarchy. And then, instead of showing up fully and powerfully, pouring themselves into the fulfillment of life on this planet (in their own unique way), they hide in self-loathing and addictive behaviors.

In general, men have been less likely than women to attend a WEI, and this is a trend we would like to change. For this reason, we will go into more detail here regarding men's issues.

In 1976, ahead of his time, Herb Goldberg wrote in *The Hazards of Being Male:* "The male has paid a heavy price for his masculine 'privilege' and power. He is out of touch with his emotions and his body. He is playing by the rules of the male game plan and with lemming-like purpose he is destroying himself—emotionally, psychologically and physically."[31]

Rule number one of the male game plan is to work. This is how most men derive their sense of self-worth. Unfortunately, in an industrial culture, there are few substitutes from which men can derive value. So compulsion to work and addictive overworking have emerged as real societal problems. It's no wonder that the presence of women in the workforce can trigger issues of power and competition between genders. And then women also start to take on these destructive patterns typically experienced by men.

Furthermore, men are historically the hunters and the warriors. While it may seem a stretch to suggest this still plays a role in a man's identity, without a healthy outlet for this archetypal energy, men turn aggressive—whether it's aimed inward or outward.

Jed Diamond, author of *The Warrior's Journey Home: Healing Men, Healing the Planet*, who brilliantly synthesizes men's trauma recovery and planetary healing, states:

In learning about the ancient hunters, I began to realize that they were the first warriors. These were men who revered life, but were not afraid to embrace death. They knew that other living things must die so that they might live. They also accepted that their own deaths were required for life to continue. It is only in our 'civilized' society that death has become separated from life, and both life and death are feared rather than embraced by men. In our obsessive denial of death we also, unknowingly, destroy life. It is no coincidence that two of the primary by-products of civilization are armaments and addictions. Young men are no longer taught to become warriors, but are trained to be soldiers whose primary purpose is to kill other men.[32]

There is still a place for "warrior" energy among men, and in society, but it is not what we moderns usually think. The late Tibetan meditation master Chögyam Trungpa says: "Warriorship here does not refer to making war on others. Aggression is the source of our problems, not the solution. Here the word *warrior* is taken from the Tibetan *pawo*, which literally means 'one who is brave.' Warriorship in this context is the tradition of human bravery, or the tradition of fearlessness ... The key to warriorship ... is not being afraid of who you are."[33]

And that bravery—to be and discover who you are—requires *feeling*. When we allow ourselves to feel, we open the door to love, and love is the most important antidote to a dominator culture. Love is the lifeblood of partnership between men and women, and between all humans.

Men have been socialized to repress and/or hide their feelings. Thankfully, a growing number of men today are realizing that this does them a great disservice and delays the creation of a more balanced culture. Absence of feeling allows untold injustice and abuse, of others and of the planet. In a dominator society, you can't have feelings of empathy or despair about what's going on. That might stop the whole engine of progress!

One of the objectives of a WEI is to help everyone to consciously *feel*. It takes a safe environment of trust and respect to honestly look inside and express what we've closed off. For both men and women, expressing deep feelings openly and then being accepted by a group may be the first catalyst to living a more empowered life—exactly what a new partnership society needs. Imagine what men and women who embody both their masculine and feminine sides, willing and able to feel fully, could offer a partnered world.

Ancient Wisdom Is Mirrored by
Twenty-First-Century Science

"The whole history of science shows us that whenever the educated and scientific men of any age have denied the facts of other investigators on a priori grounds of absurdity or impossibility, the deniers have always been wrong."[34] Alfred Russell Wallace, the British natural scientist, explorer, and geographer, made that statement in the nineteenth century, and it is still true today. We are witnessing a breathtaking development: ancient wisdom—"held in trust" over the generations by indigenous elders; the mystics of the ages; and the sages of Buddhism, Hinduism, and Taoism—is being mirrored by discoveries at the frontiers of science about the nature of reality. The rest of the world is in the process of catching up.

In the first half of the twentieth century, legendary physicists like Einstein, Heisenberg, Bohr, Planck, and Pauli rearticulated an ancient understanding and laid the groundwork for a pantheon of scientists who have followed. To do justice to these revolutionary thinkers and the impact they are having would take an entire book, and, indeed, many have been written. However, their sophisticated and awe-inspiring findings can be summarized by a few remarkable observations about the universe:

- Everything is linked to everything else, and, at the deepest level, all is one.
- There is an infinite array of processes that are characterized by ceaseless change.
- There are no discrete parts, only "wholes" that are organized into dynamically balanced relationships to which we have given names such as *molecules, bodies, ecosystems, planets, galaxies*, and so on.
- There is a manifested and an unmanifested dimension.

- Consciousness, or Spirit, is the unmanifested dimension, and its intelligent energy permeates everything.
- Human beings are not casual observers, but active participants in the unfolding evolutionary process.

These observations are part of the "remembering" of a new life-sustaining culture. After having been discarded, they have returned full circle—rediscovered at this monumental time. Going deeply into them so they are experienced as archetypal energies, rather than just abstract thoughts, helps us adapt to the disorientation and anguish we feel at having the land and sea demolished before our eyes.

Joanna Macy says it well in her book *Coming Back to Life* (co-authored with Molly Brown): "Now, in our time ... three rivers—anguish for our world, scientific breakthroughs, and ancestral teachings—flow together. From the confluence of these rivers we drink."[35] To drink of them is to be re-energized and replenished. We can go forth in dreaming a new dream, where a new science and appropriate technology are in service to the heart!

So instead of wishing for a bucolic return to a lost paradise of Paleolithic living, we can view the industrial age, and what led up to it, as a painful and destructive—yet necessary—step in planetary evolution, as a manifestation of our descent into separation consciousness. Every era on planet Earth—even the extinction spasms—has eventually led to something grander, more creative and abundant. Why should this time be any different? We can return to the Garden, but it will be a different Garden. Duane Elgin, author and scientist, adds to this sentiment in his book *Promise Ahead*:

After 13 billion years of evolution, we stand upon the Earth as agents of self-reflective and creative action on behalf of the universe. We see that we are participants in an unceasing miracle of creation. This recognition brings a new confidence that our potentials are as exalted, magnificent, and mysterious as the living universe that surrounds and sustains us.[36]

To fully embrace what Elgin is saying—which is in accordance with both indigenous teachings and the new science—involves *trusting* the very nature of the universe. Even when we don't understand why such awful things can happen in the world despite our best efforts to transform them, there is something much larger and deeper at work that can give us steadiness of mind when we align with it. This mysterious "something" is so vast and intelligent it can produce coral reefs and spiral galaxies!

Cultivating trust in the unfolding of the universe allows us to explore new, creative possibilities instead of being paralyzed by fear and despair. Even Thomas Berry, who wrote volumes on the horror of what is being perpetrated by humans against the Earth, observed:

The basic mood of the future might well be one of confidence in the continuing revelation that takes place in and through the Earth. If the dynamics of the Universe from the beginning shaped the course of the heavens, lighted the sun, and formed the Earth ... there is reason to believe that the same guiding process is precisely what has awakened in us our present understanding of ourselves and our relation to this stupendous process.[37]

---

* The ego, as defined in this book, is not synonymous with healthy self-esteem and a sense of personal power; in fact, the model of spiritual ecology prescribed here strongly encourages the development of those qualities.

Chapter 5

Getting Started: Guidelines and Overview

You never change things by fighting the existing reality.
To change something, build a new model that makes the
existing model obsolete.

—R. Buckminster Fuller

This chapter describes the sequence of elements in the first few hours of a typical Wild Earth Intensive (WEI), their tempo, and the philosophy behind them. This is a particularly important time because it sets the tone for everything that will follow. Careful oversight of these early hours by the facilitators helps get the group off to a good start, although insisting on the same degree of tight structuring for the remainder of the workshop would restrict the imagination and ease of the participants. Guides who are decisive, yet flexible, will foster spontaneity and creativity.

The key elements to include in the opening section of the WEI are:

- Welcoming and Gratitude
- Site Logistics and Agreements
- Brief Introductions
- Theoretical Framework
- Deeper Breathing
- Focused Sharing
- Intention and Dedication

It's a good idea to begin in the morning when people are fresh. The opening elements should take about three hours. Because most of this time is spent sitting, make sure there are several short breaks for people to stretch, go to the bathroom, and breathe fully. People maintain better attention when their bodies are cared for.

In general, throughout the WEI, the transitions between the various elements need to be given the same consideration as the elements themselves. Balancing the many ways human beings use their energy helps provide a healthy atmosphere in which groups can thrive. For example, if people have been listening, at some point they will need to speak. If they have been serious, they will need to play. If they have been together, they will need to spend time alone. And if they have been indoors, they will need to go out into nature.

Welcoming and Gratitude

Striking a tone of respect and caring at the outset can reverberate throughout the duration of the Intensive. When people feel respected and cared for, they feel safe. When they feel safe, they allow themselves to be vulnerable and "go deep."

If you are serving as the lead guide, ask the participants to gather into a circle, and sit among them as an equal. Welcome them warmly. You may wish to say a few words of gratitude, reminding the group that life is an amazing miracle that we can appreciate now. A sincere expression of gratitude helps participants relax, and they will be less inclined to distraction and anxiety about what will happen later. It stimulates a shift in the collective mood from the hurried, "got-to-get-to-the-next-thing" way of modern life to one of contentment with what is. The words you use could be something like this:

Out of the great mystery of existence, we find ourselves in this remarkable time and place. Regardless of our circumstances, it is good to be alive. We are grateful for all the forces, both within and without, that created this unique opportunity: the bounty of Mother Earth, which includes the fuel that brought us here; the well-wishes of others; and our own determination to do something really meaningful with our lives. It took a lot to bring us together. All the guides are glad that everyone arrived safely. We look forward to getting to know each of you in a very special way.

The exact words that are spoken are less important than the choosing of an attitude of gratitude by the facilitators. Along with treating the group with care and respect, your choice to perceive the abundance inherent in life lays the foundation for a transformative experience for everyone. Gratitude is an elixir. When we drink it, the blinders of habitual assumptions fall away and we see with eyes of wonder. We rediscover the simple things. The wind blowing through the trees, a gurgling stream in the moonlight, a robin bouncing around in a meadow, and our incredible ability to move our bodies upon the Earth are but a few of the endless blessings bestowed on us by virtue of our birth.

Living in gratitude is a resilient, expansive way of being. It can be likened to the profound qualities of water: fluidity and power. Water does not resist anything but eventually discovers a way to flow around or over all barriers in its path—and it is powerful enough to put out a fire or polish a stone. The more we can appreciate the "whole package" we are given in this life, the more we can slide around the boulders that seem to block our journey. That does not mean we don't crash into them from time to time, but when we are able to recognize the incalculable gifts we have been given, we are less likely to get stuck.

Gratitude is the basis for ecstasy,* the state of consciousness in which we fully embrace whatever we are experiencing. We say thanks to the tears of joy *and* sorrow. Both kinds of tears are part of the River of Life, which in its sheer grandeur takes us home, whether we find ourselves in a still eddy or in a raging rapid.

47

One way to make our gratitude tangible is by lighting an "eternal flame" that will burn continuously for the ten days of the WEI. Depending on site conditions and facilitator skills and preferences, this can be as simple as lighting a candle (and replacing it when it burns down, lighting the next candle from its flame) or as elaborate as starting a "tipi-style fire" with a bow drill or similar primitive fire-making method. In both cases, the honoring intent during the lighting and the commitment to keep the fire going are what is most important. After the flame has been lit, one of the guides might offer a prayer of gratitude along these lines:

> *Oh, sacred fire, you have been burning since the beginning of time. A part of the sun here on Earth, you have kept us warm in the cold and provided light in the darkness. We thank you for your mysterious, life-giving power.*

Paradoxically, we can be grateful for death as well as life. From the depths of our gratitude, we can see a totality, a sacred wholeness, in which death makes life possible. Death is the passing away of all forms—from microbes to stars. It is the exhalation of the universe, in which nothing is permanent. How truly bizarre it would be if things only arose but did not pass away, if the tide only went out, if there was only day and no night! Knowing the ephemeral nature of existence makes the gift of life that much more precious. Therefore, cultivating gratitude and appreciation for life—not just human life—is woven throughout a WEI. We begin here and end here.

Site Logistics and Agreements

There are many details specific to the site where a workshop is held that may be too cumbersome to go over at the beginning of the gathering. Instead, distribute a written handout, created by the organizers in advance. However, certain key points bear repeating verbally. Make sure everyone knows that certain tasks need to be fulfilled in order for everyone to live together as smoothly as possible. These tasks include washing dishes; preparing and cooking food (although hiring outside cooks is preferable); cleaning up; turning out the lights at night; waking the group in the morning; and so on. Part of instilling a spirit of community is getting everyone's agreement that these tasks will be divided among the members of the group. (The facilitators should not try to do everything!) One way to do this is to mention each task to the group and wait for someone to say "yes," agreeing to perform that task, before going on to the next. Then, post a list of those tasks in a visible location and ask that the participants sign up for the tasks they have volunteered to do.

After the physical logistics have been clarified, it is time to go over some group agreements. One essential agreement is that every WEI activity is optional; but when one chooses to engage in them, it is important to do so wholeheartedly. Another is that confidentiality for anything personal shared during the Intensive will be respected; nothing will be recounted to others or attributed to the person who shared it unless that person has given their permission. A third is that, although touching one another in a safe and supportive way is a normal outcome of feeling connected, anyone is welcome at any time to request not to be touched. State these agreements, and, after each one, request a nodding of heads to indicate assent.

Because of its importance, I usually present the following agreement separately toward the end of the first day or at the beginning of the second day. This agreement is to take responsibility for one's personal experience. It is an agreement that the participants make with themselves in which they consistently ask, "What can I learn from this situation?" This approach to life is empowering. Taking full responsibility means not blaming ourselves or others when we don't feel good. It means taking the necessary steps internally and externally to rectify the situation—and within a WEI, to ask the facilitators for help with any perceived problem before bringing it to the attention of the group. This kind of self-awareness goes far in creating a harmonious group environment.

The WEI can stretch everyone's comfort zone because we are exploring new terrain—physically, emotionally, and socially. Difficult feelings may arise, and that is completely natural. By stating this, facilitators can alleviate some anxiety people may be feeling about how they will come across to others in the workshop. That doesn't matter here; what we are seeking is the wonderful experience of being true to ourselves and as authentic as possible.

Brief Introductions

Asking each member of the group to briefly introduce themselves is the next step in building this new community. Let them know that they will have time to share more fully later. At this point, each person, one by one, including the facilitators, will say their name, where they currently live, and one thing, big or small, they feel grateful for.

To help everyone learn each other's name, we sometimes toss a small, soft ball to one person, saying their name as we do so. That person tosses it to someone else while saying their name, and the game continues until everyone has gotten the ball. We repeat the same pattern once or twice, tossing in a few more balls as a challenge, and thereby including that crucial dimension missing in so many adult lives: play!

Theoretical Framework

Despite the overall focus on experiential learning, an explanation of why we do this work is a valuable part of the WEI. Helping participants attain greater understanding of the "big picture" can give them increased motivation to fully participate.

Many of the participants may require an intellectual foundation in order to feel fully comfortable and to integrate the various activities. You, as a guide, can provide this by giving a ten-to-fifteen-minute presentation during the opening activities and then providing bite-size chunks of conceptual information throughout the remainder of the Intensive. While introducing the theoretical framework of the WEI, emphasize what is most meaningful for you and what evokes your enthusiasm. Expressing theory in your own words, rather than trying to mimic other leaders in this field, will be most effective. Drawing on your personal experiences while presenting this material is the best way to keep everyone engaged.

Here are the main principles I like to include in the theoretical description at the workshop's beginning. They are a synopsis of the concepts introduced in Chapter 4:

- *Human beings are one with the rest of life.* To illustrate this, you can simply draw a circle on a large piece of paper or a chalkboard. This represents the Circle of Life. Then draw a stick figure of a person outside the circle. This is how modern humans tend to view themselves. Our individual and collective mission—within both the WEI and the larger society—is to know in our bones that we never left the circle; we just had a strange dream (a nightmare!) that we did. Unfortunately, the dream seems all too real, and so we humans suffer and cause tremendous destruction in the process. The chronic feeling of being apart is something that we all grapple with, but simply realizing intellectually that "we are all connected" can't liberate us. Instead, we need to experience this connection repeatedly until it takes hold. Then we can *know* we are an essential part of creation, not more than nor less than the snails and the stars.

- *A nature-based, sustainable culture is possible.* We gather in the WEI to demonstrate precisely that, albeit for a short period. The future is created in the now through our powerful ability to dream and vision. We can be a seed for something healthy and innovative, rooted in the land.

- *We can remember an ancient way of knowing* that helped us humans thrive and develop for over a hundred-thousand years. A severe amnesia has beset modern humans, who have forgotten who they are and who believe that civilization in its most recent expression is somehow the pinnacle of human development. To recover our memory, we can take essential cues from past and present-day indigenous peoples. Their comprehensive knowledge of how nature operates—which is not restricted by conceptual thought—provides a basis for a mutually beneficial relationship between humans and the Earth.

- *Wisdom and brilliance are encoded in every human* and can be unleashed under the right circumstances. In a WEI, we are learning through direct experience and an increased capacity to feel. That means having a personal intention of fully experiencing our pain and our joy, and doing so with as much kindness and awareness as we can muster. This is the key component of reclaiming our wild souls! By supporting one another through the emotional ups and downs of the Intensive, we can draw out this wise brilliance into the open.

- *A different model of reality is emerging beneath the surface of mainstream discourse.* The frontiers of science are describing the same territory that indigenous elders, Buddhist teachers, and mystics from all the religious traditions have known for thousands of years. This territory is revelatory, numinous, and awe inspiring, and forces us to rethink everything we have been taught about what it means to be human!

The principles outlined above are inspiring, but even more basic to creating a sustainable—better yet, lasting and ecstatic— culture is the love and courage needed to make it possible. The theoretical framework is only a signpost. It has no power to change us, unless we can allow ourselves to feel and experience what it is pointing toward. This is why it is important for you to encourage a wholehearted involvement in all the processes.

After responding to any questions that may have arisen from the short presentation, it is usually a good time for a short (five– ten minute) break.

Deep Breathing

When the group returns, invite everyone to breathe more fully. You can offer your version of the following guidance:

The critical value of receiving enough oxygen into our cells should be so obvious that it's not worth mentioning, but most people in the developed world don't breathe deeply. When we are not exercising, our breath tends to be shallow and uneven. This curtails our ability to think clearly and lowers our energy level. To breathe deeply and consciously can be transformative. There is no easier or simpler way of taking in the life force, and, when done consistently, it feels so good! Let's take turns gently reminding each other to breathe during our time together.

Focused Sharing

An increased sense of intimacy and trust is one of the wonderful benefits of a WEI. One of the cultural forms that support such a sense is a talking or sharing circle (described in detail in Chapter 6) in which each person has a chance to respond, uninterrupted, to the simple question, "Why are you here?" I like to modify this first talking circle a bit from the "standard" version used at other times during a WEI, in which a single object is passed from person to person as they speak.

53

In this version, place in the center of the circle a loose bundle of sticks, containing one for each participant, which you have assembled beforehand. Then invite each person to choose a stick from the bundle. Narrow sticks about a foot long, with a variety of textures and features, are ideal, because participants will be asked to recognize theirs among the others on the last day of the Intensive.

Once each person is holding their stick, invite them to examine it closely for a few minutes and get to know its unique features. Then ask if someone is feeling brave enough to jump in by speaking from their heart. After this first person is finished talking, they pass their stick to the next person who feels moved to speak, to hold along with their own. After the second person is done speaking, they hand the two sticks to the third person, and so on, until everyone has shared and the last person is holding the entire bundle of sticks.

At that point, point out that one stick is easily broken but together they are very strong. This is a cliché, but it is true. In a society that puts so much emphasis on the individual, paying attention to group solidarity is a healthy counterbalance. Then ask if someone will volunteer to serve as a "bundle carrier," and give this person a colorful cloth and ribbon to wrap around the sticks. This person will take care of the sticks (not physically hold them the entire time) until the close of the workshop, at which time each person will reclaim their own stick as a memento of the time spent together.

To increase the meaningfulness of the general question, "Why are you here?" it is helpful to also ask the group, at the outset of the sharing circle, to consider these additional questions: "What in this world, great or small, would I take great risks to protect from harm?" "What do I care about so passionately that to see it destroyed or compromised would be unbearable?" These questions elicit an emotional response. They help the participants consider what they most want from the WEI, and for the wider world. When more fully articulated, the answers to these questions become the individual and group intentions that act as beacons for all that follows.

Here are a few snippets of what people have said in the opening circle:

My heart called me here, the Earth called me here, to heal myself, to heal the world, to heal the Earth ... The dream of us [humans] living differently moves me to no end. When I thought about the question, "What in this world, great or small, would I take great risks to protect from harm?" tears came to my eyes. Every last thing that is sacred and natural ... All living things are inherently valuable rather than needing a study to prove it ... Every last piece of Earth that is not invaded by noise, pollution, or developers, and every person who is willing to gently and ardently stand in the way of its destruction. —J. F.

When the sticks started to get passed around, and they came to me as a thicker bundle, I realized I was returning to a way of life that was slower and felt gentler, truer. I did not realize how fast I was moving ... My husband and I are thinking about having a child. I think if I go ahead and have the baby, I would do anything to make sure he or she has a good life. —N. J.

I feel surrounded by the quiet forest and I know I've come to the right place. This is an unusual feeling because things are so fragmented in my life. I really want to feel more connected. When I think about the bigger picture or even smaller things like wild animals that are in jeopardy because of the way we live, I just feel overwhelmed. I need hope. —N. F.

I am here because something deep within me called me. I don't always connect with it, yet it is something pure and true ... like watching the early morning sun sparkle across fresh snow. I am here to learn how to live from that place. From a wider angle, I am also here because I know there is something more to life than shopping malls, fancy clothes, and the gratuitous sex I see on MTV. Our consumer society encourages relentless wanting ... there is never enough. But the deep whisper of truth and purity tells me that there is another way. A way of complete abundance and unconditional love. A way where everything that I am is good enough, right now. I am here because I trust that whisper. —M. I.

What in this world, great or small, would I take great risks to protect from harm? This is a big one for me that has many layers. I would take great risks to protect the people I know and love. I would take great risks to protect my home. I would take great risks to protect the sacredness of all life, from the small snail with its slimy antennae to the coyote calling to the moon, to the sloth I have yet to meet ... the trees everywhere, the mosses on them, and the squirrels that frolic in the boughs. I believe they all should be protected from harm. But it is not only these physical manifestations of energy, but also the effortless way in which they play, breathe, live, and die. The cycles of sacred exchange, I believe, are my biggest teacher and the most important thing to help save. —M. I.

As more and more people share (and if someone prefers not to say anything, that is fine), there is a palpable shift in the group energy. A common bond begins to form, based on the times we live in, the pressure cooker of intense evolutionary change, and the desire to live in a different way. Wisdom and caring that go beyond individual concerns start to emerge. Suddenly, as a facilitator, you may realize you would not want to be doing anything else. The opening act is underway in the real-life theater that is the Intensive, and by its close, the group will be convinced this is how they want to live all the time.

Intention and Dedication

Creating a common intention to return to the Circle of Life—to really choose life with every cell in our bodies—is the most wonderful challenge of our time. Joseph Goldstein, one of America's most respected dharma teachers, echoes what Buddhists have been saying for centuries: "Choosing to formulate a wholesome intention (and then acting on it) is of paramount importance. Intention is the volitional energy that has the power to bring about either wholesome or unwholesome actions. As it is said in the Tibetan tradition, 'Everything rests on the tip of motivation.'"[1]

Ironically, by focusing on connection, a WEI can trigger the pain of disconnection. It can bring ancestral memories of a long-lost way of life into our consciousness. It can bring trauma, whether personal or planetary, into the light. We may feel grief stricken, powerless, or fearful. But when we make a point at the beginning of a WEI to dedicate our work together for the benefit of all beings, including future generations, something much larger steps in, helping us transmute difficult feelings and keep moving forward.

Our dedication, when openly declared, reinforces our intention to live a life of joy and balance, individually and collectively. This declaration, spoken now by one of the facilitators, could sound like this:

How unique it is to have the opportunity to reclaim the wild within. Let's dedicate this time together to the big dream: a truly life-sustaining culture, one that honors all creatures great and small. We open to the possibility that our Earth-honoring intention, combined with countless other acts of merit occurring all over the world, will, in Martin Luther King's words, "have the final word in reality."[2]

---

* A few more words about ecstasy: We long for it. When we taste it, we know we are home. It wells up inside of us when we least expect it. It's our natural, wild state that we dare not admit, when our souls merge with the divine mystery in a cosmic remembering: "Oh, this is way it's supposed to be." It is so ordinarily extraordinary. We feel it in the trees blowing in the wind, and it is both the wind and the space around the wind. It's oneness and diversity, our pleasure and our pain all swirling in a sacred vortex that begins and ends Now. It's the love in our hearts completely unchained—pouring out toward everyone and everything and finding out "they" were in our hearts all along.

Chapter 6

Listening

When people are listened to sensitively, they tend to listen to themselves with more care and to make clear exactly what they are feeling and thinking.

—Carl Rogers

We usually don't think that "mere listening" has the power to transform. Yet truly listening to another person—and that includes speaking at the right time—is part of sharing our love, the greatest power of all. We know the truth of this when we are on the receiving end of that love, and experience the incredible feeling of being heard and understood.

In the Native Siberian and Native American traditions, the act of listening has been elevated to an art form. While collaborating with remarkable people from these traditions and experiencing this firsthand, I was so moved that I made it my goal to study their universal teachings and pass them on to the wider world. These are cultures that genuinely value and cultivate the seemingly ordinary things of life, like simple listening, above commercial concerns. Of course, there were a few tribal members whose behavior was less than exemplary, but by and large, I was consistently amazed by the collective devotion to *healthy relationship*, of which listening is always an essential nutrient.

While with these peoples, it also became clear that I brought to our conversations ingrained preconceptions that prevented me from truly hearing them. I attempted to listen in the same way they did, but, like most of us in the dominant Western culture, I had never been taught how. In fact, the Native American and Siberian elders told me that despite a rigorous determination to free myself from the conqueror's worldview—in which an unwillingness to truly listen is inherent—it might be impossible to completely eradicate it.

However, the elders did commend me on my efforts and said that learning to listen was probably the single most important life skill anyone could develop. For them, listening meant paying attention not just with one's ears but with one's entire being, and being attentive not just to other people but to all of life. Siberian elder Danil Mamyev, a university-trained geologist and a spiritual leader in the Todosh clan of the indigenous Altai nation, explained: "From the earliest age, I was taught to listen to nature with my heart. The smallest plant and the biggest mountain were my friends. Of course, there were dangers in the taiga, so good listening also kept me alive."[1]

I tried to summarize for him why this level of listening was so difficult for me and my fellow moderns. My explanation went something like this:

With the advent of industrial society, we started to measure our worth more by our productivity and salary than by our character. Life began to speed up to meet production deadlines and the ideal of efficiency, and we internalized the belief that time is money. Today, in our hurried, competitive environment, most of us do not take the time to be truly attentive and present. The communication that does take place is focused on the exchange of mental concepts, and it is our intellects—not our hearts and souls—that most often meet when we talk to one another.

Also, we often hide aspects of who we are, for fear of being judged and found lacking, and we tend not to share deeply and honestly on a regular basis. Instead, our everyday conversations are 'newsy' and superficial. If the basis of loving is paying attention, as many psychologists such as Carl Rogers emphasize, a lot of us are left feeling unloved and disconnected.

Of course, the situation is not as one-sided as I described to Danil. There are times when we experience the wonderful feeling of being truly heard—when someone not only has comprehended the meaning of our words but has wholeheartedly received us. Then we are truly *communing* in our communication! Thich Nhat Hahn calls this state "interbeing," and explains that it is a deeply satisfying, higher level of relationship.[2] Once we've experienced it, we long for more. This is one of the reasons why romantic partnerships are so sought after: "Finally, someone will listen to me!" But the dysfunction of not listening well runs deep, ratcheting up the difficulty in many of these relationships. This dysfunction, characterized by being half there and half elsewhere, is passed from parents to their children, who in turn pass it on to *their* children.

Since the parent-child relationship is where cultural norms are shaped, we adults who wish to shape a new culture need to go deep within and cultivate attuned listening in our own hearts and minds. Consistent listening takes courage—sometimes we do not like what we hear and therefore interrupt or veer away, to quell our anxiety so that we feel more comfortable. Courage gives us the strength to stay with what's uncomfortable, and in the process, we become better listeners.

Once we muster up the courage, we need to practice. The exercises described later in this chapter are an invitation to practice listening in the friendly environment of the Wild Earth Intensive (WEI). The working assumption of these exercises is that we are much more alike than different. When we listen, we are doing more than hearing one another's truth; we are also learning about ourselves.

The following story beautifully illustrates how attuned and sensitive listening breaks down the walls of the separate self.

It is from a chapter written by Christine Longaker, a hospice founder and longtime trainer of hospice workers, in the book *The Wisdom of Listening*, edited by Mark Brady. In the chapter, Longaker suggests that, before meeting with someone whom we expect to be difficult, we imagine exchanging places with that person, as if they were "another you." We hold a strong intention to realize that they feel the same core desires and fears as we do. Like us, they want to feel happy, and are afraid to suffer. Like us, they have almost certainly experienced rejection, loneliness, trauma, fear, and grief. Like us, they have at some point felt misunderstood and unfairly judged. And, like us, they have felt anxious at the prospect of old age and death. By keeping these unifying human concerns in mind, we can listen more receptively and approach the interaction in the optimal way. Longaker also recommends daily meditation practice to activate receptivity.

Longaker is asked by Marisa, a thirty-something attractive and energetic doctor, how to cope with an ornery and bossy patient. In reply, she explains the practice of putting oneself in the other's shoes. Marisa tries this and tells Longaker, "When I exchanged places with my patient, suddenly I was this old woman who had constant pain, who felt ugly, helpless, and unwanted. And when I saw this attractive young doctor coming into my room, full of smiles, I hated her more than anything."

The next time Marisa went into her patient's room, she wasn't smiling cheerfully. Feeling genuine understanding and love for the old woman, Marisa was able to meet her gaze, even while the woman continued to scream in anger at her. "I knew just how she felt. In my heart, I told her that I understood her anger and that it was all right. She continued to be demanding, but after she saw I was not reacting anymore, her tone grew quieter. When I left her room and walked down the corridor, my mind was peaceful and calm as though the meditation was still continuing."

Longaker asked Marisa what happened when she went to see the next patient. "That man was very sweet and kind, and immediately I reacted with pleasure." She laughed. "That's when I realized I had lost my equanimity, and how important it is to keep my meditation going in every situation, whether it is difficult or pleasant."[3]

Marisa's last comment reveals how deep listening showed her both the ups and the downs of her reactions as originating from the selfsame source—reactivity! Equanimity, on the other hand, was considered one of the four divine abodes taught by the Buddha. It is a state of inner balance that is not upset by the "opposites" such as gain and loss, praise and blame, and pleasure and pain. Learning to practice deep inner listening is meditative and it cultivates equanimity.

Listening in a Wild Earth Intensive Starts with the Body

The first step in being more receptive to others and the Earth is listening inwardly to our own bodies. How can we know how to treat "out there" if we don't know how to treat "in here"?

In a Wild Earth Intensive (WEI), we take care of our bodies in a way that goes beyond physicality to a more subtle energetic awareness that nourishes the whole person. We eat healthy food (locally grown whenever possible), breathe deeply, give and receive massage, and get plenty of relaxed exercise through dance, movement, play, and nature immersion, while noticing whenever possible the sensations in our bodies throughout these activities. *Noticing* is another way of saying "being aware of." Over time, we discover that listening and awareness are synonymous!

Inhabiting the body through conscious awareness is something WEI guides practice in their daily lives. After explaining to the group the benefits of body awareness—which include relaxation, living more in the present moment, and greater connection—the guides gently activate this awareness in the participants at various times throughout the WEI by pausing and asking them, "What's happening now?" or "Can you feel the energy in your body?" When everyone understands how to do this, the guides discontinue using verbal cues and switch to a bell or chime to signal "it's time to be aware." Doing these three to four times a day can be a powerful technique for stimulating more continuous awareness and adds to the ceremonial atmosphere of the Intensive.

Practicing attentive, embodied listening while other participants speak deepens the connection among the group members. Though it may take several days for the participants to become accustomed to monitoring their own body awareness (it's rare for anyone to be engaged in it a hundred percent of the time), using the bell to gently remind everyone to bring awareness to the moment is well worth the effort.

If you are facilitating, you will want to convey early in the WEI the invaluable contribution of both inner and interpersonal listening to the Intensive, as well as to life. Your demonstrable listening skills, in contrast to the poor listening that is often the norm in social and academic settings, sets a good example. Participants may not have any idea what better listening can be like, so modeling it to the best of your ability can make a difference in their lives.

You might poke fun at the submissive style of listening sometimes demanded by our parents or teachers—spoken or simply implied, it commands, "Listen to me or else!"—or at the conversational sparring matches people can get into, where nobody gets to finish a sentence without being interrupted.

The unusual opportunity for relational practice that the WEI offers can motivate people to try different approaches to habitual patterns that no longer serve (like poor listening). Possibly the most valuable approach is simply bringing the light of consciousness to these patterns, which, in itself, helps us be more patient with ourselves and one another.

Paying attention to one another in a relaxed way and treating each other as equals not only feels better, but also creates a sacred space where everybody can realize the whole *is* greater than the sum of its parts. There is no pressure during a WEI to impress others or to be competitive in our conversations; to the contrary, it is a place to "get it in one's bones" that everyone's voice is valuable. You may wish to state clearly that we aren't gathered to compete with each other—and that includes in our conversations.

When it dawns on the group that each member will be listened to with consistency and respect, there is a noticeable sense of relief. This realization may take some time to sink in for the entire group, but when it finally does, a foundation of safety has truly been laid—a foundation that sets the stage for a deep and amazing group journey.

Introduction to the Art of Listening

As a facilitator, on the first afternoon or on the following morning of a WEI, present your version of the following guidelines:

A new, ecstatic culture requires us to learn some new habits. A really important habit is learning to listen well. When we are listened to attentively, we feel heard. And when we feel heard, we feel safe. This sense of safety slows down our pace of communication in a positive way. It enables us to hear and feel the stories of others with more presence and compassion.

Here are some effective practices for listening attentively in our time together:

- *Whether we are together as a group or in pairs, we give the person speaking our full attention, without interrupting them or talking to someone else.*
- *We keep in mind that one doesn't have to "take care of" or "fix" the speaker by offering advice or trying to solve their*

problems. Allowing people to speak what is true for them without commentary is extremely healing, even if they don't come to a resolution.

- *We listen to ourselves while we're speaking. We pause and notice our breathing and bodily sensations whenever possible. This allows us to remain aware and provides a more easeful and spacious environment in which everyone can be heard.*

These guidelines are not meant to be rules, just kinder ways of relating that teach us how to live more satisfying lives. Old cultural behaviors die hard, so be easy on yourself as you try these out. It can take time and practice to learn new ways.

After this short presentation, two of the guides might briefly parody poor communication. The speaker can attempt to get their point across while the listener offers advice, interrupts, denies the authenticity of the speaker's feelings, looks distracted, and demonstrates other examples of not being present. This always brings forth plenty of laughter as people recognize past experiences.

Practicing Listening in a Wild Earth Intensive

There are four ways of listening that are honed by the activities in a WEI. These are:

- Listening to nature (see Chapter 8)
- Listening to oneself (see above discussion on the body and Chapter 13)
- Listening in pairs
- Listening within a group

The last two items are the subject of the following exercises.

Open Sentences

Purpose: To practice listening in pairs

Duration: 45 minutes

The simple agreement "We'll take turns listening" is a gift to one another that lays a foundation for connection. We may have been taught that a deep feeling of connection is only available with romantic partners, but in fact it is a powerful element of any culture based on mutual understanding and compassion.

Ask the participants to divide into pairs. Explain that you will provide the beginning of a sentence, and one person in the pair will have three minutes to complete the sentence, while the other person listens without interrupting. Then they will switch roles as speaker and listener, and the second person will complete the same sentence. Invite them to make eye contact with each other during the process if they can. During this exercise, they will complete four or five sentences on a variety of topics, some of which are suggested below. After several rounds of listening/talking, they will form new pairs.

Structuring the listening in this way gives each person a chance to relax and absorb what the other is saying. In addition, because it is very rare that we have the opportunity to talk without interruption for even three minutes, this allows the speaker to have the experience of communicating waves of thought without somebody else editing the flow. Finally, holding eye contact for that long is also rare in our culture; some people find it hard at first, but an eye-to-eye gaze truly acknowledges another person.

As you might expect, the subject matter of the sentences used in this exercise is the relationship between self and world, and between mind and nature. These statements are designed to lead the participants into an exploration of their connection with and deep feelings toward the Earth. Here are some examples of sentences that we use:

- *A place in nature I really love is. . .*
- *One of my childhood memories related to the natural world is. . .*
- *One thing that moves me about being a human on this planet right now is. . .*
- *If I were totally in charge, humans would relate to the Earth and each other by. . .*
- *One of my favorite animals is. . .*
- *When I think of the ocean, I am reminded of. . .*
- *There is a beautiful, sacred place I've read about. I would like to visit there because. . .*

Several other paired sharing exercises are described elsewhere in this book and use this same approach of taking turns speaking without interruption and listening attentively.

The Talking Circle

Purpose: To encourage us to speak and listen from the heart
Duration: Varies depending on group size and time allotted per speaker
The talking circle, or sharing circle, is particularly powerful for building group trust and bonding. It has the same "ground rules" for listening as the paired sharing exercises. In a WEI, we use it almost daily. The creation of talking circles has been historically credited to North American Indians, but I have seen it practiced by Native Siberians and South Americans who claim they have been "doing it forever." A talking circle is where the participants take turns "speaking from the heart"—sharing their thoughts and feelings as authentically as possible—while the rest of the group listens. The practice is simple to explain but profound in its implications. It is a healing process, full of rich nuances, that helps break down some of the conditioned judgments we may have about other people based on their dress, race, politics, philosophy, class, family background, and so on.

After you have participated in a few well-run talking circles, it becomes evident that every person has something important, even profound, to say when allowed to do so in an accepting atmosphere. I am often surprised how a process so uncomplicated can be so enriching. Deep connections that may last a lifetime can emerge among those who share in a talking circle.

The combination of focused attention and confidentiality in a talking circle creates a sense of safety that enables all the members to express themselves—even those who are usually reluctant to speak. When all are heard and feel understood, individual self-esteem is strengthened, and a wise "group mind" begins to develop.

Note that, in a WEI, talking circles are not used for resolving conflict or solving problems that may arise during the Intensive. In a different context, they can certainly serve these purposes, but I have found that a group needs to be very experienced with this process in order to achieve positive results. A WEI talking circle has the overarching intentions of gaining insight, integrating what has been learned thus far, and strengthening connection with one another.

Introducing the Talking Circle
Because a "talking object"—a stone, stick, feather, or other object from nature—will be passed around the circle, that object should be at hand. Here is an example of what you might say to introduce this important group experience:

> *A talking circle is a sacred space. Each member is considered equal to any other, and each is asked to maintain an attitude of respect and open-mindedness toward the others. The circle itself represents interconnectedness, continuity, and the cycles of life. Gathering in a circle reflects the reality that no one is*

more important than another, unlike the more common seating pattern of having someone at the front of a crowd or the head of a table. In addition, sitting in a circle allows each person to see the eyes of the others—a powerful way to build trust and empathy, and to bond with one another.

In a talking circle, we pass around a talking object, which symbolizes our connection to the natural world. The talking object also serves as a reminder that we are here to honor each other with our undivided attention. Each of us may speak, without interruption from others, for as long as we hold the talking object. When we are finished, we pass it to the next person. You may opt to pass the talking object along if you do not feel moved to speak, or you may hold it for a while without speaking. The talking object will be passed around the circle twice; on the second pass, anyone who did not speak the first time may do so, if they wish.

A sense of safety and confidentiality is essential in a talking circle. For this reason, we agree that whatever is spoken in the circle will stay "within the circle" and will not be repeated to people who weren't present. In addition, if you would like to talk later with another participant about what they shared, ask them first if they want to do so. They might not want to delve into it at that moment.

In summary, these are the basic agreements and intentions we uphold:

- *The talking circle is viewed as a sacred time and space.*
- *Each person has an opportunity to speak but can opt not to.*
- *The person holding the talking object is given full attention from the group for the time allotted, without interruption or cross talk.*
- *Each person speaks from the heart.*
- *Everything that is shared remains confidential.*

It's a good idea to also make the following points about the roles of listener and speaker. Offering this guidance can prevent some common problems that might arise (e.g., people commenting out of turn, participants experiencing performance anxiety, or intellectual discussion supplanting sharing from the heart). But be concise so as not to dissipate the energy of the group before the circle even begins!

Guidance for Listeners

Listen from your heart. Learn to pay attention to what's being said without analyzing or evaluating it, or feeling that you must rescue or heal a person who is sharing difficult things.

Listen with an open mind. Even if you don't agree with the speaker, seek to understand the underlying needs and values they are trying to express.

As tempting as it might sometimes be, refrain from commenting aloud or in other ways taking attention from the speaker.

Notice what gets in the way of your full attention as a listener. Usually it's either rehearsing what you are planning to say when your turn comes or rehashing what you already said. This is a great opportunity for self-awareness. Don't berate yourself for getting distracted. Simply observe where your mind goes, then refocus on the present moment.

Guidance for Speakers

In addition to expressing your thoughts and ideas, take this opportunity in a safe environment to share your feelings as well. When you are as authentic as possible and trust your own spontaneity, you enliven the process for everyone.

Speak the truth of your own unique experience, using "I" statements. Besides typical prose, you can express yourself in a variety of ways: sharing a personal story, using movement or metaphors, reciting a poem, or even singing a song.

Since time is limited, ask yourself, "What most needs to be said at this moment?" or "What is most alive in me right now?" If the answer doesn't correspond to the topic chosen for the circle, that's okay.

Take the risk to share vulnerably, and to say difficult things without self-judgment and without blaming others.

Stretch your comfort zone. If you are shy, try speaking loudly enough that the trees and rocks can hear you, not just the circle of people, and take the full time you are allotted. If you tend to be wordy, try allowing some silence during your sharing as you choose your words concisely and precisely.

There are two other ways to pass the talking object, instead of around the circle in a predictable sequence. In one method, whoever wishes to share first does so, and then spontaneously carries the object to someone who has not yet spoken. This increases alertness and spontaneity and has the energetic effect of weaving a web. Another method (which takes more time, and so may be best suited to small groups) is to place the talking object in the center of the circle and allow each person, as they feel moved, to claim it and speak, and then return it when they are done. This allows each person's organic impulses to be the motivation for speaking. It also tends to interject some moments of silence between speakers, which can deepen the impact of what has been shared.

Tips for the Talking-Circle Facilitator
If you don't have experience leading a talking circle, don't worry; with practice, you will get better at introducing the concepts and holding the kind of presence that inspires rich sharing. In fact, a talking circle is a good opportunity for less-experienced facilitators to learn to be more attentive and responsible within a group. In addition, it is likely that some participants will have

been in a talking circle before and will automatically infuse an ease and eagerness into the circle.

While a talking circle can't really go wrong as long as the basic principles are followed, I have learned from my experience with facilitating or participating in many circles that certain things will enhance the experience. The tips that follow don't need to be explained to the group, but hopefully will offer a deeper foundation for the facilitator.

Choose a meaningful topic to discuss in order to provide focus and clarity. There are countless topics to choose from, and they will vary based on the priorities of the group. A few topics we often use in a WEI, depending on when during the Intensive we are doing the circle, are:

- What brought you here?
- What are some of your impressions after connecting with the natural world?
- How would you summarize what you have learned so far?
- How do you *feel* about this time on Earth?
- What makes you laugh?
- What is your relationship to your ancestors, the land where you live, and your tribal/ethnic background?

Begin the talking circle with a simple ritual. Include some or all of the following elements: Take a moment to be silent and breathe deeply. Express gratitude for the blessings of life. Light a candle and/or burn some sage. Create a modest altar in the center with flowers and a few sacred objects belonging to each of the participants. Ask to be guided by love and wisdom.

Consider time constraints in advance. Whenever people are invited to share, the issue of time limitations may come up. It would be delightful never to restrict what people have to say because a certain number of minutes have ticked by. After all, a culture that lasts is not in a hurry. Its members value being deeply present for each other, and that can take time. In fact, a talking circle is a tool that can help free us from a perceived scarcity of time. One comment often heard after a talking circle is: "When I was really concentrating on what each person was saying, time seemed to stand still." In some other settings, talking circles can be so enthralling and healing that, with breaks for food and sleep, they can last for hours, or even days!

However, since most WEIs have other activities planned, a time frame for the talking circle must be devised. A balance has to be struck between the needs of the individual (to be heard) and those of the group (to do a variety of activities). In addition, if each person has a very long time to speak, others may find their own energy and inspiration waning before the talking object reaches them.

Plan how much time you want to spend in the circle and set an appropriate time limit for each person. For example, say you want to allot an hour for a group of ten people. One hour (sixty minutes) divided by ten people gives six minutes for each person—but subtract a minute each because most people need to wrap up their comments when their time limit is reached. So that's about five minutes per person. Let everyone know during your introduction how many minutes they each will have, and that time will be kept in the following way: A watch or other timepiece will be passed along the circle, and the person who has just spoken will keep track of time for the current speaker. The timekeeper will gently touch the speaker when about thirty seconds of their speaking time remains. If the speaker continues much past the time allotted, the timekeeper can hand them the watch, indicating it *really* is time to finish.

At the outset, ask for brevity. Mention the concept of lean expression: What is lean does not have anything extra on it!

That means using only those words necessary to get your point or story across. Wonderful "gems" of great value can be shared in short periods.

Halfway through the circle, remind people to be brief—and tell them before you start the circle that you are going to remind them, so the person who has just spoken before the reminder does not feel criticized.

For larger groups (thirty or more), it will save time to form an inner circle and an outer circle. Whoever is sitting in the inner circle can speak while those in the outer circle listen. The two groups switch roles at a later date. Alternatively, two or more talking circles can run concurrently in different spaces. The advantages of concurrent circles are time savings and a more intimate feeling during sharing; the disadvantages are the need for more space, additional facilitators, and a feeling of having missed some people's sharing.

Participants in smaller groups, after some practice in holding talking circles together, often attune to one another so well that the time management techniques mentioned above are no longer necessary. Each person can sense the rhythm of the circle and "wind down" their sharing after approximately the same amount of time.

Many Native Americans and other indigenous people frown on the use of a timepiece during a talking circle because they feel it is an artificial imposition on an organic process—and it is. In a larger WEI group, however, it is a practical tool that allows us to hone our listening skills and experience being in sacred time together, yet still have plenty of time to explore a variety of other meaningful activities.

Gender Medicine Circles
Purpose: To gain renewed appreciation and respect for the unique qualities of one's gender and, in so doing, receive healing
Duration: 4 hours

In Chapter 4, we discussed the critical importance of a true partnership between men and women. One of the ways that partnership can be strengthened, paradoxically, is by making time to be exclusively with those of one's gender. Without exception, the times I have spent with just men, with the intent of connection, healing, mutual support, and/or just plain fun, have been tremendously enriching. Most of the women I know who have experienced "intentional" time with just women have told me they have felt similarly. Gatherings of men and of women bring a certain kind of medicine that cannot be experienced in any other way.

What is taking place at the deepest level during these gatherings is listening to the unique qualities and energy of your gender. However, "listening" during these times may or may not involve focusing on words. At some point during a WEI, men and women will divide into gender circles, which are held in separate locations. It is helpful if they are far enough apart so as not to be seen or heard by the other group. Although sharing one's thoughts and feelings verbally is important, other activities can also create a sense of closeness and solidarity with one's gender. These can include singing, spending time in nature, massage, cooking, playing games, movement and dance, drumming and making music, yoga, and hiking. The activities are decided and led by the group. The WEI facilitators add gentle guidance only if necessary.

This experience can end with a ritualized coming together of the men's and women's circles, with special songs or gifts given to the other gender. The intention is to create appreciation both for one's own gender and the opposite one. This can be expressed in any way that feels appropriate.

Some people do not identify themselves as one gender or another but may feel as if they are neither or both. If this is the case, a third group can be formed if there are others who feel similarly, or that person could join either group. The most important thing is to acknowledge this group and not assume that everyone feels comfortable with their societally defined gender role.

Chapter 7

Feeling and Healing

Let everything happen to you: beauty and terror. Just
keep going. No feeling is final.
— Rainer Maria Rilke

We modern humans have a peculiar relationship to feeling. A huge spectrum of sensations and emotions is available to us, but we have been trained to be comfortable within only a narrow band. The dominant culture, which acts as a kind of collective parent, domesticates us into consuming and self-medicating as a way of coping with life. If that process of domestication had a single voice, it would say: "Don't get too happy, but don't get too depressed, either. You might travel too far outside the box and no longer be a productive citizen. Be a good consumer and never question the temporary satisfaction you receive from each new purchase. Whenever the pain comes, reach for a drink or a pill or some other way to avoid it."

Most of us have been well-behaved and have gone along with this program. Yet, deep inside, there is a longing to stretch ourselves far beyond what we have been told is safe and acceptable. We long for the wild within and the full palette of feelings that goes with it. This is evidenced by the widespread fascination with sexuality/romance, "extreme" sports and outdoor activities, and the perennial quest for attaining altered states of consciousness by whatever means available. Those experiences aren't "wrong" or "bad," but they shouldn't be a substitute for the joy and wonder of ordinary life, especially life that is connected to the natural world. The task for most of us is to relearn how to feel more fully and to enjoy the magic available in every moment, whether the feelings that arise are pleasant or unpleasant.

We have learned to fear powerful feelings. Because it's socially frowned upon to show them or we are afraid they will overwhelm us, we avoid truly opening to them. We tend to close off whenever we reach a certain threshold. The truth is it takes tremendous energy to stay confined within an emotional and sensory box. It's exhausting. And there are few resources readily available that support us in feeling more fully and releasing pent-up emotions, whether it is joy, anger, or sorrow. This is particularly true for the resolution of emotional pain; in a society that has developed remarkably effective care for mending physical damage, such as broken bones, there is not nearly enough care and thoughtfulness when it comes to treating emotional difficulties.

This inadequacy is even more evident when the pain is in response to what is happening in the larger world. There is a subtle but powerful taboo against verbalizing such pain and finding out what it is trying to tell us. A good example of this is presented in the opening scene of the movie *Sex, Lies, and Videotape*. A woman tells her psychotherapist that she is very anxious about all the garbage that is piling up all over the world, and she wishes she could do something about it. Her therapist responds, "Tell me more about your marriage."[1]

Pain for the Earth

I discovered in scores of "deep ecology" workshops that the participants tended to feel alternately overwhelmed, afraid, trapped, hopeless, and deeply despairing about the environmental crises in our world. They were having heart-based, emotional responses to the tragedies unfolding around them, but they had little or no outlet to express these powerful feelings. What they needed — and what was always included in the workshop schedule—was the opportunity to allow these feelings to bubble up and out, and to honor and validate them. Individually, they always received an empathic response from the group, because there was a willingness in most of the other participants to open to feeling pain rather than avoiding it.

When it comes to feeling pain, especially pain for the world, we may fear that if we uncork the well of despair, we will drown in it. But it is this fear that prevents us from fully experiencing our aliveness. Nobody explains this better than Joanna Macy:

> Our experience of pain for the world springs from our inter-connectedness with all beings, from which also arise our powers to act on their behalf. When we deny or repress our pain for the world, or treat it as a private pathology, our power to take part in the healing of our world is diminished. This apatheia need not become a terminal condition. Our capacity to respond to our own and others' suffering—that is, the feedback loops that weave us into life—can be unblocked. Unblocking occurs when our pain for the world is not only intellectually validated, but experienced. Cognitive information about the crises we face, or even about our psychological responses to them, is insufficient. We can only free ourselves from our fears of the pain—including the fear of getting permanently mired in despair or shattered by grief—when we allow ourselves to experience these feelings. Only then can we discover their fluid, dynamic character. Only then can they reveal on a visceral level our mutual belonging to the web of life.[2]

In other words, feeling our personal pain and our pain for the world is natural and healthy. To block these feelings is to diminish our capacity for aliveness and to deafen ourselves to one of our most powerful forms of innate wisdom. We cannot hope to create a sustainable culture if we don't allow ourselves to feel our feelings. Another way of saying this is that we "moderns" don't really listen to our hearts (and plenty of people will say they don't know what "listening to one's heart" means). We've been taught to *think* our way through life instead of using the other dimensions that make up our larger intelligence: feelings, intuition, awareness, and imagination. Taking the time to really learn about these powers is, in essence, trusting the intelligence of the universe. This is the key to unleashing the love and creativity so necessary at this crucial time in human evolution. But we can't do so if we repress our feelings. Trusting what our pain is telling us is often the entry door to an empowered relationship to the world.

Sharing Powerful Feelings

In 1989, I experienced for the first time the power of sharing raw, uncensored feelings in a group setting. This took place in a workshop called "The Council of All Beings," guided by John Seed. Through this amazing process—co-designed with Joanna Macy—John encouraged us to actually *feel* what was happening to the natural world. Although we were excited and open-minded about the invitation, we were nervous about opening up in this way. Much of what we knew about the health of ecosystems worldwide was bad news, and it evoked gnawing despair, fear, and anger that we usually stuffed down in order to carry on in our lives. If we invited those feelings out, where would it end? Might we go crazy with the depth of our anguish? Would others be shocked or judgmental at unrestrained tears or rage?

But forge ahead we did, both in small groups and as a single large group. We took turns describing and feeling our way through such horrific problems as the lethal consequences of plutonium; deforestation on every continent; the pillaging of the oceans; strip mines leaching toxins, like oozing sores;

and "smaller things" like wildlife being hit on the roads and gasoline leaking into the groundwater. Fear, grief, and anger poured out. John saw to it that everyone received some form of empathy or support, so that we each felt safe to reveal our forbidden secrets—not the information itself, but how strongly we felt in response to that information.

Years later, one person who participated in a similar exercise at a Wild Earth Intensive (WEI) put it this way: "Finally, I felt safe enough to talk about all the painful stuff I was pushing down. The fact that the animals are going extinct because of our stupidity still makes me nuts, but at least I saw I was not alone in feeling this way. Afterwards, I realized I could be part of some greater healing that I don't understand but I know is happening."[3]

The whole plate of feelings that could generally be called "loss" is very strong. Whether it's the loss of a child, the losses suffered during childhood, or the loss of the Earth's biodiversity, it really hurts. After participating in many "despair and empowerment" processes like the Council of All Beings and the exercises described in the second part of this chapter, I discovered that feelings of loss are never purged completely. They continue to arise naturally throughout our life journey, but they need expression in protected settings like a WEI, so that they do not choke off our life energy. Opening the inner pressure valve allows us to redirect that energy to useful action rather than being paralyzed with some form of depression.

Numbness

However, a welcoming space for authentic, powerful feelings to be shared is only an invitation. Often, some people in these groups are silent and tearless, and, of course, that's completely fine. Even when deeply compelling issues that need our attention are spoken out loud, not everyone is going to call forth emotional fire and express their feelings overtly. Some people may feel unable to let go, or are not ready yet, or don't feel anything at all. Sometimes they become angry at themselves for being unable to emote as others are doing.

Feeling emotionally numb is understandable; the more you know about the destructive momentum on planet Earth, the more likely you are to have periods of feeling frozen with despair. It is very common—universal, perhaps—to have times of burnout and hopelessness. Any one of us deeply committed to positive change may throw up our hands and say, "I just don't care anymore!"

I have had this experience myself and have seen it in others many times, and, fortunately, it's temporary. It's a symptom of overload, of too much time alone with the burden of a world in crisis. A powerful prescription for recovery is to come together to witness others' feelings or others' numbness.

It's just plain helpful to be around people who are expressing deep feelings that we share. It's good for our hearts. It reminds us of our kinship with them. At the same time, it helps us see that it's possible to allow the full force of sadness, fear, or anger to wash over us, and then watch hope and joy arise once again.

Personal Stories and Group Connection

Many of us carry in our personal history one or more painful chapters. During a WEI, when remembering our ancient bond with nature and community is the main focus, these stories and their accompanying feelings come closer to the surface. In a life-affirming culture, revealing and healing our personal stories is a life-giving process. Those who listen to these stories accept the sacred responsibility of hearing them without judgment. This responsibility is born not out of obligation but out of compassion. Many of us carry wounds that chronically plague us, and we wish for others what we would like for ourselves: freedom from the grip of those old wounds. As we tell our stories in the presence of supportive companions and allow our feelings to emerge authentically, the toxic influence of those stories dissipates. We then become emotionally available to one another and live more in the present moment.

It may seem paradoxical, but a healthy, nurturing environment where feeling our feelings is encouraged may evoke painful feelings we didn't know we carried. For instance, many WEI participants suddenly realize that the human support and connection of the group is poignantly missing from their "real life." Or a flood of feelings—perhaps based on childhood trauma—may surface, after a lifetime of avoiding them. Although a WEI is not focused directly on healing childhood trauma, it provides a space where adults can feel kinder towards the child that lives within them.

There is no hard boundary between the personal and the collective. As Joanna Macy explains, "Because we are all interconnected, suffering in our personal lives always has roots in our collective lives, and the suffering of each of us compounds in turn our collective pain."[4] The empathic attention of others, during a process or a workshop as a whole, can help us in a powerful way to access the reality of interconnection. In a WEI, there are many other opportunities to access interconnection besides the sharing of feelings: ceremony, play, meals, and other activities engender feelings of camaraderie, especially when we are immersed in nature.

Compassion

The following are key assumptions about my fellow humans (and myself!) that I keep in mind as I facilitate. I am not a psychotherapist, but I find these assumptions support my intention of having an open and compassionate heart and helping the group navigate their emotional territory:

- People are inherently good, regardless of their behavior.
- People act in irrational ways because they are wounded.

- People cannot heal unless they can feel their feelings. Their ability to cry, express anger, laugh, and tremble with fear is essential to the healing process.
- People are always attempting to meet their fundamental human needs (e.g., trust, sustenance, and understanding), but are often unable to communicate these needs.

When facilitators work from these assumptions, an atmosphere of compassion arises. Compassion is the essential healing balm that helps people feel heard and understood. This extraordinary quality is not something that certain people have and others do not, though some people draw from it more consciously than others. Compassion can be developed and strengthened in anyone's innermost being. One of the most important ways to do that is the willingness to open to pain.

Opening to pain could be described as an inner "edge." Like an edge in the natural world—where the terrain changes and we move from the familiar to the unfamiliar—the emotional edge of allowing pain in, instead of blocking it, is like a journey into the unknown.

A WEI invites everyone to explore their inner edges. Besides feeling pain in a safe setting, other edges are plentiful in the Intensive. They can be almost anything that raises energy: relating to others more authentically, walking in the forest at night, altering one's consciousness, being still and quiet, playing, and doing without the comforts of home. Each one of these edges evokes a variety of feelings. The more we allow these feelings to flow through us without resistance, the more alive we feel.

Each person who has been attracted to this process of coming together and exploring edges has an adventurous, courageous soul as well as the tenderness of a young child. Looking upon others and ourselves with as much love and compassion as we can muster—knowing deep down we are beautiful human beings who are doing the best we can—is the most powerful tool we have to make positive change.

Working with Strong Emotions

Experiencing strong emotions is new terrain for lots of people, especially with an unfamiliar group of people. *If you serve as a facilitator, you cannot guide participants in exploring this terrain unless you have spent a good deal of time there yourself.* To validate powerful feelings of fear, anger, despair, and grief in others, you must have already discovered for yourself the strength and healing that comes from truly experiencing their depths. If you have done so, you will:

- Ensure no one feels pressure to display emotion. The outward expression of emotion is no indication of its inner intensity.
- Realize that you cannot rescue anyone, convince them that "all will turn out OK in the end," or resolve their emotions by trying to comfort them. Your accepting presence is comforting enough.
- Trust the process. At the very beginning of a WEI, you are inviting larger, life-giving forces to assist you and the group. You are an agent of these forces.
- Participate fully. This means do not stand aloof. You will feel whatever emotions are evoked in you by the process, while simultaneously keeping an eye on the group. The ability to focus inside and outside increases with practice.

Sensations

Sometimes we can get so swept away with our thoughts and emotions that we forget that we are also awash in many different ordinary sensations. We experience the sensations that are evoked by the outer world through seeing, hearing, tasting, touching, and smelling—*and*, seemingly out of nowhere, through the rich interior of our body/mind. We can choose to pause and become aware of this entire realm that is often ignored in favor of the thinking mind, and by doing so, gain another method of tapping into our aliveness.

With practice, focusing attention on our sensory experience opens us to a pulsating, dynamic, and ever-changing world abounding in energy. When we also allow thoughts and emotions into our field of awareness, each new moment gifts us with a rich energy tapestry. As young children, we primarily experienced this tapestry as an uninterrupted flow. Once again, if we are willing, we can feel the life energy pour through us unimpeded.

Freeing Emotional Energy in a Wild Earth Intensive

In one way or another, all the activities described in this book are aimed at encouraging us to feel more fully and with more awareness. The exercises described below specifically serve to unblock repressed emotional energy, with a particular (but not exclusive) focus on feeling our pain for the world. Undoubtedly, painful "stuff" will show up during these processes. Keep in mind that one of the reasons for welcoming and expressing these so-called negative feelings is that it is healthy to do so. Feeling what is genuinely true for us provides a much-needed dose of reality, and it's a key component of an inspired culture of authenticity, compassion, and interconnection with all life.

Each of the first three exercises below has been designed to help us express and honor our feelings. These may be done singly, but in WEIs, it has been quite powerful to do them in sequence. Together they offer a quick way to build trust and safety within the group, as each person gradually opens to deeper levels of feeling. If they are done as a trio, take a five-minute, silent break after completing Eco-Milling and Voices of the Earth. (The silence serves as a container for the building emotional energy.) All three can be completed in a morning or afternoon.

Start by encouraging everyone to spread out so they have space to stretch and move, and then put on some lively music for a few minutes and let them get their energy flowing. This puts people in a more open space for listening to an explanation of the reasons for doing these exercises. It can be helpful to include the following concepts in the explanation:

- We can't heal what we can't feel.
- Unblocking painful feelings is healthy and natural.
- Our pain for the world has its roots in our passionate caring about, and our unbreakable connection to, our larger body, the Earth.
- All feelings are acceptable, including numbness.
- Openly sharing feelings creates the space for greater intimacy.

Eco-Milling

Purpose: To provide a non-verbal and active way to begin experiencing interconnection
Duration: 15–20 minutes

This exercise has five phases that flow together and build on each other, taking participants from feeling like individuals locked in their own stories to experiencing the interconnected beings we really are. Each phase of the process has a different focus:

1. Helping people connect to their bodies and surroundings and become more present.
2. Evoking first the uncomfortable rush of industrial time (through parody) and then the intention for gathering together at a WEI.

3. Encouraging participants to "breathe through" a few of the stark realities of this planet-time, from the vantage point of caring about the person standing before them.
4. Assisting people in expanding their sense of self through awareness and imagination.
5. Inviting participants to look with fresh eyes at reality and open to the inspiration that a new perspective brings.

This exercise is best done in a spacious room or outdoors. Before beginning, make sure there is an even number of people. (This is another place assistant guides can be helpful; one of them can join in the activity to make an even number.) Explain that everybody will be "milling" about: silently walking randomly in the space, with no apparent purpose or direction. Start the process by modeling it yourself. Then invite people to start milling about. Guide them through each phase, with words similar to the following:

Phase 1

> *Look down with a soft gaze. Walk in any direction that pleases you. Don't focus on getting anyplace or making eye contact with anyone.*

If outdoors, you might continue with:

> *Feel your body and the Earth beneath your feet. Notice the beauty around you as you move through the air, each leg clearing a space for the next step. Take your time. Breathe a little more deeply.*

If indoors, you might substitute:

Wherever you are, the Earth is making herself known. She is manifest in the man-made objects in the room and the room itself. Feel her presence among you as you walk.

When you are finished speaking, give them some time to enjoy the exercise in silence. After a couple of minutes, prompt everyone to stop walking:

Now, wherever you are, just stop. Look at the person closest to you and silently form pairs. Turn toward each other. Greet and acknowledge one another silently, gently gazing at your fellow human, a wondrous part of creation.

Phase 2

Now continue walking, but this time a little faster. Pick up the pace. Gotta get moving. Gotta check e-mail and phone messages. "Time is money," you know. You're in a hurry, so you may accidentally bump into your competitors. You have very important things to do and you have to keep busy. Maybe you have to get into your car and drive somewhere.

Most people express nervous laughter at this all-too-familiar way of being. Let this go on for just a minute or two, so that the participants have time to sense this unpleasant energy. Then transition with something like this:

Glance around at your fellow humans under this burden of busyness and stress. No time to talk, no time to say what is really going on in their minds and hearts. But they are not always like this! Now let the tension in your body dissipate, and slow down ... slower ... and stop in front of the person closest to you. Take a deep breath. Notice each other while you also notice your own body. Neither of you is alone. Reach out a hand to each other. Engage the other's eyes — these true portals to the soul — and take in their presence. This person you are with loves the natural world and cares passionately about her well-being, just as you do. They want to live in a culture that honors the Earth. This person could have been doing many other things right now, but has chosen to be here, doing this important work. Nonverbally express your thanks to this person for their caring.

Phase 3

Begin walking again, but this time move playfully. Maybe brush against someone as you pass. Become aware of the child who still resides within each adult around you.

Let this playful phase continue for a minute or two and then continue thoughtfully with:

Slow down again, find yourself in front of someone, and stop. Look at each other's face and consider the fact that we are living in a time like no other. This person knows the pain of a world that is dangerously out of touch and feels it ... knows about the destruction of the rainforests and the oceans ... knows about the exploitation of animals. They know about war. They may even die of some environmentally related disease. Let whatever feelings you have arise, and truly feel them.

Pause to let this sink in.

As you fix your gaze upon this person, reflect on how they could have shut down to all of this information, but have not. Experience your admiration and respect for this person, and express it nonverbally in whatever way feels appropriate. Nod goodbye and move on.

Phase 4

Start milling about again. Notice your fellow travelers as you pass them, and recognize the courageous journey you are on together. Again, find yourself standing in front of someone, and take a few moments to register their presence. Reach out and touch each other's left hand. Now close your eyes and feel the hand. Touch it gently with great care. Notice how it is strong and durable, yet fragile and vulnerable. Explore this hand. Feel its texture and temperature. Is it moist or dry? Explore it with great wonder, as if you've never felt anything like it before. Touch the skin, the bones, the knuckles, the strong opposable thumb. Reflect on the millions of years of evolution it has taken to get to this point. Now see what this hand can teach you of its history. Is this a hand that has done a lot of manual labor? Allow this hand to take you back in time, and see if you can feel the child's hand that became this hand. Now take a leap and go even further back, back into the history of life. Can you feel the paw in this hand? Can you feel the claws that led to these nails? Go back further. Can you feel the fin that existed before this hand emerged from the oceans? Perhaps now you can feel the very stardust of which this hand is composed? Now, with your eyes still closed, without words, say goodbye to this hand. Acknowledge nonverbally your amazement at the person attached to this hand before you move on.

Phase 5

Start the final milling. Open your awareness to the Earth in all her grandeur, whether it's right in front of you or in your mind's eye. Feel the strength of your heart and the hearts of those who pass you, who are able to hold all of it: the miracle of life on Earth, and the painful realities of our current time.

Once again, for the final time in this process, come to a stop in front of someone and look with fresh eyes at the being before you. Take them in. Notice their goodness. Wouldn't it be great to work in some creative way with this person?

Eco-Milling is the perfect beginning to a wide diversity of deep ecology processes. If you are going to transition directly into an activity that involves pairs, like the one below, let the pairs just formed find a comfortable place to sit down together.

Voices of the Earth

Purpose: To allow people to verbalize their ecological concerns in an intimate, safe setting and embody those concerns in a creative way
Duration: 30 minutes

This exercise brings abstract information into the heart and expands one's sense of self. It enables people to better trust their "gut" and experience a variety of perspectives in a short period.

Have people pair off if they have not done so already. Partners sit face to face with enough distance between pairs so they won't distract each other during the process. Have each pair choose who will go first, and explain that this person will be the "speaker" responding to a series of prompts spoken by the facilitator. The other person will listen with full, silent attention to what is being said. This is not a conversation! Then the partners will trade roles.

Ask everyone to take a minute to reflect on an ecological area of personal concern and the feelings that it evokes.

Offer prompts similar to the following and, after each, remain quiet while the speakers respond. Let them know they'll have about four minutes for each prompt, but give a little more time to the first one. Toward the end of each segment, ask the speakers to "bring your sharing to a close."

1. *Passionately describe an ecological problem. This is an opportunity to let go of your inner censor. Experience yourself speaking; feel what you are saying.*

2. *Become the voice of a plant, an animal, or a part of Earth that is affected by this problem. Identify with this being. Tell your partner what you feel like as this being, describing both your inner and outer experiences. If you can, try speaking in the first person (using "I"). For example, you might say: "I am a raccoon. I come out at night. I need to cross a road to find food, and I'm scared because big metal boulders with bright lights move very quickly and have killed members of my family."*

3. *Speak in the voice of someone you think is the cause of an environmental problem. For instance, become a corporate executive for a large oil company, or a logger, or a nuclear plant worker. Again, speaking in the first person, explain who you are and what you do, feeling that you are completely in the right. Use your flexible intelligence to "become" that person. Really get into it.*

Have the partners switch roles, and repeat the series of prompts for the new speakers.

The Truth Mandala

Purpose: To provide a ritual structure for owning and honoring our pain for the world, and the solidarity it can bring

Duration: 1 hour for small groups (twenty or fewer); up to 1½ hours for larger groups

I have participated in and led dozens of these powerful rituals. The Truth Mandala is one of the most moving practices Joanna Macy has created. As she says, "Truth-telling is like oxygen: it enlivens us. Without it we grow confused and numb."[5] The Truth Mandala provides an opportunity to express more fully what has been bubbling to the surface in the preceding two exercises. This sequence ensures that people will have had an opportunity to relate to one other in some depth, allowing for a more authentic voicing of concerns. In this exercise, ecological, social, and even personal issues are welcome.

The following description is from Macy's book, *Coming Back to Life*, co-authored with Molly Brown. Some minor modifications have been made to adapt it for a WEI.

This practice emerged in 1992 amidst a large, tension-filled workshop in Frankfurt, on the day of reunification between East and West Germany; since then, it has spread to many lands. To a large number of participants, it has been the most significant experience in a workshop, if not in their lives.

People sit in a circle. They sit as closely packed as possible, for they are, as we often put it, creating a containment vessel — or an alchemical vessel — for holding and cooking the truth. The circle they enclose is divided into four quadrants (visible demarcations are not needed), with a sitting cushion in the center. In each quadrant is placed a symbolic object: a stone, dead leaves, a thick stick, and an empty bowl. Entering each quadrant, the guide holds the object it contains and explains its meaning. Here are some words we have used:

This stone is for fear. It's how our hearts feel when we're afraid: tight, contracted, hard. In this quadrant, we can speak our fear.

These dry leaves represent our sorrow, our grief. There is great sadness within us for what we see happening to our world, our lives, and for what is passing from us, day by day.

This stick is for our anger, for there are anger and outrage in us that need to be spoken for clarity of mind and purpose. This stick is not for hitting with or waving around, but for grasping hard with both hands — it's strong enough for that.

And in the fourth quadrant, this empty bowl stands for our sense of deprivation and need, our hunger for what's missing — our emptiness.

You may wonder: Where is hope? The very ground of this mandala is hope. If we didn't have hope, we wouldn't be here. And we will see, as we proceed, how hope underlies what is expressed in each quadrant.

We will begin with a dedication and a chant, because this is holy ground. Nothing makes a place more holy than truth telling. Then we will step in one at a time, spontaneously. We will take a symbol in our hands and speak, or move from one [quadrant] to another. We may come in more than once or not at all; there is no pressure on us to enter. Even if you stay on the periphery, you will find that, as each person enters the Mandala, you are in there, too. We will speak briefly. In brevity, words are powerful."

Now the guide, entering each quadrant, demonstrates how its symbol can be used for speaking the knowing and feelings we carry. For example, holding the stone of fear:

I'm scared by the spread of cancer and AIDS. Will my lover be next? Will I? Where can I go to escape from the poisons? They are everywhere — in our air, our water, our food.

Holding the dry leaves:

I feel sorrow for the people of Tibet and for the loss of all the old indigenous cultures. Now when we most need the wisdom of their ancient traditions, we wipe them out. So I weep for us, too.

Holding the stick:

Oh, the fury I feel for our war on the poor! What will happen to the women, the children? What kind of jobs can they get?

Holding or pointing to the bowl:

I don't know what to do. I recycle, I take the bus, I change my diet, but in truth I don't know what can save us. I am empty of ideas, strategies, confidence.

Then offer the group some general guidance:

Since we are not used to talking like this in public, we need the support of the whole group. After each person has spoken, let us all say, "We hear you." That's enough. Your agreement or approval is not needed—just your hearing and respect. And let us pause for three breaths in silence between speakers.

Maybe there's something you'll want to say that doesn't fit one of these quadrants, so this cushion in the center of the mandala is a place you can stand or sit to give voice to it—and it could be a song or a prayer. In the Truth Mandala, we speak not only for ourselves, but for others, too. It is the nature of all ritual that it allows us to speak archetypally—not just as separate individual selves, but on behalf of our people, our Earth. Let the ritual object—stick or stone or leaves or bowl—focus our minds. We don't enter the mandala to perform or explain or report to the rest of us, but to let that object help us voice the truth of our own experiences.

The ritual time then begins with a formal rededication to the welfare of all beings and the restoration of a vibrant, lasting human culture. A simple chant or the beating of a drum starts the proceedings.

One at a time, people enter the Truth Mandala and tell their truth. Usually, there is a tremendous amount of energy that is verbally released in small, powerful bursts from most participants. The energy tends to reach a crescendo about midway through the group process and then stabilizes, allowing the softer or more tentative voices to come forth, if they so choose.

Trust yourself to sense the moment to draw the ritual to a close. You will read clues in people's body language and the energy of the group, or from utterances that seem to provide an appropriate note to end on. As you prepare to close, tell people, so that those who have been holding back and waiting to speak can seize the chance to do so. We often say:

> *The Truth Mandala will continue in our lives, but this chapter of it will soon draw to a close. Let those who wish to, enter it now and speak.*

After a few drumbeats to formally close the Truth Mandala, you can seize the moment to enlarge the group's understanding of what has transpired. Speaking generally and on behalf of all honors the truths that have been shared:

> *Truth telling is like oxygen: it enlivens us. Without it, we grow confused and numb. It is also a homecoming, bringing us back to powerful connection and basic authority.*

Then you can point out the deeper import of each quadrant in the mandala:

> *Each symbolic object is like a coin with two sides; the courage to speak our fear, for example, is evidence of trust.*

Indicating one object after another, we say, in effect:

Please notice what you have been expressing and hearing. The sorrow spoken over the dead leaves was in equal measure love. We only mourn what we deeply care for. "Blessed are they that mourn."[6] Blessed are those who weep for the desecration of life, because in them life still burns clear. And the anger we heard, what does it spring from but passion for justice? The empty bowl is to be honored, too. To be empty means there is space to be filled.

Honoring Our Losses

Purpose: To integrate the emotional content evoked in the previous (or similar) exercises
Duration: 30 minutes

Like the Truth Mandala, this is not a stand-alone exercise. It builds on the work that has taken place so far. After several hours of focusing on painful events and the feelings they evoke, there is a short but significant period of "wobbliness" before a sense of empowerment takes hold. A skilled guide understands that when people travel through rugged emotional terrain, they cannot be rushed into feeling hopeful or positive. They are naturally inclined in this direction, but they need time to integrate what has transpired and to "lick their wounds." Honoring Our Losses provides the space to do so.

This exercise is imperative because the losses "out there" are also "in here." It is best done outside because the natural world is always awash in healing energy. When we are raw and vulnerable, we can be very open to this energy. This is especially true after the Truth Mandala, which is usually held indoors. (Remember to give participants a fifteen-minute break between the two exercises.)

Find a place different from the one where the morning's exercises were held, but not so far of a walk as to dissipate the introspective and reflective mood. Going there in silence is a good idea. A large, flat boulder or a rock outcropping is ideal, but the ground is fine. This site should allow the group to comfortably form a circle or semicircle where everyone can see everyone else. After arriving at this site, ask participants to take five minutes alone and each find an object that represents some loss that was highlighted for them during the Truth Mandala. This loss does not have to be obvious or "huge" — such as the loss of topsoil, the loss of someone close, the loss of indigenous peoples — but could be more subtle, like the loss of silence, community, or a slower pace of life. And the word *loss* is really too narrow here. When individuals are looking for their objects — an acorn, leaf, flower, stone, etc. — they are simply remembering anything that was particularly meaningful and that affected them deeply. Gather the group back in this special place. The open area where the objects will be placed does not need to be very large; a square yard (3ft by 3ft) should be sufficient. Begin this simple ritual with words such as these:

> *We have been through a lot together in a short period of time. We've explored territory many people fear to tread. We've felt a lot of different things. Now we have an opportunity to honor something we have heard or said that made an impact on our hearts. In front of you is an empty altar. One by one, express whatever words of respect and appreciation come to mind, and then place your object on the altar.*

Here are a few things that participants have expressed during this exercise:

"With this leaf, I honor the loss of the coral reefs. Their beauty is so amazing and unique."

"This stone represents the difficulty I felt doing these processes. It was really painful. I want to honor that part of myself that does not want to face any of this."

"I place this small flower on the altar to represent my love for trees. I want to honor their patience and strength."

"The lobes of this pinecone represent a few of the many starving children. May they find something to eat."

"This branch honors my father. He was tough, but he taught me a lot."

Whale Wash

Purpose: To allow full body relaxation while increasing trust and intimacy between participants

Duration: 45 minutes

This "lighter" process goes well after deep, cathartic exercises, as long as some time for physical activity has elapsed. It is best done in the evening, when group energy is winding down. Whale Wash is essentially a relaxing group massage that focuses loving attention on one person at a time, either energetically or through physical touch. It is important to introduce this exercise only after the group has already bonded with a certain degree of intimacy.

The participants and facilitators divide into "pods" of five to six people with enough space between each pod to create a more intimate feel. Each pod sets up a comfortable place for the "receiver" to lie down, preferably with cushions or a mat. Each person receives an equal share of time, usually five to six minutes. Longer periods make it difficult for the receiver to then give, because they are so relaxed! Timekeeping is also equally shared. Someone in each pod volunteers to be the first receiver and requests what form of nurturing they would like. They may be specific: "I'd like someone to rub my feet and neck and lower back" or "I'd like the group to focus on me without touch."

However, most people will request some kind of massage, and the pod will quietly work together, often switching positions to focus on various parts of the receiver's body. The receiver can make additional requests during that time, such as asking for deeper work in a particular area or saying that something doesn't feel good.

Shortly before each round comes to an end, the pod raises their hands a few inches above the receiver while continuing to channel loving energy. After a few minutes of this, the receiver is gently notified that it is time to make the transition to the next person (or that the final round is over). Between rounds, participants should energetically cleanse their hands in some way, such as shaking out the energy.

Chapter 8

Nature Connection and Immersion

Look deep into nature, and then you will understand
everything better.

— Albert Einstein

As is well known, several hundred years of rapid industrialization have produced many negative social and environmental effects. One effect that is frequently overlooked is the increasing human sense of separateness from nature. Accelerating technological "progress" has only intensified the illusion of an isolated self. This false perception considered normal by most people—"I'm in here and everything else is out there"—has led to an acute physical and psychological disconnection from the land. It's a negative feedback loop in which we retreat further and further from our core nourishment, the natural world.

The absurd idea that we can be fully human without a deeply felt kinship and intimacy with nature could only have been created by an alienated society. Richard Louv, author of *Last Child in the Woods*, who coined the term *nature deficit disorder*, said this about our societal condition on National Public Radio:

> Our kids are actually doing what we tell them to do when they sit in front of that TV all day or in front of that computer game all day. The society is telling kids unconsciously that nature is in the past—it really doesn't count anymore—that the future is in electronics, and besides, the bogeyman is in the woods.[1]

One of the key functions of the Wild Earth Intensive (WEI) is to create the time and space for a sustained, conscious relationship with the natural world. A wide variety of people of different ages, races, and classes have consistently told me that when they nurture this relationship, even just a little bit, they are quenching a deep thirst.

Moving from the stance of an *outside observer* (our role when we watch nature films or take the occasional walk outside) to that of a *participant*, experiencing full immersion in the natural landscape, is necessary to nurture this primal connection. A dip here and there does not produce the results we seek, because reconnecting to nature is like any other skill. The more we do it, the more adept we get and the easier it becomes. By exercising our million-year-old nature connection "muscle," we redevelop an emotional and spiritual kinship with the land. To do this is to come home to ourselves. We then feel rejuvenated and alive and experience a sense of belonging to something very old and very familiar. Feeling this innate connection allows us to break free from the narrow confines of the self-absorbed human world, and suddenly we find that we can really breathe.

Trees, bushes, rocks, bodies of water, animals, and even those otherworldly insects start to take on special significance when we take the time to really *be* with them. Strengthening this mode of perception stimulates a crucial shift, in which getting to know a place goes beyond the collection of data and becomes a sacred communion with living beings and energies. This is when the mythic, animistic character of the land can reveal itself—the utter mystery and intelligence found in every part of the natural world.

Paul Devereux spends three hundred pages making this point in his book *Re-Visioning the Earth*. Here is one cogent paragraph:

Place is not passive. It interacts with our consciousness in a dynamic way. It contains its own memory of events and its own mythic nature ... which may not be visible but can be apprehended by the human ... especially in the appropriate mental state ... On a less dramatic level, the forms, textures, smells, sounds, or light of a particular place can trigger associations within us that another place would not. It can bring things to the fore, into awareness, that were until then existing in the unconscious mind. Place can therefore illuminate us, and provoke mythic imaginings within us.[2]

When this visionary geography is as obvious as the tip of one's nose, it can be developed into an ongoing, living art form. A glowing example is the "dreaming tracks" or "songlines" of the Australian Aborigines, which epitomize their special relationship to the land, a relationship that evolved over tens of thousands of years. British novelist and travel writer Bruce Chatwin describes the songlines as "the labyrinth of invisible pathways which meander all over Australia."[3]

But these numinous landmarks are invisible to the eyes only. The Aborigines bring them into the realm of the heart through storytelling, dancing, singing, and painting. The songlines also provide them with subtle tracking mechanisms vital for navigation and survival. Like so many aboriginal peoples the world over, they believe the land was created through sound and vibration—as they themselves were. Sound and vibration came from "the Ancients," who gave the people life. When the Ancients walked over the land, those ancestral beings looked around and sang rocks, animals, plants, and streams into existence. Wherever they walked, Chatwin writes, "they left a trail of music."[4] The Aborigines still hear these songs, which are "stored" in the countryside. This is the heart of their culture: a sacred symbiosis of land, people, song, dreaming, and art.

This mythic understanding is not extinct in modern humans but smolders within us, waiting for the right combination of intent, circumstances, and practice to fan it into flame. Paul

Devereux interviewed Australian poet and writer James Cowan, who has spent considerable time with the Aborigines in the outback.

Devereux: "To take a hypothetical case, let's say the Aborigines disappeared altogether in a particular area, and another tribal people eventually came and lived in that landscape. Do you believe that a similar mythic relationship would build up between them and the land?"

Cowan: "Yes, I do."

Devereux: "In the sense of it [the mythic relationship] being seeds dormant in the earth?"

Cowan: "Yes. Provided that the people were amenable to that land as a non-material concept ... I do believe that if what you are trying to say, that the landscape has its own, let us say, metaphysical data imprinted in it which is unchangeable, my answer is yes. And, moreover, that that information could be invoked now or 20,000 years from hence."[5]

In other words, the landscape can always express itself through human beings if we possess strong intent and genuine receptivity. There are thousands of tribes throughout the world that have left and continue to leave, similar legacies. They remind the rest of us that developing a spiritually connected relationship with the land is not only possible but essential.

Connecting to Nature at a Wild Earth Intensive

The two fundamental qualities of nature connection that are emphasized during a WEI are *knowledge of place* and *awareness of place*. These are subtly distinct yet equally important aspects of nature connection, and they are mutually reinforcing. When both of these aspects are fully integrated in an individual, that person can truly embody the landscape. Embodying the landscape is a key part of reclaiming our true power as humans and developing the kind of ecstatic culture we long for.

The great American farmer-poet-writer Wendell Berry said, "If you don't know where you are, you don't know who you are."[6] Geography is more than the study of maps. It begins with a living, breathing understanding of where one is standing. During a WEI, we cultivate this understanding by exploring the immediate environment in which the Intensive is held. The appreciation and gratitude toward nature that emerge when we do this can transform our lifelong relationship to the outdoors. This is especially true when we invest our energy in both aspects of nature connection. To begin, let's discuss these aspects and put them in context.

Awareness of place happens only in the present moment through bare observation without interpretation, and it allows us to perceive more deeply and accurately because abstract thinking is put temporarily on hold. Tracker, writer, and photographer Paul Rezendes puts it this way:

Your sense of an individual self will be removed through direct observation/awareness of the inner and outer landscapes. It sees things as they are, not wanting them to be other than what they are. This awareness or intelligence is the basic consciousness of all beings. I call this Wildness because it is totally uncultivated. This is our true nature and place. Being is Wildness—that is the "place" common to all nature.[7]

This direct way of knowing is also the primary step in learning nature's language and patterns. That language and those patterns are the basis for an in-depth knowledge of place, which includes the diverse fields of natural science. However, because natural science is well established, knowledge of place in a WEI emphasizes the mythic and energetic. As this type of knowledge of place deepens, the "dreamtime" consciousness described in the previous section takes hold. Experiencing this state of consciousness is one of the goals of a WEI. Then, when geographical, geological, and ecological concepts are introduced, they take on a fresh meaning.

When both awareness and knowledge of place are developed, and then coupled with the shamanic journeying skills described in Chapter 11, even urban environments can be experienced in a new and profound way. We come to realize firsthand that everything—in both our inner and outer environments—is made of energy and intelligence. This realization is a vital part of a new sense of self that is at the heart of a WEI.

Knowledge of Place

A thorough knowledge of place requires extensive observation and practice. Because the knowledge of place that is emphasized at a WEI is mythic and energetic, our immersion in the landscape is not focused on the discovery of features that would support sustained physical living on the land. (This is one of the worthy goals of permaculture design.) Nature immersion during the Intensive also does not stress wilderness survival skills. However, if a group is gathered for more than ten days, elements of these disciplines will be included, as they are important parts of a comprehensive understanding of place.

Like many permaculture and wilderness survival courses, nature immersion at a WEI does start with orienting to our surroundings. One or two of the facilitators provide a short geographical overview based on site research done ahead of time. Instead of simply feeding information to the participants, you can arouse interest by putting forth questions such as these (written on a large sheet of paper and meant to be explored in the field): Where are the nearby bodies of water? Where are the major rock outcroppings? What are the keystone species? What animals make their presence known? What, if any, is the archeological evidence of human interaction with the land? Where are the prevailing winds coming from, and what are the typical weather patterns of this particular season? In which direction is the water flowing?

Of course, there are many more questions of this type than could be covered in a lifetime, let alone an Intensive. Feel free to choose from the questions above and add any others that seem important to you or that are relevant to the site (e.g., if you are at high elevation, ask about the major characteristics of the mountains). Again, these questions are not meant to be answered comprehensively but are intended to focus the group's attention on the land.

This also involves frequently drawing out the curiosity of the participants throughout the program with comments like: "Hey, look at that track! Wow, I wonder what made it? Did you notice the nail marks in it?" or "Check out that bunch of white fungus that looks like miniature trees. What is going on there?" This way, the questions regarding the ecology of the landscape don't come off as dry and abstract but are made tangible in the present moment. They serve as a "launching pad" for making the perceptual transition from the purely physical into the energetic. A follow-up question guides often ask repeatedly after it's clear the participants are beginning to feel more connected to their surroundings is: Where does the energy appear to be flowing and what does it seem to be saying?

Although the guides may have more ecological knowledge than the other participants, it is important to let everyone share what they know. Fresh insights always seem to abound as we journey deeper into the living library that is nature. For example, one WEI participant in the northeastern U.S. pointed out that the antidote to poison ivy is jewelweed, which usually grows right next to the poison ivy. Another participant saw a squirrel burying an acorn and commented that these animals are "scatter hoarders" that don't put all their acorns in one place, in order to avoid catastrophic loss to their entire cache during the winter. The squirrels won't find and eat all the buried acorns, resulting in many new oak seedlings in the spring. She then said, "I've heard this is a very old relationship going on for more than five million years." And then, to everyone's surprise, she asked, innocently yet wisely, "Where does 'squirrelness' end and 'oakness' begin?"[8]

Human language is the amazing "translation device" that helps us communicate these concepts to each other. The naming of things and their relationships can lead to a deeper appreciation of the natural world, as well as an understanding of how to survive in it. However, we can, and often do, get carried away. Naming a thing without really being aware of its unique essence and intelligence can objectify it and reinforce the mistaken sense that nature is separate from us. When we are precise and state, "This tree is *called* an oak," we are not confusing the name of the tree with what it is *to be* an oak.

The first set of exercises below can help us deepen our knowledge of place and lay the foundation for an increased familiarity and ease with the land. They are also designed to motivate the participants to take the necessary time to develop this familiarity beyond the container of the WEI. It may be helpful to remember that although knowledge and awareness of place are distinct aspects of nature connection, they are not separate. Whenever we focus on one aspect, the other is present to a lesser degree. Thus, participating in these activities will also enhance our awareness of place.

In addition, these exercises stimulate awe and appreciation, which are the basis for overcoming our fears of "the wild." For example, many people are afraid of the dark. Time spent outdoors in the dark lessens or eliminates this fear. And most people tend to be fearful of getting lost "out there." Learning basic orienteering skills (using map and compass, following waterways, and developing a relationship with the sun and other distinguishing landmarks) builds confidence in being able to comfortably navigate unknown territory, both externally and internally.

With increased familiarity comes a deep knowing that we humans are completely dependent on the Earth for our lives. There is no mystique about being connected to nature. It's just the way things are. Occasionally, when a WEI guest facilitator with wilderness survival skills shows how to make a fire by friction (e.g., using a bow drill) and that first spark ignites the tinder, I look around and see the awe—even primal vulnerability—that is on everyone's faces. I sense that a long-buried memory of how our ancestors learned to survive the cold, damp, and dark has been jarred loose.

Basic Orientation

Purpose: To orient one's body on the land
Duration: 10 minutes

An important part of knowing where you are during the Intensive (or anytime, for that matter) is being able to determine where you are in relation to the four cardinal directions. Many people are not aware that if you live in the northern hemisphere, you can follow the arc of the sun during the day and know that the top of the arc is south. When you know south, you can locate the other directions. Not only is this helpful in a practical way, but when you know the location of the directions, you have a vantage point for exploring the larger "medicine wheel" of life. Every part of the wheel, including above and below, has a different spiritual meaning or archetypal energy, according to many indigenous cultures. Thus, learning how to locate one's physical body in space can be the beginning of a deeper relationship with the Earth and the cosmos. When you know the directions, you can also find your center. You are not just floating in space. You can "ground" and be present.

In your role as a guide, provide this overview to the group and then ask them to practice noticing the sun's passage throughout the day and to orient themselves accordingly. Have them observe the changing intensity of the sunlight and how it reflects off the trees, rocks, and water. It can be helpful to tell them that, unlike reading a compass, the ability to find the cardinal directions is not learned instantly but is acquired gradually through repeated observation.

Basic Orientation is a left-brained complement to the Calling in the Directions invocation that begins the Intensive.

The Embrace of Life

Purpose: To make the transition from talking about the landscape's features to experiencing them animistically
Duration: 10 minutes

Gather the group outside. Slowly and meditatively speak words such as the following, pausing between declarations to allow participants time to do what is suggested:

Look around you. Slowly rotate, taking in the beauty before you. Now, standing still, feel your feet rooted in the Earth. Feel the Earth holding you, holding us. Really ground yourself in this place and take a few deep, healing breaths. Feel the exchange of vital gases with the plant world, breathing in the life-giving oxygen the plants give so freely. Bask in the light from the sun no matter how bright or dim. Feel that light in your body. Feel its heat as your inner fire. Now, make the leap from the seen to the unseen. Feel the presence of the people who were here before and who took care of this place. Imagine how they honored the land in their unique way. Now go back further and imagine a few of the past myriad life forms that shaped this place: the ancestral bacteria, the fish, the amphibians, the reptiles, and the animals that made it the way it is. Sense their incalculable influence. Now, taking another deep breath, feel the mysterious intelligence behind it all. Perceive that in your own way. Thank it silently.

This basic exercise may seem awkward to some because it's so outside the usual way of interacting with the world. That's OK. If you can lead this with a certain amount of authority (derived from your own experience and using your own words), this way of perceiving and knowing will become, over time, more accessible and even pleasurable to the participants. It will lead to trusting the more "shamanic" ways of interacting with the landscape in a WEI.

Anchoring the Attraction

Purpose: To anchor our inherent awe and connection to nature
Duration: 15–20 minutes

Find an outdoors area that has some variety, perhaps with an edge where there is openness on one side (like a field) and more density on the other side (like a forest). Ask the group to spread out, remaining within sight of each other, and to observe their surroundings silently for several minutes—not just what's right in front of them but also what's overhead and behind them. Their task is to find something that particularly attracts their interest and inspires some sort of feeling. Let them know that *any* part of nature is acceptable. It could be the sky, a bird, a pebble, or a clump of soil. Call the group back together after they have a few minutes in which to locate something. Then invite them to describe it—and the feeling it inspires—to the group. When everyone who wishes to share has done so, ask them to take a minute to reflect on what they observed and to silently anchor this feeling in their body, so that in the future it will be more accessible. *Anchoring,* in this case, means to give focused attention to the feeling and then set it to memory so it can be recalled more easily.

Solo Time

Purpose: To create the habit of connecting to the natural world without the support of other people
Duration: 15–30 minutes

The WEI is a time to build true community, but we can't do that without creating "space" from one another. Taking a break from the intensity of human relationships and letting the natural world nurture us is a form of medicine. Making a habit of connecting with nature by oneself builds inner strength. This quiet time gives participants another way to tune in to their senses and observe changes in weather, wildlife, and plant communities. Done repeatedly, Solo Time offers each person a chance to get to know one area really well and, in so doing, increase their ease with it. This will also create greater ease when they are in other places.

Early on in the WEI, invite everyone to find a spot that they will return to almost every day (even if, at first, the spot appears less than exciting or glamorous). Their only instruction is to relax, pay attention, and let their spot embrace them. Tremendous richness, stillness, and subtlety can be found almost anywhere!

Dancing the Landscape

Purpose: To embody part of the landscape and feel its unique energy
Duration: 30 minutes

Gather everyone and explain this fun and creative exercise. Each person will go out onto the land "solo" for about ten minutes and wander on their own, staying within hearing range of your call to return. During that time, the participants will look, listen, and "feel" the general features and overall qualities of the landscape. As they wander, they will endeavor to discover how the whole place "moves" them. They might choose to stop and "ground" to a particular spot. They will keep energetically sensitizing themselves to the landscape until they can feel a movement, sound, and/or dance in their bodies that best represents their experience. In your explanation, encourage them to follow their first spontaneous impulse about what moves them. They should practice the sound or movement for a while, allowing it to become an organic, natural part of them. They will then come back into the circle, and those who wish to share will each take a turn expressing their sound or movement to the others. It's important for you to emphasize that any expression is welcome and the more dramatic ones are not better, just different.

[Thanks to John Mosimann for this exercise.]

Poet-tree

Purpose: To experience nature as poetry
Duration: 1–1½ hour

Before the exercise, choose three trees of different species that the group will visit, not far from the main meeting space. (If trees are not present on the site, select three shrubs, large rocks/boulders, or other landscape features.) Prepare three sets of paper slips (e.g., 8½in by 11in sheets cut into quarters), one set for each tree, so that everyone in the group will have a slip at each tree. Then take three envelopes and mark each of them 1, 2, or 3. Place one set of slips in each envelope and leave it at the corresponding tree.

Gather the group and hand out pencils then explain the exercise. Walk together with the entire group to visit the three trees. At the first tree, ask the participants to each take a slip of paper from the envelope. Invite them to silently observe or otherwise perceive the tree's essence for a few minutes, and then write a word or phrase (fewer than five words) to describe the tree in a poetic fashion. Collect the slips and return them to the envelope, then lead the group to the next tree, to repeat those steps, until all three have been visited. Allow about ten minutes per tree and five minutes between each one.

When that is completed, bring the group together and divide the participants into three roughly equal-size groups. Give each group some full sheets of paper and one of the three envelopes. From what is written on the enclosed slips of paper, each group is to create a poem about the tree, trying to be as true to the original phrases as possible but adding a few new ones if necessary. When they are finished, each group reads their poem aloud for everyone to enjoy.

[Thanks to Julie Hawkowl for this exercise.]

The Four Elements
Purpose: To connect with the four essential elements on Earth
Duration: 45 minutes per element; can be done at separate times or in a sequence of 4 hours

Water
Find a body of water—a stream, pond, or lake—or if none is available, have each person fill a bowl with water. Ask that the participants take the time to silently explore the miracle of water as if discovering it for the first time: touching it, observing it, drinking it (if it's clean enough), and even wading in it (but not taking a swim just yet). They should notice its depth and mass, not only its surface, and imagine what is below the surface, unseen. About midway through the allotted time, invite the participants to describe their experiences, if they so wish. Did they notice anything unusual? What feelings did this exploration evoke? (Sharing impressions in this way reinforces the connection with the element.) Reflect on the yielding fluidity yet tremendous power of water. Thank water openly for its gift

of life. Then go for a swim! Play like dolphins, beavers, otters, and other creatures that clearly love water.

Air

Begin by inviting the group to consciously breathe together. Then ask them to take deeper breaths, feeling the life energy in each breath. Ask them to "look" at the air, the invisible substance between all things, and then to breathe that in. Next, have everyone hold their breath until it starts to feel uncomfortable, then have them notice the relief of the exhale and really savor that first in-breath. Offer the suggestion: *Inhale with gratitude. Exhale with love.* You might mention how air, along with the precious oxygen contained within it, is an inestimable gift from our earliest bacterial ancestors. Life as we know it began with them. Thank them for this essential miracle. *Inhale with gratitude. Exhale with love.* Suggest that the participants notice the birds and the insects and how they can "swim" in the air. They might take some time to observe how flying is a highly unusual and wondrous ability and feel any wind or breeze. Again: *inhale with gratitude, exhale with love.* Invite the participants to share their experiences. What did they notice? What are they feeling? Thank the air for its direct, boundless inspiration.

Fire

On a clear day, invite the group to notice the sun, the great primordial fire in the heavens, the fire that begets all fire on Earth. Have everyone greet the sun. Speak to it. Thank it. Feel its warmth and the life-giving qualities of fire.

A variation at night is to make a campfire. Ask people to be silent, to heighten awareness, and to carefully notice the lighting of the match (or if someone is knowledgeable, the spark and subsequent fire created by a matchless method!). When the fire is going strong, offer it a pinch of tobacco* or scented oil, or even a few spoonfuls of milk (a favorite Siberian method). These are ancient methods of acknowledging the mysterious transformative power of fire. Invite each person to place a small piece of wood in the fire as they invoke something in their life which is meaningful to them or with which they want to deepen their connection. As they do so, they may choose to say out loud: "I bring my passion for _____. Thank you, fire, for helping that passion burn brightly within me."

When this little ritual is completed, have each person reflect on the wonder of *this* fire and what makes it special, such as the constantly changing shapes of the flames, the intensity of its warmth, and the different types of light it emits. At this point, if you don't switch into another activity, such as general storytelling, invite each person to share any impressions "popcorn" style ("popping" happens when an individual's urge to share becomes so strong that they voice their thoughts). Because enthusiasm, like passion, is a fiery emotion, you can ask the group to share what they are feeling enthusiastic about or simply how fire enriches their lives.

Earth

Have everyone explore the soil or the ground. If there is a garden and a place within it where people can sit or lie down, all the better. Invite them to take the time to crawl, touching and delving into the earth like young children. Perhaps there are some small rocks in the soil. If so, they might play with them. Let each person's sensual nature express itself. Encourage them to notice the plant world in its variety and glory, and to observe how each plant depends on the earth, with which it is connected through its roots. Then suggest that they mimic the roots with their fingers and feet, drawing in the grounding, stable energy of earth as it makes its way into their bodies. Guide the group aloud through the process and do it with them. Close the exercise by inviting everyone to kneel and thank the Earth for her balance and abundance, and to kiss the ground if they wish. Have everyone share whatever impressions come to mind.

Mythic Landscape Map

Purpose: To outline some of the outstanding features of a particular landscape artistically, and in so doing, to go beyond ordinary mapping and chart its "mythos," a good exercise when it's raining
Duration: 30 minutes at a time

On a large sheet of paper, sketch a boundary to represent an area that extends roughly half a mile in all directions from the main indoor meeting place for the Intensive. Ask participants to share aloud the significant impressions they have received thus far from interacting with specific places in the landscape. This will be easier if they have been asked to notice these places as they walk the landscape from the beginning of the Intensive. What moved them and why? How might they describe that place using a verb or colorful phrase in an evocative way? A few examples are Wailing Rock, Bright Doe Meadow, Dripping Moss Staircase, and Courageous Creek (or humorous ones like The Humping Hemlocks).

Ask whoever feels called to sketch a miniature representation of these places on the map, writing the names underneath. This can be done by one or more people. Try to keep these places proportionally distant from one another so that the map is roughly to scale. A person who knows the land well will need to advise this process. If someone becomes particularly enthusiastic about the exercise, they can spend time embellishing the map, refining the sketches with detail and color, and adding in any roads or trails. Display the map in a central, easily visible location.

This mapping process, which can be quite whimsical at times, may continue spontaneously throughout the Intensive. You might remind people to add to the map if they wish, or even set aside additional times to do so as a group. Toward the end of the WEI, the map can provide an easy way to tell a retrospective story of the time spent outdoors. One or two people can volunteer to narrate the story, using the map as a visual aid.

Awareness of Place

Humans are highly sense-oriented beings, but the prevailing cultural norms have relegated most sensory input to a low priority or have even deemed it something to be blocked out. We can relearn how to use our senses for the purpose of knowing and feeling the natural world in a new, yet ancient way, by developing our awareness of place. This can lead to a profound vitality that participants may never have felt before. To achieve this, the five senses of seeing, smelling, touching, hearing, and tasting, and the "sixth sense"—intuition—are placed center stage.

The strengthening of sensory awareness is a form of active meditation. The aim is not to force ourselves into being aware of our surroundings, but to relax and allow what exists to make its presence known. This is done by the simple yet profound act of paying attention, and by bringing the attention back when it wanders into distracted thinking. We could also call this the act of pure observation, but it is done with our whole being, not just our eyes. The rewards for doing this are immense. When we slow down, become silent, and let nature reveal herself, in her time frame, we begin to feel the essential miracle of life. To do so is to begin to live in balance.

Joseph Cornell, the world-renowned naturalist, writes about this in his book *Sharing Nature with Children*:

> When a person becomes harmoniously attuned with the world, feelings of harmony with other people are intensified, too. Through watching nature in silence, we

discover within ourselves feelings of relatedness with whatever we see—plants, animals, stones, Earth and sky. The American Indians knew that, in silence, we can feel that all things are expressions of a single Life, and that we humans, too, are children of that Life.[9]

In the past few decades, Cornell was joined by a whole generation of "tracker-educators" who made full-bodied nature connection their life's work. Three of the most well known are Jon Young; Tom Brown, Jr.; and Paul Rezendes. Their masterful teachings, based on indigenous wisdom, include more than instruction in physical survival skills and animal tracking; they are about making that crucial connection between nature and spirit. They have attracted thousands of people in the process. Some of the exercises below, designed to strengthen one's awareness of place, are adapted from those teachings. The effectiveness of these exercises stems not only from the various techniques but from the innocence, openness, and wonder that arise from within oneself during practice.

Eckhart Tolle explains this well in his book *Stillness Speaks:*

> To bring your attention to a stone, a tree, or an animal does not mean to *think* about it, but simply to perceive it, to hold it in your awareness. Something of its essence then transmits itself to you. You can sense how still it is, and in doing so the same stillness arises within you. You sense how deeply it rests in Being—completely at one with what it is and where it is. In realizing this, you too come to a place of rest deep within yourself.[10]

This kind of peace with nature can only happen when one is paying attention to what is actually happening in the immediate environment. The large body of nature awareness literature contains a wide variety of field exercises, but they all start by honing one's attention. Those chosen for a WEI have been included because of the guides' familiarity with them and because they all include the following components that provide an optimal learning experience:

- Awakening energy and interest
- Sharpening attention
- Experiencing without abstraction
- Sharing inspiration as a group

What Colors?
Purpose: To help us break out of conditioned ways of perceiving the world
Duration: 15 minutes
Do the following preliminary exercise to demonstrate the difference between abstract thinking and seeing what is. This can be conducted indoors, if necessary. Prepare in advance a poster board or sheet of paper large enough for all to see. Paint or use colored markers to draw the words *yellow, black, blue, red, green, orange,* and *brown* on the board—but do not paint them in the colors they represent. For example, paint the word *red* with blue paint or any other paint but red. Gather the group and show them the board, asking them to quickly call out the colors they see—not the *words,* but the *colors.* Most people will not be able to easily say the colors but will confuse them with the words. They will laugh! Then you can point out that when they are outside, they can mistake the name of a tree—for example, an ash—for the unique, living being *called* an ash.

Fully Present
Purpose: To deepen our basic experience of nature by tuning into the present moment with concentrated awareness
Duration: 20 minutes

This four-part exercise includes grounding one's energy, using peripheral vision, and walking with awareness. Ask each person to focus intently on the micro-moments of the practice so that with a few repetitions they will be able to do it on their own as a regular routine. Participants usually report a greater sense of power and connection following the exercise. The increased concentration that is called forth puts the busy thinking mind on hold and releases more life energy into their bodies.

Guide the participants through the exercise as follows, pausing between sentences:

1. *Begin to ground your energy in the Earth by putting complete attention on the body. See if you can feel the precise place where your human body ends and the Earth body beneath you begins. Now include the act of breathing in your awareness. Close your eyes for a minute. Breathe a little deeper than normal, imagining the breath flowing down through your torso into your legs and down past your feet like roots. Sink your roots deep into the Earth. Do this for several deep breaths. Feel the life energy course through you, and notice how it connects your body with the Earth's body. Now inhale, and feel the energy emanating from the ground coming into your feet, legs, and body and rising up to your head. Do this a few times at your own pace.*

2. *Now open your eyes and raise your hands to the sky. Use the space between your outstretched arms like a telescope, looking at the vastness before you. Then, eyes wide open, practice the same kind of breathing and energy exchange with the sky that you experienced with the ground. Take your time.*

3. *Now spread your arms apart, parallel to the ground. Use your peripheral vision by extending your sight as far as possible in both directions (without overdoing it), taking in the whole view. Then move both arms in wide, scooping motions toward*

your heart and "breathe in" the surrounding environment.
Again, do this a few times at your own pace.

4. *Start moving slowly, feeling your feet and imagining them*
   as webbed sensors that are always connected to the ground,
   even when one foot is in the air. Bring renewed awareness to
   the simple act of walking—first in this exaggerated way and
   then normally, but without losing the intense awareness. Keep
   walking, remaining highly alert to your surroundings. Focus
   for a few minutes on just seeing whatever is in view. Slow
   down and focus on hearing, and then, while continuing to
   walk, switch to touching various parts of nature, followed by
   smelling and even tasting things.

To finish, call the group back together, and ask them to share reflections on what they experienced.

Variation: Suggest that each person begin their Solo Time by beginning with steps 1–3 above.

The Camera Game

Purpose: To open us to the sheer wonder and beauty of the natural world as well as to build trust between participants
Duration: 30 minutes

Have people pair up and decide who goes first. That person will agree to be led, with eyes closed, around the immediate vicinity—say fifty square yards—by their partner. The person being led will be the "camera," and the guiding partner will be the "photographer." Of course, it's important to emphasize that the guiding partner should be gentle and walk slowly with their camera! The job of the photographer is to find interesting things to show the camera and to take "photos" of them by tapping gently on the camera's back. The possibilities are almost infinite, as the photographer aims the camera up and down, simulates use of micro and macro lenses by focusing on close or distant subjects, and takes pictures of animals, plants, minerals, etc. With each tap, the camera will open their eyes a few seconds to enjoy the sight, and then close them again, like a camera shutter. (Demonstrate this beforehand with a volunteer from the group.) Give the first pair about ten minutes to take several photos. Then have them switch roles. Leave a little time at the end for spontaneous sharing among the group.

Tracking 101

Purpose: To cultivate a deep and penetrating awareness of the natural world. This is the central exercise for doing so in a WEI.

Duration: 45 minutes–1 hour

Sit down with the group and give each person a printed copy of the list below. Explain that each of them will be selecting a spot within a hundred-yard radius, close enough to hear your "wolf-howl"† when it is time to return. They will spend some time alone and out of view from the others. Ask them to select a spot they have not visited before or one that especially calls to them. Once there, they will focus on "tracking" the things on the list. This list is not to be followed rigidly or in order, but is meant to serve as a handy tool to connect with nature in new and creative ways. It suggests aspects of the natural world for them to observe and feel during the exercise:

- Color and shading: What are the subtle differences you notice between similar colors?
- Water and air flow: Where is each of these coming from and where does it go?
- Grouped relationships/communities: What is growing in relationship to what? What animals, insects, or birds seem to be connected to what plants?
- Patterns (pronounced areas of growth, branches, spirals, stress marks, odd and even numbers of things): Can you see any underlying similarities in design?
- Edges: Where does one system meet another?

- Limits: What seems to be held back from full expression? Why might that be happening?
- Effects of past events (the smoothness on a rock, tooth marks on a downed tree, new plants growing out of a stump): Can you visualize what happened?
- Opposites (hard and soft, light and shadow, high and low, far and near): How do they relate to each other?
- Energy: How are light and heat coming into and leaving the system? Can you feel that in your body?
- Change: Where isn't there change?
- Your inner world: What are you are feeling? Is there an inner story?

Point out that different kinds of inner stories about who they think they are may surface during this process and they should track these as well. *Tracking* really means to observe thoroughly—and that includes observing the thought process. It does not mean chewing the thoughts over and over, but just noticing them as dispassionately as possible. Examples of possible stories they might track are:

"I am an expert nature observer. I can do this better than the others."

"I can't pay attention. I am the worst."

"When I'm alone in nature, I feel lonely/scared/bored/restless."

"Some event happened an hour ago (or years ago), and I must figure it out right now."

"There are so many things I need to be doing after this retreat is over."

There are countless inner stories like these, and most of us have experienced a wide variety of them. In a sense, they are all attempts at avoiding the present moment. They are not problematic if we simply notice them without getting caught in them. Of course, we do get caught sometimes. Turning our attention to the list, and what it points to, is an excellent way to not get lost in a story.

When you call the group back together, invite them to share their experiences. Be sure to convey your appreciation not only for the sharing of impressions regarding the outer world but for any inner stories revealed and the vulnerability that entails.

Supplemental Nature Awareness Exercises

Depending on the inclinations of the group, the total amount of time allotted, and the weather conditions, the following additional exercises may be offered at the Intensive. These can also be substituted for the simpler ones described above.

Aimless Walking

Purpose: To renew a childlike and lighthearted bond with the natural world

Duration: 1–2 hours

The participants each take a walk alone without a purpose. They have no direction and no goal. They are free to wander wherever their inner compass takes them. They each bring a map and an outer compass and check their bearings before they leave. (They must know basic orienteering skills and be familiar with the landscape before doing this.)

Offer the group suggestions such as these:

Once you begin walking, allow your sense of wonder to guide you. What do you smell? What's behind that rock? Where does that exposed root lead? What's in the clearing? Be playful and explore the Earth in a way you always dreamed of. You are not trying to get anywhere, but at least for the first fifteen to thirty minutes, keep moving. Do you want to take your shoes off and feel the moss or water directly on your feet? Do you want to hang from that branch or look in that animal hole? Keep engaging your senses without pushing too hard. Breathe more deeply. Feel your body. Touch natural objects in different ways. Sense the life energy all around. Have fun! Return refreshed, ready to engage with others and share some highlights.

Widening Circles

Purpose: To enlarge our sense of self beyond the boundary of our skin
Duration: 15 minutes

We are so much bigger than we think we are! When used deliberately, vision can be a wonderful aid in knowing our larger bodies. Choose a spot in which the group can sit comfortably with the widest, farthest view possible and an interesting foreground. To begin, lead them in an abbreviated version of the "grounding" segment in the Fully Present exercise. When they open their eyes, have them pause and look at what is closest to them, taking a few minutes to fully receive what is offered by nature. This immediate view of their surroundings—let's say at five feet—will be the first of several widening bands that they will slowly scan horizontally for at least a full 180 degrees. Each succeeding time, they will look a little farther and wider, moving toward the horizon.

Provide guidance such as this:

Take the time to look deeply at the grasses, small bushes, flowers, stones, and insects close to you. Scan this visual band slowly. Extend a sense of empathy and kinship to whatever you behold. (This may seem contrived at first, but that's only because our cultural conditioning says that each of us ends at our skin. Eventually, it will feel natural.) ... Now extend your vision by focusing twenty feet away and scan again, making sure to receive and let go of each image in turn ... This time, focus forty feet away ... now eighty feet ... pause, breathe in, and savor each band of nature. Now look as far as you can. See where the land and the sky meet and feel that edge where they "kiss."

Meet-a-Tree

Purpose: To enable us, using senses other than sight, to locate and connect to a tree

Duration: 45 minutes

Give a brief overview of what is to follow. Obtain from all participants permission to blindfold them and ask them to trust the process—setting aside expectations and beliefs for the time being. Then have people pair up and decide who in each pair will go first. That person will agree to be led blindfolded by their partner out into the woods, within prearranged boundaries. The sighted person holds the hand of their partner and walks carefully to any tree that is neither too close nor too far away from the starting point. About twenty to thirty feet away is a good distance. The sighted partner should proceed in a meandering, indirect way to the tree, where the blindfolded partner is left for two or three minutes, giving them sufficient time to "greet" it. Silently, the blindfolded partner may introduce themselves to the tree, feeling its bark, smelling its aroma, hugging it, visualizing it in their mind's eye, sensing the rhythm of its energy, or in any other way connecting to it. (It is useful to suggest these means of connection during the overview.) The sighted partner moves a few yards away while this is taking place, so as not to interfere, distract, or—by their presence—encourage any conversation. When the time is up, the sighted partner leads the blindfolded partner back to the starting point, using a different route.

When they arrive back at the starting point, the facilitator asks the tree "greeter" to remove the blindfold but before looking around to just stop and concentrate. Instruct the greeter to *see* that tree in their mind, visualize the way back to it, and, when ready, walk out and find it. As the greeter moves off to locate the tree, their partner follows along about five yards behind, to not influence their movements. It is only after the greeter declares, "This is my tree," that their partner will confirm or deny that it is the right tree.

The partners switch roles and repeat the exercise. After it has been completed, ask the participants to take a few moments to reflect upon their experiences and then to share with the group what they learned/experienced.

---

* Tobacco is considered a sacred plant in many indigenous traditions. It is used in a wide variety of ways, for blessing, healing, prayer, and making offerings.

† The "wolf-howl" is a fun and effective way to get the attention of your group and call them back to the meeting place. As members return to the meeting place they, too, can begin to howl with the guides. With each additional member of the "pack," the sound gets louder and louder until everyone has returned. Your pack is back together again, ready to share their reflections and insights on the exercise just completed or go on to the next practice.

Chapter 9

The Power of Story

The universe is made of stories, not of atoms.
                                        —Muriel Rukeyser

The true storyteller teaches the cultural values [and]
passes on knowledge and the beliefs within the stories to
the next generation ... The true role of the storyteller is
to pass on the lessons from the beginning of time.
                                        —Pauline McLeod

We like to tell stories. Long before television, movies, and the
Internet, people sat around campfires and used language to
share the pictures they saw in their minds. Over time, these
pictures became collective agreements about how things are.
They were dreamt and spoken, and then told and retold.

Today, few cultures pass on stories this way. But every
culture continues to shape reality through storytelling. The
question is: *What kind of stories do we want to tell?* Do our stories
leave us inspired or drained? Are they life-enhancing or life-
destroying? Are they functional or dysfunctional?

What's in a Worldview?
In his remarkable novel *Ishmael*, Daniel Quinn makes the
distinction between "Leavers" and "Takers."[1] The Takers are the
people often referred to as "civilized" who formed a culture out
of an agricultural revolution* that began about ten thousand
years ago in the Near East. The Leavers are the people of all
other cultures, referred to by the Takers as "primitive."

The Leavers and Takers have very different stories. Each of
these stories contains a core worldview that forms the basis of

their respective cultures. As Quinn's character Ishmael puts it: "The premise of the Taker story is *the world belongs to man.* The premise of the Leaver story is *man belongs to the world.*"[2] These premises make all the difference, defining whether people live in balance or imbalance with nature.

Currently, here on Earth, it is the era of the Takers, and their habitat is the entire planet. The Leavers still exist here and there, but their humble voices have been nearly silenced since the onset of the industrial age. The Takers who make up most of humanity have taken almost everything. They have steadily increased their dominance, not because their story is better or more adaptive than that of the Leavers, but because it has been backed up by superior firepower. That's the stick behind the Takers' success. The carrot, now sustained by a dizzying amount of technological innovation, is the seductive illusion that industrial civilization can keep growing forever, and that population and consumption on Earth have no limits.

Those of us who seek to create an Earth-honoring culture are drawn to the Leavers' story, adapted for new circumstances. We grapple with what it means to live sustainably while thoroughly embedded in a Taker world. Let's look at some of the crucial differences between the Taker and Leaver worldviews.

The foundation of the Taker worldview is that humans are apart from, and superior to, the rest of the web of life. The pillars of this worldview are:

- The world revolves around humans.
- There is not enough to go around.
- The Taker story is the only story that is real.
- Humans are inherently flawed.
- Nature is our supply house.
- The present moment is a means to an end.

Many other assumptions reinforce the Takers' belief in separation and superiority, but these six are the meta-beliefs that hold all the other assumptions in place.

Everyone born in the modern world has been steeped in this story. We absorb it from the Taker culture, whether we grow up with a scientific worldview or a religious worldview (or neither). In fact, the story is so widespread and "normal" that even if rejected intellectually, it is firmly rooted in the subconscious and is a strong determinant of our behavior. Indeed, cell biologist Bruce Lipton points out, "Cognitive neuroscientists ... conclude that 95% of our decisions, actions, emotions, and behaviors are derived from the unobserved processing of the subconscious mind."[3] We can verify this by looking at our own experiences and noticing the difficulty we often have in changing undesirable patterns of thought and behavior, even when we are committed to doing so.

The Leavers are not more valuable or worthy than the Takers, but Leavers see the world quite differently. They believe that *humans are embedded in, and inseparable from, nature.* They also have been around a lot longer than the Takers. The Leavers' life-affirming perspective includes:

- Humans are no more or less important than other creatures.
- The universe is an abundant place.
- There are many different stories and ways to live.
- Born from the Earth, humans are just fine the way we are.
- Everything is alive and we are in relationship with it.
- The present moment is where life is lived.

Spanning the globe, from the Hopi of the American Southwest to the Ittelman of Kamchatka, Russia, there remain a few thousand Leaver tribes.[4] Many of these tribes are relatively small. Each speaks a distinct language and does its best to maintain its traditions, embodying the tenets listed above. The shamans and medicine people I've met from various Leaver tribes emphasize that they are not engaging in philosophizing: "We don't just believe these things, we experience them!"

While I have great respect for these Leaver societies, it won't be possible (or desirable) for Taker society to abruptly dismantle its social and economic structures and copy existing Leaver ones (as compelling as that may sound). As humans, we have already experienced the majority of our history as hunter-gatherers. We are again poised for a different culture and lifestyle—one that is neither hunter-gatherer nor based on domination, but instead infuses the Leaver story into the next phase of human evolution. A story to help us make this epic transition might go something like this:

For many years, those of us who fervently loved the Earth thought the situation was hopeless. Now, after a long and difficult journey, many of us have begun to remember the old ways. We sense a quickening into something mysterious, and through observing the life cycle of a butterfly, we know that transformation is possible. Our focus is on celebrating life, and we remain steadfast in an attitude of cooperation and gentleness. We insist on seeing the world as our animistic ancestors did and imagining it from the vantage point of our thriving descendants. Banding together, we nurture love and creativity because they are the basis for the kind of world we want to live in. We have no idea about the outcome, but we ask the forces of nature to help us. Demonstrating the beauty and functionality of a new culture—and the joy that brings— is our passionate calling. We realize we are not helpless; we are powerful agents of change because we are made of Earth and stars. We reinforce this worldview with one another while accepting what is honorable from the dominant society. To the best of our ability, we love fully and live lightly on the land.

Imagine that this story is told and retold by aspiring Leavers and that it gains power not by coercion but by attraction. Imagine that it dovetails perfectly with the relocalization movement, in which local populations determine their economies, energy sources, and food supply, including trade and integration with the larger whole. Such a vision is not an unattainable fantasy. It is the outcome of transitioning from a culture of separation to one that is rooted in nature's design: a mutually beneficial exchange between humans and the living systems that sustain them, and amongst humans themselves.

The Hero's Journey

Changing the Taker story takes courage and determination. We can't just think about it. We need to *experience* the ecstasy that is possible in a new Leaver lifestyle. Only through repeated, formative experiences can we "reprogram" our story with functional beliefs that will settle into the subconscious. (All the exercises in this book are aimed at just that!)

Telling a new Leaver story means discovering who we are. We can't fake it. It means understanding clearly how the sacred path we are walking as individuals corresponds with our collective destiny. It's not about acquiring elegant ideas or convincing others of anything. It's about investigating our life experience with resolute honesty to find out what works and what does not.

Deciding to live with this level of self-awareness is what the great mythologist Joseph Campbell called the "hero's journey."[5] Whoever chooses to live outside the Taker worldview is on a hero's journey. To take that risk requires willingness to experience the fear of being between stories. The old one does not work, and the new one has not yet materialized. This is just the place in which to draw strength from each other as we learn not only about our fears but about the beauty and courage, we each possess.

One WEI participant put it this way: "We were sitting around the campfire and time seemed to stop. Everyone looked ancient, far wiser than one lifetime. In an instant, I felt what it meant to rely on each other as if our lives depended on it and was ashamed because I always thought I could get by solely on my own."[6]

Choosing a different worldview and doing one's best to live by it can be daunting and personally painful at times. To live with gratitude and keep an open heart even in the worst of circumstances is heroic. That kind of radical decision has been written about extensively by Bernie Siegel, an oncologist who is an authority on the role of attitude in getting and staying well. In his bestselling book *Love, Medicine, and Miracles*, he cites numerous examples from Nazi death camps and other extreme circumstances in which fortitude and flexibility made the difference between life and death. The survivors whose stories he documented categorically contradict the idea that external conditions solely dictate a person's sense of well-being. His conclusion: we are not victims of a cold world, fundamentally helpless to improve our life situation and attitude.[7]

However, it takes practice to decondition our minds from the helplessness and despair we learned by being steeped in Taker society. This is especially true when contemplating the destruction of the natural world. Joanna Macy writes: "When you look at what is happening to our world—and it is hard to look at what's happening to our water, our air, our trees, our fellow species—it becomes clear that unless you have some roots in a spiritual practice that holds life sacred and encourages joyful communion with all your fellow beings, facing the enormous challenges ahead becomes nearly impossible."[8]

The story "Jumping Mouse," told by Hyemeyohsts Storm in his book *Seven Arrows*, beautifully represents the hero's journey each of us must take if we want to return home to our aboriginal nature. This is the story of a heroic mouse who shows that courage, determination, and generosity can lead to greatness. This mouse ventures away from his small world of mice to follow a sound that he, and only he, hears. Despite his fear of the unknown, the mouse persists in his journey. He meets Raccoon, who leads him to the river and introduces him to Frog, who gives him the following advice so that he can gain Medicine Power: "Crouch as low as you can, then jump as high as you are able."[9] When he does this, he glimpses the Sacred Mountains and earns the name of Jumping Mouse.

He returns to the world of mice, but he cannot forget his vision of the Sacred Mountains. So, Jumping Mouse courageously ventures off again. He meets Old Mouse, who warns him of dangers and tries to convince him to forget his quest and stay where it is safe and predictable. Determined, Jumping Mouse continues his journey and meets Buffalo, who is sick and dying and can only be cured by the eye of a mouse. Jumping Mouse cannot let such a great being die, so he gives him one of his eyes and Buffalo is healed.

In gratitude, Buffalo leads him to the foot of the Sacred Mountains where he meets Gray Wolf, who has lost his memory. Jumping Mouse gives his other eye to the wolf, who is then healed. Gray Wolf takes Jumping Mouse into the Sacred Mountains to a Great Medicine Lake. The mouse drinks the water from the lake while Wolf describes to him the beauty that is there. After Wolf leaves, Jumping Mouse is blind and alone and trembles in fear. He feels a shadow on his back and hears the sound that eagles make when they strike, and then he goes to sleep. When he awakens, his vision is clear and he sees his old friend Frog on a lily pad on Medicine Lake. "You have a new name," calls Frog. "You are Eagle!"[10]

For children and adults alike, stories like "Jumping Mouse" light the way. Their innocent but penetrating wisdom underscores a universal theme: to change what we have been taught and to live authentically can be scary. The journey is filled with challenges and difficulties, but the reward is transformation. If we take these stories to heart, they can help give us the courage to birth a culture that is in alignment with the rest of Life.

A New Science as Part of a Leaver Worldview

Science permeates the modern world. In almost every country with more than a rudimentary educational system, a very similar science is taught, and its application has been the handmaiden of industrialization. Science has been brilliant at analysis, observation, measurement, and description but has failed to adequately incorporate subjective experience and consciousness into its story. (Science is, after all, also a story!) However, a more exciting and imaginative vision of reality is being presented by the leading edge of the scientific community. This vision suggests that the universe is not a random and meaningless interaction of mostly "dead" parts, but is laden with meaning, purpose, value, and life!

There are thousands of scientists at the forefront of creating a new scientific story, but two are particularly good at articulating a warmer, life-centered cosmology. They are Brian Swimme, a mathematician and astrophysicist, and Robert Lanza, a cell biologist and medical doctor.

During an interview, Swimme, in his inspired way, said:

This is the greatest discovery of the scientific enterprise: You take hydrogen gas, and you leave it alone, and it turns into rosebushes, giraffes, and humans.

Life begins around three and a half billion years ago, and then it began to complexify around seven hundred million years ago. And then, one strange little lineage forms—the worms. The worms develop a backbone and a nervous system. We're so impressed by brains. The worms created the brains. You see the theme I'm developing here? Hydrogen. It becomes us. All of matter is spiritual. And if the worms can create the brains, then creativity is everywhere![11]

He explained:

> The point is that if humans are spiritual, then hydrogen is spiritual. It's an incredible opportunity to escape the traditional dualism—you know, spirit is up there; matter is down here. Actually, it's different. You have the matter all the way through, and so you have the spirit all the way through.[12]

Lanza shared another part of the story:

> In daily life, space and time are harmless illusions. A problem arises only because, by treating these as fundamental and independent things, science picks a completely wrong starting point for investigations into the nature of reality. Most researchers still believe they can build from one side of nature, the physical, without the other side, the living. By inclination and training these scientists are obsessed with mathematical descriptions of the world. If only, after leaving work, they would look out with equal seriousness over a pond and watch the schools of minnows rise to the surface. The fish, the ducks, and the cormorants paddling out beyond the pads and the cattails, are all part of the greater answer.[13]

To re-emphasize: science is just now beginning to recognize what indigenous people, Eastern religions, and mystics have understood for millennia. At the beginning of the twenty-first century, the cherished foundations of Western civilization that seemed immutable are cracking, as life pours through human vessels (us!) like plants shooting through abandoned concrete. The new sustainable cultures born out of this pressure cooker will undoubtedly tell a story that includes a science that honors nature's design. It's an empowering story that places humans inside nature, not as distant observers.

Story in the Wild Earth Intensive

The Wild Earth Intensive (WEI) is an invitation to tell and experience a different story. By the end of the ten days, some version of a new Leaver story inevitably begins to emerge. Since the WEI is not a course in philosophy, psychology, or anthropology, this does not show up as a tidy group thesis, but in laughter, connection, and celebration. When the story is spoken, it comes out spontaneously in small phrases, such as "We can live in a new way that is very old," "Slowing down and living in the now makes all the difference," and "When our hearts are open, we just don't need so much stuff."

This kind of insight and openheartedness occurs naturally as a result of the group's strong intention to create a lasting, healthy culture, and the vigilance on the part of the guides to harvest stories—both inside and out of the Intensive—that support that intention. By taking a sustained break from the information glut of the modern world, we learn what oral cultures have always known. This enables us to tell stories that are nourishing and adaptive—those that make us feel better and allow our tribe to run more smoothly.

During a WEI, a new cultural story is explored and embodied throughout the various program activities. This is done both directly and indirectly, personally and transpersonally. If you are facilitating and are ready to engage the participants in overt story changing, you can do so in the following ways:

1. Explain the power of story.
2. Summarize the stories of the Leavers and Takers and the new scientific story (using several videos if you wish), so that participants can see the larger picture.
3. Ensure that each participant has an opportunity to voice their pain.
4. Tell the story of Jumping Mouse or a similar story that illuminates the sacred path we are walking and the courage it takes to keep going. Invite each person to take a turn reading a paragraph or two until the story is finished (usually after two consecutive evenings), and then have the group reflect on the following questions:

   - How do you relate to the story?
   - What did it teach you?
   - What do you think the various metaphors mean? For example, "Crouch as low as you can, then jump as high as you are able."
   - What are your sources of support?
   - Who helped you and how?
   - Where do nature and the animals fit into your story?

Option: Invite a guest facilitator with expertise in storytelling and the hero's journey to spend a day focusing on this theme.

5. Engage in several exercises that bring forth and focus upon the gifts of each participant. A person in touch with his joy, expressing his talents and abilities, is demonstrating a great story!
6. Glean the empowered stories that emerge. As the participants feel more connected, they gain a clearer perspective on their lives. For example, one man said, with tears in his eyes, "I live alone and always felt more

comfortable that way. Now, I've become aware that I'm afraid of people leaving me, because my anxiety is growing at the thought of our group breaking up in a few days. I realize I need to get closer to people anyway."[14] This man was very openhearted, but his self-image was that of a recluse. It is important as a facilitator to validate this newfound story with some kind of acknowledgment, either privately or publicly.

7. Sit around a campfire or inside a round structure such as a yurt for a few evenings because these settings energize the act of storytelling. Ask participants to share a highlight of the day: "What did the land, sky, or the animals whisper in your ear?" "When you took your solo time, what was different or new about your special spot?"

8. Notice the unique tone and characteristics of the collective story that is created by the group during the time they spend together. Find out if one of the participants wants to encapsulate this time with a song or a poem.

9. Make the distinction between formal and informal storytelling. Formal storytelling is an art form that takes years to perfect, while telling stories happens all the time. However, you may want to bring attention to the recipe for any good story: plenty of conviction and a touch of humor, spiced with colorful imagery. Point out that stories are not only told through speech but may be chanted, sung, or even danced.

10. Change the negative stories we tell ourselves (see the last exercise of the chapter).

A Treasure Chest of Gifts and Talents

Everyone possesses life-enhancing qualities. Many of us can demonstrate several of these qualities in our daily lives consistently. For example, one person may have the ability to be patient and peaceful in stressful situations, while another may uplift a group by being cheerful and positive. Another may have a great sense of humor or may be particularly sensitive and kind. Others can be "coyote like" and, through their contrarian nature, can draw out a higher truth in a group. And still others are organized and demonstrate clear thinking. These qualities could be considered our rich interior gifts. Some people are fortunate enough to embody many of them.

On the outer level, most of us express or would like to express, our natural beauty and unique perception in a particular way. There are gifted builders, healers, musicians, potters, athletes, naturalists, actors, and social innovators of all types, all of whom enrich the lives of others. The list is almost endless and, of course, none of us is limited to one role. Our outer gifts are an expression of our inner essence.

Expressing our inner and outer gifts is one of the most important contributions we can make as human beings. We tend to feel most alive when we do. WEI guides aim to put these gifts in clear sight, so everyone participating can witness them like sparkling jewels.

When people feel safe and relaxed, these gifts usually are made visible, but without being given conscious attention by others, they may not have the opportunity to flourish. About three-quarters of the way through the Intensive, we offer three exercises in a row (with plenty of time for movement in between) that invite the participants to image and list their gifts and appreciate others for theirs.

Imaging Our Gifts
Purpose: To image our gifts through artistic expression
Duration: 30 minutes
Drawing colorful images that are based on feeling and spontaneity can help us tap into the creative Source of our gifts which is beyond words. This exercise gets people to make the

intuitive link between identifying (and strengthening) their innate gifts and tapping into the flow of life force energy—true power—that is always available.

Lay out drawing materials (large paper, crayons, oil pastels, and/or nontoxic markers). If outdoors, invite the group to listen to the wind in the trees; if inside, play soft music in the background. Have them work in silence. Remind people that they are not being asked to show artistic mastery, and request that they express their responses to the following question, using color, in whatever way seems appropriate:

> *When you think of a time when you felt powerful, or when you were clear that you made a difference in somebody's life, or when you felt really happy doing something you loved (or all three), what does it look like? (Don't ponder it too much, just draw it!)*

Option: Use clay instead of drawing materials.

Speaking Our Gifts
Purpose: To identify and/or reinforce our gifts
Duration: 15 minutes

Have people bring their drawings (or clay sculpture) from the previous exercise and then divide into pairs. The drawings will be used as a touchstone to reflect upon while the participants verbally list their inner and outer gifts as self-appreciatively as possible. You can remind everyone that appreciating oneself can be difficult but very rewarding. Have paper and pencils on hand.

While one person is speaking, the other writes the key phrases they are hearing. The speaker is asked to say whatever comes to mind in a free-associative, spontaneous manner. If the speaker gets stuck, the listener, acting as a good coach, just reminds them to keep breathing and does not intervene in the content. After about five minutes, gently ask all the speakers to wrap it up. The listeners then read back to the former speakers what they heard and wrote down. It can be quite powerful for a participant to hear what they have just said, now spoken lovingly by their partner. Then the pairs switch roles.

This simple exercise increases the spiral of appreciation for oneself and others that has been building from the start of the WEI. It also forms the basis for preparing the participants for "visioning" (see Chapter 17)—the exploration into how to use one's gifts for the benefit of the community—which takes place near the close of the Intensive.

The Gifts I See in You

Purpose: To change ingrained patterns of self-condemnation
Duration: 1½ hours

Often, we fear that if we are truly seen by others, they will notice that, underneath our personality, we are insufficient, bad, or ugly. On the contrary, being "mirrored" by others can be remarkably transformative. It is transformative because, after growing close to one another over a series of days, what we hear from others tends to be both authentic and uncannily accurate. This exercise, on the heels of the preceding two, usually leaves the participants in a state of awe from the sustained love and appreciation.

The group sits in a circle and, one by one, each person is *briefly* appreciated for their gifts by all the others. If more than fifteen people are participating, divide them into two groups. It can be helpful for the "appreciator" to start with the sentence, "The gifts I see in you are ..." After a dozen or more of these acknowledgments, the "receiver" has been given a fairly comprehensive dose of reality. After one person is mirrored by each of the others in the circle, move on to the next person to the left.

Every statement of appreciation will vary, but here are a couple of examples:

"The gifts I see in you, [person's name], start with tenacity. It is clear you have the ability to get things done, no matter the level of difficulty."

"When I heard you play guitar the other night, I noticed a wonderful passion came through you that was filled with wisdom and sensitivity."

[Thanks to Cathy Pedevillano for this exercise.]

Healing the Stories We Tell Ourselves[15]

Purpose: To tell a life-affirming story
Duration: 1½ hours

When we access our gifts and feel the power that naturally flows into our being as a result, often a pernicious inner "voice" will come along and try to diminish that power, making us feel small and inadequate. At other times, while we are simply relating to friends or taking a walk, a similar voice may block our life energy and we may feel disconnected and pessimistic. The messages conveyed by these voices are only stories created in our minds, yet in the words of singer, songwriter, and musician Mother Turtle (Marsia Shuron Harris), who designed this simple but powerful exercise, "they are toxic."[16] Unfortunately, they are all too familiar: "I'm no good"; "I'm not worthy of love"; "I'm not good enough"; "I'm not smart enough"; I'm not pretty/handsome enough"; "I can never do this." Fortunately, these stories, born from a culture of separation, can be changed — particularly if we are highly motivated to do so.

The supplies needed for this exercise are: feathers and stones (about the size of a human head) for each participant, sage for smudging, a shell or bowl for the sage, and paper and pencils. To start, gather everyone in a circle and create a sacred space. In the center of the circle should be a pile of stones, of sufficient number that there will be at least one per person. Pass around the shell or bowl filled with burning sage and invite the participants to smudge themselves.

Then explain the power of story for good or ill and give examples of stories you have been working with from your own life (this is very important as it creates safety in the group and enables them to access inner places that may have felt shameful). Affirm and receive agreement that everything shared will be kept confidential.

When you are done, ask that they each write down one personal story that is clearly not working and causes pain, and that they are ready to shift and/or release. The story should be relatively concise, no more than a page. Seeing it written down has the power to create distance so we can see that the story is not concrete reality but merely a collection of thoughts. Also have them imagine, and then commit to paper, what it would look like if they continued to live that way. Then, point to the pile of stones. Invite the participants each to walk up and grab one. Ask them to feel the weight of their stones, and to consider that they are carrying them around in the same way they have been carrying around their toxic stories. At this point, each person should take some quiet time (while holding their stone), and reflect on their strong desire to shift and change the story.

Then you, as the guide, need to bravely declare your new story in front of the group. For example, when Mother Turtle was developing this process, she realized it was essential that she turn around the story that she had held since childhood of feeling unattractive and unworthy. She now says to herself and at her workshops: "I'm a bold, beautiful woman worthy and capable of great things."[17]

When you are done sharing your new story, bring out the paper and pencils again. Invite the group to put their stones aside and write down their new stories. Make sure they include the "core belief" — the life-changing nugget of the story, like the one shown above: "I'm a bold ..." You might say something like:

> *Are you ready to claim your new story, the one that is healthy, that you really want to live into, and that feels great? If so, write the new story down in a pithy, uncomplicated way — a way that your subconscious will really hear.*

When they are finished answering that question, give them each another sheet of paper and invite them to use their imagination to bask in what their life could actually look like if the new story were lived. Mother Turtle, when asked about this, said: "I think it's easier to let go of the old story, or at least be willing to, because the new story looks so desirable. The person starts to realize: 'I would be free'; 'I would be able to do this or that'; 'I would be able to speak clearly'; 'I could receive love and respect'; or whatever it is ..."[18]

When both parts of the exercise are completed, there should be a noticeable change for the better in the group energy. Now is the time for the participants to stand up and tell their new stories aloud. This takes courage. Respect the fact that some people may not want to share. Let them know that they can voice their new stories at another time before the close of the WEI. To conclude, have the group sit down, close their eyes, and silently give thanks for a new way of seeing things. Give everyone a feather to symbolize the lightness of a new, life-enriching story.

Mother Turtle emphasizes that changing stories is a process: "We can say to ourselves, 'I commit to no longer telling myself this toxic story and I commit to replacing it with the new, healthy story,' but it still takes practice. As we decide to tell the new story (e.g., 'I'm a beautiful, worthy woman'), we'll find that the old story will keep knocking on the door — 'Hey! What about me?'—and you just have to be determined not to carry that around anymore."[19]

---

* The agricultural and industrial "revolutions" are defined as such by the Taker story only. The axiom "History is written by the victors," attributed to Winston Churchill, makes this point well.

Chapter 10

Ceremony

What we call their "ritual and ceremony" was a sophisticated social and spiritual technology, refined through many thousands of years of experience that maintained their relationship with the land.

—Dolores LaChapelle

The only cure I know is a good ceremony.

—Leslie Marmon Silko

Imagine an open field with large standing stones placed in the cardinal directions: east, south, west, and north. A circle of people has gathered there. The smell of wildflowers mixes with the thick scent of burning herbs. Birds make short, graceful appearances on top of the stones. It is the time of the summer solstice, and the rich, luxuriant exuberance of nature's bounty is all around. A man and woman have been chosen to help guide the circle in a ceremony that has been anticipated for weeks. Each member of the group brings a unique gift to the unfolding ritual, whether through spoken words, song, movement, or silence. They are collectively expressing gratitude and respect to the Earth and the Spirit that flows through all things. Sometimes the people hold hands, and, at all times, they are deeply at ease.

The whole mood is pure theater, and the cast is also the audience. There are no strict scripts or rehearsed lines. What unfolds is sometimes reverent, sometimes humorous, with an easygoing yet fierce spontaneity that springs forth from each heart, guided gently by the cues of the land. The land, as always, is filled with the visible and invisible, the audible and inaudible. All the people are dressed in ways that reflect the beauty they see within and without. They are paying attention. They are present to life.

Although this ceremony has a pagan European flavor, its overall style and intent can be seen in various types of rituals conducted throughout the world for thousands of years. These unpretentious ceremonies and festivals are the predecessors of most of the organized rituals in modern religious and secular life. Unlike most contemporary rituals, they include both Earth and Sky, the masculine and the feminine, the immanent and the transcendent—and they are done outside whenever possible. They are about each person gathered with others, aligning with the powers of the universe. There are no human intermediaries to this alignment. Everyone feels the Spirit in different ways. Everyone is honored.

As Elizabeth Rose Babin, an Anishinaabe elder from northern Canada, once told me, "We were created to offer ceremony. This is what the people do."[1]

A ceremony that gathers people into a circle honors the circular shape of reality. Black Elk, a revered holy man of the Oglala Lakota, shared the following in 1930, as recounted by author John Neihardt:

> You have noticed that everything an Indian does is in a circle, and that is because the Power of the World always works in circles, and everything tries to be round.
>
> In the old days ... all our power came to us from the sacred hoop of the nation, and so long as the hoop was unbroken, the people flourished. The flowering tree was the living center of the hoop, and the circle of the four quarters nourished it. The east gave peace and light, the south gave warmth, the west gave rain, and the north with

its cold and mighty wind gave strength and endurance. This knowledge came to us from the outer world with our religion.

Everything the power of the world does is done in a circle. The sky is round, and I have heard that the earth is round like a ball and so are all the stars. The wind, in its greatest power, whirls. Birds make their nests in circles, for theirs is the same religion as ours. The sun comes forth and goes down again in a circle. The moon does the same, and both are round. Even the seasons form a great circle in their changing and always come back again to where they were.

The life of a man is a circle from childhood to childhood, and so it is in everything where power moves. Our teepees were round like the nests of birds, and these were always set in a circle, the nation's hoop, a nest of many nests, where the Great Spirit meant for us to hatch our children.[2]

Nature-Based Ceremonies

Nature-based ceremonies or rituals (these terms are used interchangeably in this book) honor the mysteries and forces of nature. They are a celebration of the ecstatic because they reconnect us to the Earth, her creatures, and the deeper dimensions of reality. Nature-based ceremonies are as natural as breathing.

There are an almost infinite variety of forms for their expression, yet each of them helps us to remember the ancient knowledge of the wild, indigenous soul that lies deep within us. They draw us back to the body of nature, the body that constantly nurtures us and that, somehow, we tricked ourselves into believing we could abandon. The rebirth of nature-based ceremonies counteracts a trend that has increased over the past two thousand years within the dominant cultures: the movement away from our biological origins, and the separation of the realm of the Spirit from Earthly matters. But where is the Spirit more evident than in the body of Earth—in the resplendence of nature?

These ceremonies can also play an important role in healing the destruction of the natural world. The Tuvinian shaman Moonheart (Ai-Churek Shiizhekovna Oyun), the most well-known shaman in Russia, spoke passionately about the need for us to "perceive the Mother Earth returning to full health." She stated: "People must come together, respect the Earth, and make ceremonies. It will be good for them. I want people to stop killing one another."[3]

In stripping things down to the basics, Moonheart acknowledged that we humans are inextricably tied to the land and that nature-based ceremonies facilitate reconnection and restore balance—between people and between the land and the people. Such ceremonies are healing in the broadest sense.

John Seed states:

> We modern humans are the only culture as far as I've been able to find out who have ever attempted to live without these ceremonies and rituals as an integral part of our societies. The people who place great importance upon such rituals and ceremonies are people who live in very, very close connection with nature, hunter-gatherer societies for instance, where people are immersed, imbedded in nature all of the time. If we consider that they find it necessary to guarantee that connectedness by performing such ceremonies, how much more we, living such denatured lives, must need to do this.[4]

Unfortunately, the dominant society has not heeded Seed's call, and we have become increasingly disconnected. But it is never too late to return to our roots — to realign ourselves with nature and our indigenous souls.

Dolores LaChapelle, one of the first deep ecologists in the twentieth century, understood that it would take more than legislation and appropriate technology to establish a truly sustainable relationship with the natural world. In the following passage, she emphasizes the degree to which indigenous cultures inextricably combine nature-based ritual and sustainable living:

> Most Native societies around the world had three common characteristics: they had an intimate, conscious relationship with their place; they were stable "sustainable" cultures, often lasting for thousands of years; and they had a rich ceremonial and ritual life. They saw these three as intimately connected. Out of the hundreds of examples of this, consider the following:

> - The Tukano Indians of the Northwest Amazon River basin, guided by their shamans who are conscious ecologists, make use of various myths and rituals that prevent over-hunting or over-fishing. They view their universe as a circuit of energy in which the entire cosmos participates. The basic circuit of energy consists of "a limited quantity of procreative energy that flows continually between man and animals, between society and nature." Reichel-Dolmatoff, the Colombian anthropologist, notes that the Tukano have very little interest in exploiting natural resources more effectively but are greatly interested in "accumulating more factual knowledge about biological reality and, above all, about knowing what the physical world requires from men."
> - The Kung people of the Kalahari desert have been living in exactly the same place for 11,000 years! They have very

few material belongings but their ritual life is one of the most sophisticated of any group.

- Roy Rappaport has shown that the rituals of the Tsembaga of New Guinea allocate scarce protein for the humans who need it without causing irreversible damage to the land.

- The longest inhabited place in the United States is the Hopi village of Oraibi. At certain times of the year they may spend up to half their time in ritual activity.

- Upon the death of their old cacique (religious leader), Santa Ana Pueblo in New Mexico recently elected a young man to take over as the new cacique. For the rest of his life he will do nothing else whatsoever but take care of the ritual life of the Pueblo. All his personal needs will be taken care of by the tribe. But he cannot travel any further than sixty miles or one hour away from the Pueblo. The distance has grown further with the use of cars but the time remains the same; his presence is that important to the ongoing life of the Pueblo. They know that it is ritual which embodies the people.[5]

All these examples point to a core understanding that reciprocity between humans and nature is the norm when that relationship is not distorted by human illusions of dominance and separation. People are able to restore or—if they have been doing it for millennia—*maintain* balance with the land through giving back, and one of the ways to do so is through ceremony. Just as a river irrigates the landscape, the love within each of us needs to give back to the universe from which it sprang. Our love, expressed in myriad creative ways, feeds the unseen energies (the spirits) that give rise to the manifested world. During ceremony, we make a conscious and deliberate effort to honor and embrace these energies. This is, of course, in contradiction to the Western worldview—and that's just the point. The Western worldview has not exactly scored high marks in nature protection. Those of us who are passionate about restoring balance are eager to make offerings to everything that gives us health: the wind and the waters, the plants and the animals, the fire and the rocks, and the ancestors who are praying for our safe passage through life. Throughout my travels to Siberia, I witnessed the shamans making ritual offerings to all these aspects of nature. Why not take their cue and reestablish the circle of giving and receiving? In the simple but powerful words of Elizabeth Rose Babin, "We need to get the love out and do it together."[6]

Elements of a Nature-Based Ceremony

There are almost as many kinds of nature-based ceremonies as there are human activities: marriages, celebrations of celestial/seasonal events, recognitions of births, rites of passage, and rituals for planting/harvesting, to name some of the major ones. When the community involved puts in the time and energy, each ceremony holds the attention of the participants in the present moment—the place of power. Being fully present while archetype and myth reveal themselves shifts us out of our customary ways of seeing things. This process is as old as human culture.

The concept of nature-based ritual may seem serious, but in practice it can sometimes be anything but. For example, the Lakota have the *heyoka*, or sacred clown, a person who has a certain kind of spiritual power and sometimes enacts it in an entertaining and comic way. One of his roles in ceremonies is to poke fun at everything and everybody, in order to help maintain the harmony and balance of the community. Part of his message is, "Lighten up. Don't take things too seriously." The *heyoka* fulfills a highly respected role that requires great dedication. Many other Native American tribes have something similar.

Nature-based ceremony practiced in any culture may combine one or more of the following elements: singing, praying, drumming, silence, poetry, art, dancing, ritual attire and other body adornment, and the spoken word. These ceremonies are not necessarily complex. Some are as simple as dancing around a fire or making an offering to one of the four elements.

Rituals are adaptable and can change over time and with different circumstances. They may also be influenced by the traditions of other cultures. A few years ago, I overheard an Apache elder speaking to a younger Pueblo man in northern New Mexico. He said, "About eight hundred years ago, my people came here from the north and we witnessed your ceremonies. We realized they were based on this land, so we incorporated a lot of what you do in yours into ours."[7]

Blindly clinging to the past leads to boredom and cultural sclerosis. The props and protocol of living ritual are always changing and evolving, although the universal truths — such as love, balance, and the celestial rhythms — will always be present. In shamanic cultures, tradition provides the framework but is subservient to the spontaneous and creative needs of the moment. Recognizing this is important, so that as we make new culture, we honor, but do not duplicate, ancient practices.

Three key attitudes that make for memorable nature-based ceremonies are: (1) gratitude for and celebration of life, (2) relinquishment of the need to control, and (3) acceptance of one's personal responsibility to connect directly with the Source of Life.

Let's briefly take them in order:

1. To live on a planet that sits in the middle of mostly empty space and yet teems with life is to know a profound and unlikely miracle. But sometimes we forget. Expressing gratitude reminds us of the sheer abundance that we are born into. One conscious breath can jog our memory, and an entire ritual with this intent can fortify us for weeks. Whether the ritual is somber or lighthearted, taking the time to celebrate our existence and all the things that bring it about reconnects us to our larger self.

2. Letting go of the need to control anything—from our environment to the living beings around us—brings us true freedom. In a nature-based ceremony, the participants engage with the larger forces of nature without trying to dominate or control them. These forces are intelligent, and by opening to their guidance—or even letting them direct our actions—we can learn to open to the deep wisdom that lies within ourselves. Even the simplest of ceremonies, when done with this sense of allowing, can bring about a sense of humility. Given the tremendous power modern humans have to alter the environment, isn't this something we need to cultivate?

3. Accepting personal responsibility to connect directly with the Source is empowering. We can discover our own spiritual truths without needing a human intermediary to tell us we are doing so correctly or to interpret our experience. This view is in sharp contrast to the message from the dominator cultures, which have thrived for centuries partly by mediating and controlling the spirituality of the masses. When people have a direct, ecstatic experience of the divine—especially the divine in nature—they are not under the spiritual control of

others, and they may even be perceived as a threat by religious or secular authorities, who cannot predict what they will do.

Ceremony in a Wild Earth Intensive

In a Wild Earth Intensive (WEI), ceremonies are usually held outside at ceremonial sites that have already been created on the land, unless the group feels especially called to make a new site. Each ceremony draws on a variety of the elements mentioned above. Each is an invitation to journey deeper into the Great Mystery and to be nourished in the process.

Although the entire WEI could conceivably be viewed as a ceremony, we have enjoyed at least three "formal" rituals in each Intensive: the Opening Ceremony, the Sweat Lodge or Medicine Lodge Ceremony (with guest facilitation), and the Closing Ceremony. Each is described below. In addition to these, guest facilitators often offer other ceremonies with which they are familiar.

Opening Ceremony

Purpose: To enter into the mystery and power of sacred space
Duration: Approximately 1 hour
Prepare the site in advance. In a large open space, create a U-shaped "gate" of saplings and flowers (or other natural materials). Place the gate in the east, with the two ends held up by stones or set into the ground. Inside the gate, using cornmeal, stones, or evergreen branches, mark out a circle large enough to include all the participants standing comfortably.

To begin the ceremony, invite people to line up in front of the gate. Ask them to enter slowly and silently, one at a time. Two guides will smudge each person with sage or cedar (or another purifying herb) and then, using flowers or evergreen boughs, sprinkle some drops of water (from a small bowl) on them as they enter. The guides will let each one know firmly but softly how glad they are for their presence, saying something like: "Welcome, we are glad you are here. Enjoy the mystery." One by one, the people will take their places around the circle, and the guides will take turns smudging each other before "calling in the directions."

This next step requires some explanation. To "call in the directions" means to invoke the forces of the universe. This very powerful act sets the tone for the remainder of the ritual, as well as the entire WEI. At its essence is the acknowledgment that we are all kept alive and guided by these forces, whether we know it or not. If we are wise, we approach them with gratitude and humility. Each of the seven directions (the cardinal directions; Earth; Sky; and Within, or Center) represents an archetypal energy. Indigenous traditions throughout the world honor these energies differently. In the WEI, we have used the following "amalgam" given to us by Cathy Pedevillano, a shamanic practitioner who has been taught by a variety of indigenous elders over the past twenty years. This is only one possible model for honoring the directions.

The facilitator(s) who are calling in the directions step into the center of the circle and explain what is to happen next. They ask the participants not only to focus on the archetypal energies being invoked but also to fully experience the qualities of the physical environment as they turn and face each direction. Then they and the group begin drumming and rattling to raise the energy. Participants can bring drums and rattles with them when entering the circle or the instruments can be placed there ahead of time. The lead facilitator calling in the directions slows down the drumming after approximately five minutes, and then faces East and invites the group to do the same.

The invocation for the East is spoken loudly and clearly, after which the group responds, "Spirits of the East, welcome." The group then turns clockwise to face the South (then West and then North), and the invocation for that direction is spoken. When invoking the Sky, the Earth, and Within, the group will, in turn, look up, kneel, and place their hands on their hearts, respectively. The process is complete when all seven directions have been called in and welcomed.

The ceremonial words proposed below may serve as a guide to invoking the essence of each direction, but the actual words spoken during the invocation are best uttered spontaneously and from the heart.

Thank you, powers of the universe, for the gift of life. We honor you and pray that we may align ourselves more fully with you.

East
We call forth the Spirits of the East, the power of dawn and new beginnings, the Eagle that flies above to help us see from a higher perspective. Thank you, Spirits of the East, for the light of a new day and the energy to begin again in each moment. Thank you for illuminating the path before us. East—place of the children and the springtime—we are so grateful.
[The group responds, "Spirits of the East, welcome!"]

South
We call forth the Spirits of the South, the power of growth and vigor. Thank you for the innocence of Porcupine and the scrutiny of Mouse. We thank you, Spirits of the South, for both passion and integrity to lead an active, healthy life. South— place of young adults and the summertime—we are so grateful.
["Spirits of the South, welcome!"]

West
We call forth the Spirits of the West, the power of transformation. We thank you for the Bear and his nighttime dreams of grace.

West — place of the setting sun, of adulthood, and the autumn —
we are so grateful.
["Spirits of the West, welcome!"]

North

We call forth the Spirits of the North, the power of insight and
spiritual understanding. Thank you for the cold that keeps us
awake and alert, and the Wolf that teaches us wisdom. You are
the place of the elders and the ancestors who guide and protect
us with crystalline clarity. We are so grateful.
["Spirits of the North, welcome!"]

Sky

We call forth the Spirits of the Sky, those that watch over us
from above, Grandmother Moon, the Stars and Planets, the
Star Beings, the Rainbow Warriors, and the Cloud People.
We welcome the expansiveness of Sky to open us to our own
expansive, eternal nature, and we are so grateful.
["Spirits of the Sky, welcome!"]

Earth

We honor and thank you, Mother Earth, for your beauty and
abundance, for providing us with food, water, and shelter
so that we may survive. We welcome the Nature Spirits and
energies of this place, the animals, plants, trees, insects, all
those who teach and guide us from the Earth Realms. Thank
you, Mother Earth, for grounding and healing us.
["Spirits of the Earth, welcome!"]

Within

We welcome the Spirit within each one of us, the Spirit that
brought us here today, the Creative Intelligence that is so
vast and mysterious. We thank you for this awesome power

that dwells in our hearts and enables us to uplift and nurture
ourselves and one another.
["Spirit within, welcome!"]

The lead facilitator then may allow time for participants to call in their own personal allies or any other energies they wish to honor, which they may do by either naming the energy out loud or focusing on it silently. After sensing that the group has finished, the facilitator will announce that the ceremony is complete. Sometimes, the facilitator will invite the group to make offerings of cornmeal and/or tobacco before they leave the circle. Little bowls containing the cornmeal and tobacco will have been placed near the eastern gate, and participants may choose to take a pinch of either (or both) and give it to the Earth as an offering of gratitude before leaving. People then move out of the circle through the gate.

Sweat Lodge or Medicine Lodge Ceremony

Purpose: Purification of the mind and the body
Duration: Timeless, but usually 2–3 hours

Different versions of the sweat lodge or sweat bath have been conducted all over the world by indigenous cultures. Their most basic common element is the use of heat for purposes of physical and spiritual purification. Sometimes known as a "medicine lodge," the sweat lodge is so primal that it peels away our layers of resistance to simply experiencing our aliveness. Letting go of that resistance provides healing on spiritual, emotional, and physical levels.

In North America, different Native peoples have variations both in the structure of their sweat lodges and the format of their ceremonies. Whenever possible, a WEI sweat lodge ceremony should comply with local tradition, to honor both the Native people of the area and the spirits of the land on which the Intensive is being held. To respect that tradition, it can be beneficial to invite a trained Native American ceremonialist to lead the sweat lodge, if you are meeting in the Western hemisphere. However, more and more non-Natives are also able to "pour a lodge" in a skilled way. Those who practice a sweat lodge tradition respectfully and competently need not be ruled out as ceremonial leaders in a WEI.

In the foreword to his book *Mother Earth Spirituality*, Oglala Lakota ceremonialist "Eagle Man," Ed McGaa, writes:

> A question that will be asked is why I am willing to teach non-Indians about Native American spirituality and about my spiritual experiences. I believe, like Fools Crow, Eagle Feather, Sun Bear, Midnight Song, Rolling Thunder, and a host of other traditional peoples, that it is time that spirituality is shared. Frank Fools Crow, an Oglala holy man and ceremonial chief of the Teton Sioux, said in reference to the pipe and the sweat lodge, "These ceremonies do not belong to Indians alone. They can be done by all who have the right attitude ... and who are honest and sincere about their beliefs in Wakan Tanka (Great Spirit) and follow the rules."[8]

I've been in numerous lodges throughout North America led by many Native leaders, some of them quite well known. Without exception, all of them said approximately the same thing: "It's time. These powerful Earth teachings must be shared and they must be done right. They are not for sale. They are for the good of future generations."

Each of these lodges taught me some valuable aspect of returning to the Source. Some were long and extremely hot, and some were short and, sometimes, cooler. Some had a lot of singing and an upbeat quality, while others were quiet and somber. They were as different as the people running them, but they all followed the same basic protocol: rocks or stones were heated in a ceremonial fire and then respectfully brought into the lodge structure where the people were gathered in prayer.

Jamie Sams, a well-known Native American author and medicine woman, writes in her book *Sacred Path Cards* about the deeper purpose of the stones:

> These Stone People are the carriers of Earth-Records and release ancient lessons through the steam. We need to reconnect with these ancient lessons in order to aid in the continuation of life on this planet. As our perspiration returns to the Mother Earth in the form of water, the Earth is again nourished. When the door of the lodge is opened in between endurances, or rounds, the steam travels to Father Sky to take our prayers home to Great Mystery.[9]

Apprentice sweat lodge leaders in certain Native traditions may train for years before starting to lead a "sweat," in order to safely navigate the powerful spiritual realities that the ceremony may induce. For this reason, and out of respect to the sacredness of the ceremony, this book does not include instructions for conducting a sweat lodge. Instead, we encourage you to invite a trained sweat leader to your WEI (see Chapter 14).

Please note that alertness to safety—essential in all WEI activities—is especially important during all aspects of the sweat lodge ceremony, including construction of the lodge. For example, materials must be used that will permit sufficient oxygen flow. If the site of your WEI does not already have a sweat lodge built upon it, it would be wise to consult the ceremonial leader for instructions in how to construct one.

The sweat lodge ceremony has endured and has been passed down for generations. Perhaps the Ancient Ones knew that there would come a time on the Earth when purification was essential for survival. Perhaps they saw in the light of the sweat lodge fires that this time is now.

Closing Ceremony

Purpose: To provide closure at the end of the WEI by honoring and thanking the land, the spirits, and all the people who contributed to the richness of the Intensive

Duration: Approximately 2 hours

It is important to end the WEI with a sacred ceremony, just as it was begun. If possible, have the closing ceremony at the same place on the land where the opening ceremony was held, to provide continuity. Below is a suggested format for the ritual. Although the guides will keep track of the process and lead transitions, it is most empowering to involve everybody in the process.

Quiet Reflection (Part 1)

The group gathers together in a circle at the special place where the WEI began. Everyone then takes some "solo" reflective time to offer gratitude to the land, the spirits, and the people who assisted them. Bowls with loose tobacco and cornmeal are available for offerings. This period, lasting five to ten minutes, is also a time to feel the stillness that penetrates every part of our being, inside and out, and to let it wash over us. People sit in one place or walk around inside the circle.

Praise for the Elements (Part 2)

Earlier in the day, before entering the ceremonial circle, each person chooses the element—Earth, Air, Fire, or Water—they most strongly embodied during the ten days of the Intensive. Of course, all four elements will have played a role in each person's experience, but one of them will have stood out. The facilitator may suggest that if a person is not certain what to choose, that person can ask one of the elements to choose them! If they are still uncertain, they can ask their fellow participants for feedback as to which of the elements "came through" them most strongly.

When everyone has decided, they form into four groups—one for each element—and collectively decide how they will want to thank this element publicly during the ritual. This can be quite a creative time, as people create short "skits" on behalf of these elemental mysteries, each of which corresponds to one of the four cardinal directions. In this part of the ritual, the correspondence between the elements and the directions follows the Anishnabe tradition.[10] East is Fire, the beginning of all that is. South is Water, which nourishes all growth. West is Earth, from which the harvest is reaped. North is Wind/Air, which provides continuing life.

By the time this segment of the ritual begins, each group will be clear about what they are going to do. The following example illustrates one possible form that Praise for the Elements can take.

The Fire people in the East light a small fire in that part of the ceremonial circle (or if that is impossible because of rain or fire danger, they light covered candles or matches). They start out by making passionate fiery movements and/or sounds, embodying the qualities of the element, before lighting their fire. Once it is burning, their spokesperson(s) can say something like:

We so appreciate you, fire, for your tremendous power. You are the sun that shines on us every moment, night or day. You are in our cells. Your light gives us life. Your heat keeps us warm. We offer praise and gratitude for your fierce, wild ways. Thank you for helping us to transform our lives.

The Water people in the South swish around, mimicking streams, waves, and rain. They *become* water. Their fluid dancing movement demonstrates the human power to shapeshift. The Water people will have actual water handy in some containers. They may be playful and spritz everybody with it and/or sip it with the reverent attention given to only the most precious of substances. The spokesperson(s) can say something along the lines of:

Water who carves the banks of rivers and who smoothes boulders with your waves, we give you great gratitude. We thank you for your power to nurture and sustain us through your rain. By flowing along the path of least resistance, you show us how to live. We drink of your healing wells and are blessed by you constantly. Thank you for teaching us flexibility. May we ensure that you are clean and run free!

The Earth people in the West kneel and pat the ground with their hands, gently but firmly "drumming" the rhythm at the heart of Creation. They are feeling the core vibration emanating from the Earth's crystalline center[11] and bringing it to the surface. They caress and knead the soil, acknowledging how it is the basis of growth for plants, and therefore food. They make whatever other movements or sounds the Earth whispers to them, and then the spokesperson(s) can say:

Mother Earth, your power is indisputable. Beneath our feet, we feel your flesh as our flesh, your bones as our bones. You give your unconditional love in so many ways. We thank you as you show up as rock, as animal, as insect, as soil, as plant, and on and on. It's a miracle to behold, and we offer great praise. May we learn to honor you once again in word and deed.

Air/Wind people dance in wavy motions, making "whooshing" sounds, and when they are done, their spokesperson(s) can say something like:

We have been breathing you in our whole lives. You flow in and around us, giving life to all beings. We offer infinite praise for the way you teach us lightness and ease. Thank you for the way you soar across all obstacles and purify everything in your path. You are a miracle, and we will not take you for granted.

Blessing One Another (Part 3)

This is a process where each person asks the group to bestow a blessing on them, focusing on a particular intention that can be either general or specific (e.g., "I would like a blessing for the publication of my new book" or "Please bless my health and well-being"). The group forms two lines facing each other about three to four feet apart. This formation can be likened to a birth canal. One person at a time (or two together if it is a large group) stands at the head of the lines, facing the group, and makes their request. That person then begins walking down between the lines, being sure to glance at as many as possible of the smiling faces they pass. As they walk, their fellow participants may bless them with words or energy from upheld hands or may touch them in a reassuring way. When the person finishes, they take their place at the far end of the line they began in, so there is a continuous flow of people to the front. Then the first person in the opposite line takes their turn. Facilitators take their turns in asking for blessings as well.

One-Word Appreciation (Part 4)

The group forms a circle, holding hands. Each participant looks at the person to their left and thinks of one word that captures a positive quality of that person. Then the guide asks someone to go first. This person pauses, turns left toward the person he wants to appreciate, and says one word like: "wise," "caring," "authentic," "sensitive," etc.

The person receiving what was just said takes a brief moment to silently acknowledge that quality within and then turns to the left and does the same for the next person. The process continues around the circle until everyone has been appreciated, including the facilitators.

Thanking and Releasing the Directions (Part 5)
At the beginning of the WEI, the powers and spirits of the seven directions were called in. It is important to thank these energies and to release them, simply and briefly. Seven people volunteer to thank and release a direction (e.g., "Spirits of the North, we thank you for your wisdom and guidance and we release you"). If the directions were called in the order of East, South, West, North, Sky, Earth, Within, then to close they would be thanked and released in reverse order: Within, Earth, Sky, North, West, South, East. This can be followed by drumming and rattling and sounds of gratitude.

Closing Words (Part 6)
Offer some parting words of encouragement to not let go of this way of life no matter where we find ourselves. Often, participants leave the circle on an empowering phrase, such as "From my heart to your heart," "Yes to Life!" or "We are One!"

Group Hug (Part 7)
Enjoy a final group hug to feel and embody the closeness that was cultivated throughout the Intensive!

Option: As part of the closing ceremony plant an actual tree and water it. This symbolizes watering the Tree of Life.

Chapter 11

Altered States of Consciousness

Then I was standing on the highest mountain of them all, and round about beneath me was the whole hoop of the world. And while I stood there I saw more than I can tell and I understood more than I saw; for I was seeing in a sacred manner the shapes of all things in the spirit, and the shape of all shapes as they must live together like one being.

—Black Elk

Our normal waking consciousness, rational consciousness as we call it, is but one special type of consciousness, whilst all about it, parted from it by the filmiest of screens, there lie potential forms of consciousness entirely different.

—William James

We change consciousness all the time. We sleep, we dream, we use alcohol and other consciousness-altering substances. Yet in the words of writer and consciousness researcher Ralph Metzner:

Culturally, we tend to be focused only on the value of one consensual state, and we don't value other states as much as cultures of other places and historical periods have. There is a strong bias within the dominant paradigm that all valuable learning must happen during the normal waking state, using cognitive methods.[1]

To create a viable culture, our basic assumptions need intense re-examination—and that includes the assumption that only cognition in the waking state will give us answers.

Trying to learn by looking through only one of countless lenses is constricting. Intense re-examination involves going beyond the surface of things and challenging unhealthy social conditioning. To do so requires courage. One of the ways "to break out of the box" is to seek out healthy altered or non-ordinary states of consciousness. I am not implying that a Wild Earth Intensive (WEI) should or does use drugs to induce altered consciousness. During the program, we use methods that gently nudge the human mind and body out of their habitual modes of operation without the ingestion of any substances. In fact, almost every activity in the program has either a mild or strong power to elicit a shift away from rote perception. This chapter focuses on one of the strongest, yet completely safe, methods of doing so: shamanic journeying.

Before describing that process, it is important to explain what "altering consciousness" means, and to discuss the shamanic heritage that is our most ancient cultural source for such an exploration.

A first step is to emphasize the naturalness of seeking non-ordinary states of reality. The pioneering holistic physician Andrew Weil, who has been at the forefront of integrating the best in allopathic and alternative medicine, states in his groundbreaking book *The Natural Mind:*

It is my belief that the desire to alter consciousness periodically is an innate, normal drive analogous to hunger or the sexual drive. Note that I do not say "desire to alter consciousness by means of chemical agents ..." Furthermore, the need for periods of non-ordinary consciousness begins to be expressed at ages far too young for it to have much to do with social conditioning.[2]

Non-ordinary states are not simply changes in mood and emotion, or new ways of thinking. They are changes in feeling and thinking, combined with an altered perception of space, time, and the body. They are also navigable, in that we can maneuver within them to acquire knowledge or to effect healing. When we have a strong intention to glean their teachings, they do not happen *to us* but *through us*. With practice, we can learn to navigate more effectively, and can explore different versions of reality in order to tap into wellsprings of creativity and insight.

Starhawk, the well-known pioneer for the revival of Earth-based spirituality, makes this point eloquently:

> When I began studying magic, ritual, and psychic development, the first thing my teachers told me was to stop using drugs. They got in the way because they took me into the states without control, and I needed to learn to enter many kinds of altered states by choice, deciding where to go. And where to go depends on what you're looking for. There are states of pure ecstasy; states that help you clarify your perceptions; states that help you get information unavailable to normal consciousness; and creative states wherein you create seeds of what you want to happen. Now my way is through ritual — which is a whole complex of methods — and through visualization, drumming, and breathing. The art of ritual is that as you use certain visualizations, meditations, or rhythms repeatedly, they become anchors for particular states. The more practice you have, the easier it becomes to enter a state and know where you're going ahead of time.[3]

The practices that Starhawk refers to above are part of the dynamic, animistic, and ancient way of life called shamanism. The ability to navigate in and between various states of consciousness — to journey to other worlds for the benefit of the community—is the mark of the shaman, and all humans have this ability to greater or lesser degrees. *Shamanism*, an anthropological term derived from the Siberian Evenk language, is not an ideology. It's not concerned with accepting any particular set of beliefs but with accessing our genetically coded relationship to the Earth and Cosmos. These are our original instructions! According to Thomas Berry, "Our bonding with the larger dimensions of the universe comes about primarily through our genetic coding."[4] Instead of our DNA enslaving us to predetermined patterns of thought and behavior, consciously accessing our original instructions frees us to embody the larger knowing that everything has spirit, that nature is alive and sacred, and that we can navigate this deepest of realms with our hearts. Shamanism is the original deep ecology. Through direct experience, it shows us how the intelligence in nature and the intelligence in us are one and the same.

Leslie Gray, a Native American shamanic counselor with a doctorate in clinical psychology, adds:

Shamanism is based on a sophistication about mind-body healing that was lost in the handful of years when humankind became industrial and technological. I'm now convinced that human beings are built in such a way that certain circumstances result in our entering into non-ordinary, spiritual consciousness. In other words, we are literally wired so as to connect with Spirit.[5]

D. Patrick Miller also underscores the value of accessing non-ordinary reality, and provides motivation for the whole undertaking of re-visioning culture from the inside out:

Fortunately, the known rewards of transcending normality are experiences of bliss, ecstasy, inspired creativity, and spiritual communion. And even those experiences may merely be maps to a different everyday way of being — a new "human nature." When that term can be used as an affirmation rather than an excuse, the learning potential of altered states will be fully realized.[6]

By changing our consciousness in a deliberate manner and with positive intention, we have potent means to work with, not against, the flow of life.

Shamanic Journeying

Shamanic journeying is one of those potent means. It was considered by religious historian Mircea Eliade to be a "flight of ecstasy."[7] Although possible to do alone, it is usually done in pairs or groups. One or more people, using a drum, a rattle, the voice, or some combination of these as a sonic driver, act in the role of guides. The sound is either repetitive or possessing very little variation, but it has surprising power to nourish and invigorate our psyche and awaken our hearts, especially when done for extended periods.

For example, while co-leading a journey to visit some of the shamans of Tuva, Siberia, in 2002, I was seated in the center of a large room with my new companions, a dozen other Westerners. We had just arrived. The head shaman, a woman, asked us to close our eyes. Then, with no forewarning, about a dozen Tuvans, wearing traditional attire complete with feathered headdresses (as I later saw), started drumming together to the same rhythmic beat. They circled us steadily, blessing us with a radiant enthusiasm, for about twenty minutes. Afterwards, some members of our group agreed that they felt a tremendous healing energy was at work. Tears were evident on many faces. When the head shaman asked us to share what we had experienced, two people described almost identical "journeys" in which they had traveled to inner landscapes that they (and we) would later see for the first time in the steppes of Tuva!

While shamanic journeying is probably thirty thousand to forty thousand years old, it has recently had a resurgence and has been embraced by thousands of Westerners since the 1970s. Drumming, rattling, and singing allow for a temporary relinquishment of the compulsive thought process and induce relaxing alpha and theta patterns in the brain. They move an individual away from the cognitive state and into the mythic roots of reality. Shamanic consciousness is none other than the waking form of the dream state. This altered state is safe and natural, and there are even documented health benefits, such as reduced stress, enhanced immunity, and increased control of chronic pain.

There are many forms of shamanic journeying employed throughout the world. The methods I will describe in the pages that follow are derived from my experience with Siberian and Native American shamanism, and my apprenticeship with John Perkins.

The Wild Earth Intensive Journeys

In a WEI, we try to include journeys to the seven major realms of the shamanic universe. They are the lower world, the upper world, the four elements of the middle world (Earth, Air, Fire, Water), and the realm of the ancestors. We include as many of these as "feels right" over the ten days.

First, however, we take two foundational journeys of approximately ten minutes each to help participants more effectively navigate the realms mentioned above. The first one is to find (or reconnect with) a *sacred place*; the next is to find (or reconnect with) a *spirit guide*.

A sacred place is any place that feels safe, loving, and peaceful, which becomes the departure point and return point during subsequent, longer journeys. It could be a real, physical place on Earth or someplace imaginary. Often people find themselves seeing (or feeling, hearing, or otherwise sensing) a place in nature, perhaps surrounded by close friends. As a guide, you may suggest this idea ahead of time but encourage people to trust that whatever place they discover is most suitable for them. It might be a physical location in a city, a place from one's childhood, or a fantastic place — the key is that it feels nurturing and that they can imagine themselves there easily and consistently.

A spirit guide is any aspect of the universe, human or non-human, living or non-living, which offers a sense of protection and wisdom to the journeyer. It will become a companion for the other journeys during the Intensive. Before beginning the journey to seek a spirit guide, encourage participants to allow themselves to *be chosen* by a guide, rather than consciously conjuring up one. You might suggest that the journeyers watch for things such as a flower, another human, an animal, a radiant ball of energy, or even a stone cliff or a pool of water.

Whatever the spirit guide is, it must feel like a real ally in the journey of life. Also, people tend to accept more readily a spirit guide that already exists on the Earth, instead of something unfamiliar that bends all known physical laws — but again, trust whatever guide "arrives on the scene." It is possible to befriend many spirit guides over the course of one's life, and to have many show up for a journey, but asking just one or two to come along at a time eliminates confusion.

Choosing a Setting for the Journey

It is best to select a space in which all participants will have enough room to lie down comfortably. You may wish to provide mats for this purpose, or to ask people in advance to bring their own.

It can also be beneficial to select a setting that is as peaceful and quiet as possible, although you don't need to be too concerned about this. Healing and the retrieval of beneficial information are commonplace during shamanic journeys regardless of setting.

It is the intention of the journeyers, coupled with the integrity and skill of the leader, that is of paramount importance.

Leading a Shamanic Journey

A shamanic journey can be divided into three parts:

- Introductory explanation (5–10 minutes)
- The journey (10–20 minutes)
- Sharing and integration (15 minutes)

The duration of these parts can be varied depending on the mood, energy level of the participants, and any particular sense of alignment with the topic of the journey, based on the preceding activities (for example, an hour spent with an actual pond or stream particularly lends itself to a "journey to the waters").

Introductory Explanation

As you settle in to do a shamanic journey with your group, it will be helpful to offer an opening explanation emphasizing that we are stepping into a different way of perceiving reality that has ancient roots and has been practiced in various forms across the globe. It is not necessary to spend too much time explaining why you are journeying; simply let the participants know they have an opportunity to access more of their aliveness, to merge with parts of themselves they hardly knew were there, and to strengthen their connection with those parts. Perhaps you might want to add a quote like one of those given earlier in this chapter, citing the value in journeying.

There are some misconceptions about what a journey actually is, so it is also important to assure people that they will not lose control or go into some bizarre hypnotic state. Nobody will do anything to them or make them do things. It is a safe, personal experience whose boundaries are always within the control of the journeyer.

Also, you might reassure your group that there is no "correct" journey or "successful" experience. Everyone has a different experience that is right for them. For instance, they may have a journey of sounds, devoid of recognizable visual images. Or they may only experience a feeling or a progression of them. Those experiences count as journeys! All feelings are acceptable, too. The main goal is trusting in one's own journey experience. By the way, normal physical laws such as gravity do not apply in a journey—anything is possible in the non-ordinary realm!

It can also be helpful to mention that the same skills of awareness and focus that are used for outer tracking in nature can be used for shamanic journeying. This means using the same power of attentiveness to detail inside one's mindscape as one would in an outer landscape. Observing colors, shapes, and textures can add to one's level of concentration and can be most helpful at the beginning of a journey, when one is getting one's bearings. After that stage, most people will want to simply let go and follow the energy.

Finally, briefly explain the steps you will be leading them through: relaxing, journeying with some initial verbal guidance, traveling with the sound of the drum(s) or rattle(s), coming back from the journey, and then having a period of silence for writing or illustrating their journeys. There will also be a time for sharing their experiences with the group, if they so wish.

The Journey

Many different kinds of journeys are possible, far more than the ones mentioned above, but in this style, the basic format for each is the same, and guiding participants through the following steps may help maximize their shamanic experiences.

1. Suggest that people find a relaxing position. Lying down, with eyes closed, seems to work best.
2. Begin a slow heartbeat rhythm with a drum and/or rattle as you verbally guide participants to their sacred places from which to begin the journey.
3. Verbally help them each connect with a spirit guide.
4. Send them off on their journeys, stop speaking, and then gradually speed up the drum and/or rattle rhythm* to three or four beats per second, building to a crescendo, and keep it constant throughout this phase of the journey. This is the time in which each journeyer learns how to navigate without facilitator guidance.
5. Slow the rate of the drumming rhythm, and quietly invite them to return from their journeys.
6. Finish with four distinct drumbeats and welcome them back to physical reality.

Note: Beginning journeyers will particularly benefit from inclusion of the foundational steps—beginning the journey from a sacred place and connecting with a spirit guide—but when participants are more experienced in journeying, you may find that these two steps can, at times, be omitted. Also, the sacred place and spirit guide journeys are shorter than the others—approximately ten minutes each, instead of fifteen to twenty—but the faster rhythm employed in step 4 is the same in each of them.

Beginning the Journey
After each person is lying down comfortably on a mat or a blanket, invite the group to prepare to journey, with words such as:

Get settled in. Close your eyes. Tune into your body and relax any areas of tension. Take a few deep breaths and, as you exhale,

sink into the Earth. Feel it supporting you. Let go of having to
figure anything out.

As you begin slowly drumming or rattling, be sure to synchronize the heartbeat rhythm with any assistants who are drumming/rattling along with you. Then, in a gentle voice, begin to offer participants verbal cues to help them on their journey.

The following paragraphs provide samples of verbal cues that can aid participants in getting to their sacred places, finding spirit guides, and starting journeys to each of the seven realms (upper and lower worlds, Earth, Air, Fire, Water, and the ancestors). Make sure you pause between cues to give the journeyers time to make the inner transitions. Don't worry about getting the verbal cues just right. By leading a journey with the intention of connecting to these realms, you are opening up to huge wellsprings of creative power. You will intuitively find the words that best convey how to begin and end each journey.

Sacred Place

> *Scan your inner horizon. Let yourself go anywhere and in any*
> *way you choose. Feel the freedom of inner space. Look for a*
> *place you really love, or a place that you imagine, in which you*
> *feel safe and alive. Perhaps you have close friends there with*
> *you. Take your time and enjoy exploring this place, until you*
> *feel a certain familiarity with it. Know it, feel it, look around*
> *with keen interest. Bask in it. Drink in the feeling.*

Spirit Guide

> *Return to your sacred place: walk down a path or in some other*
> *way make your way to the edge of your sacred place. Look around*
> *for signs of a spirit guide to be your ally on the upcoming*

journey. Feel your eagerness to meet this being. Allow yourself to sense its presence. Whoever or whatever appears, be open to receive the gifts your ally has to offer. Spend time relating and asking questions, such as, "Welcome. Are you my guide?" and "Will you accompany me on my journey?" Take the time you need to discern whether the being gives you a feeling of connection and trust.

The Lower World

Return to your sacred place and, after taking some time to bask in it, look below you for an opening. Perhaps it's an entrance to a cave or maybe a whirlpool or some kind of tunnel. Before entering, pause and find your guide. Make your way together through the opening and downward to the lower world. At some point, you will see light appearing. Go toward it. It is your entry into the lower world. It is a place vibrant with life. Get to know it.

The Upper World

A journey to the upper world may be experienced as only space, light, and energy, but it may also contain object such as stars, temples, planets, moons, etc.

From your sacred place, find your spirit guide. Communicate with each other. . . Look out at the horizon. Go there together. Watch this expanse get wider and wider, where there is now open space all around you. Form the intention that you want to expand and rise up! Maybe there is a large tree or mountain nearby to assist you in getting off the ground. Let the drums (and/or rattles) propel you and your spirit guide faster, higher, and higher. You are flying. You are open to the wisdom and guidance from above.

Journeys to the Elements: Earth, Air, Fire, and Water
While the elements intermingle in our world and are not really separate, we journey to experience each one individually and learn about its essence. However, journeyers should not feel restricted to focus on the element itself, but free to use it as a touchstone to deeper levels of being.

Earth
Feel the womblike essence of Earth. Pay attention to whatever part of this miracle attracts you. You are exploring your larger body—you are part of Earth through and through. Notice that beneath the apparent solidity of physical reality, everything is pulsating with different kinds of energy. Relate with your heart to all that you see.

Air
Take a deep breath. Feel the air as it enters your lungs. At another moment, this same air could be the wind blowing through the trees or near the ocean. Sense the mystery of this invisible element. Go into it. Explore it. Where does it want to take you?

Fire
See the sun in your inner eye. This is the source of all fire on Earth. Feel the warmth. Feel the heat. How is it flowing in your body? Is it passion? Is it anger? Go into the energy of fire fully. What does it want to show you?

Water
Feel the water flowing throughout your body. There is so much there. How does it feel? What is the essence of this life-giving liquid? This water flowed in rivers and streams. It was part of the body of beautiful lakes. It is as old as the Earth. Merge with it. Where does it want to take you? What does it want to show you?

Ancestors

Our ancestors include both human and non-human ones. They may have been alive recently, or they may be as ancient as the Earth or older! Human ancestors fall into three categories: 1) mentors and teachers no longer alive who have helped shape your spirituality, 2) deceased family members you are related to by blood or adoption, and 3) mythic heroes and heroines who are part of your cultural or spiritual heritage.

> *Put your hand on your heart. Feel the lifeblood pulsing. Feel how strong that heart energy is. Now use that energy to guide you to an open landscape. Take some time to explore this new place. Look all around you. Ask to know what ancestors would like to make their presence known. Whoever or whatever appears is fine. Feel them radiating this same heart energy toward you. Some are more visible than others. One or more of them wants to communicate with you. Accept their company and their words with gratitude. Travel together wherever they wish to take you. They have lots to show you.*

Maintaining the Rhythm

After you have finished offering verbal cues, allow the drum or rattle to build to a graceful crescendo, and then "coast" on the plateau of rhythmic waves "coming into the shore." Again, it will be important to synchronize changes in rhythm with any assistants. You may find yourself embarking on your own journey during this time; this is quite common and may provide you with useful information and insights regarding the group.

Maintain the fast drumming/rattling rhythm for the journeys described above for a period of time that is usually between ten and twenty minutes (journeys to establish a sacred place and find a spirit guide are shorter than the others). You will probably not need to look at your watch because you can sense a natural unfolding; listen for a gentle inner prodding that it is time to wrap things up. However, glancing at your timepiece is a good idea if another activity is scheduled on the heels of the journey.

Returning from the Journey
To gracefully end the journey, gradually slow the rhythm of your drumming/rattling. If you have assistants, look at them and synchronize the process of slowing down. Gently guide the journeyers:

> *Wherever you are, it is time to return from your journey. Find your way back the way you came, or another way if it seems appropriate.*

Continue drumming at the slower tempo for another few minutes, and then slowly come to a halt. Before stopping completely, glance at your assistants again, perhaps give a nod, and then conclude with four clear, distinct beats.

Allow a few moments of silence. Invite people to silently offer gratitude for any and all spiritual assistance they have received. Then offer a final cue:

> *Feel your body. Wiggle your toes. Come back into awareness of this place, here and now.*

Sharing and Integration
Central to the shamanic journey is the retrieval, from non-ordinary reality, of gifts that are brought back to this plane. A gift may come in the form of a drawing, a poem, a song, a story, or simply a deep feeling or intuition. These are bejeweled messages from the Dreamtime. Following a journey with a period of time that allows for quiet reflection and then sharing of one's experience with others is a way to illuminate these jewels. The post-journey period can also be a sensitive time

(people need to reorient to physical reality), so be conscious to move and speak a bit more slowly than usual.

This mood is usually very conducive for artistic expression. Have art supplies and writing materials available. It can be helpful to remind everybody this is not an art course or exhibit: whatever they put on paper is just fine.

After either a few minutes of quiet reflection or a longer period (twenty minutes) for artwork, call the group together and encourage each person to describe something about their journey. Most people find that sharing verbally is supportive in integrating their experiences. During the sharing, listen for:

- Each individual's developmental "edges" and places in need of healing
- Clues to any unexpressed talents ready to be revealed more fully
- Impressions, symbols, and archetypes that two or more people make known. (If these are pronounced and repeated several times, they may turn into a group theme and provide important information in deciding future activities. For example, one group had journeyers who saw repeated images of petroglyphs and then decided to visit pre-Columbian features on the land.)

Give everyone a chance to share but let them know that it is fine to remain silent, if they choose. As a facilitator, you may find yourself sharing an insight or impression that was related to their experience, as well as sharing a little bit of what it is like to guide. These non-evaluative insights can help them assimilate their experiences and can provide support to each individual. As you continue to facilitate journeys, your ability to offer helpful insights will improve.

Sometimes a journeyer will ask, "Did I do it right?" The answer is that because journeying is an entirely subjective experience, there is no "right." Typically, some people in the group will report a vivid, visual journey with an extensive plotline and will draw it with detailed imagery, while others will have little to verbalize or draw. Those people may need encouragement to trust in their own style, timing, and inner guidance. They also need to know it takes practice to access and feel comfortable with this unseen dimension, which is discounted by the dominant culture. As children, many of us tapped into non-ordinary reality with ease, but as we grew up, we quickly learned that only the seeable, the solid, and the physical are "real." As adults, we can learn to embrace the unseen dimension as a source of wisdom.

Concluding Thoughts on Guiding Shamanic Journeys

You may not have time for all of the journeys described above during a single WEI, but I strongly recommend that you make the sacred place and spirit guide journeys priorities. And if you decide to do the journeys to the elements, try to do them all. (They do not need to be done back to back but can be spread out through the ten days.)

Shamanic journeying is an invitation to let go of accustomed ways of thinking and perceiving and tap into tremendous power and intelligence. It's another method of reclaiming the wild within.

---

* An experienced shamanic singer, having skill with vocal styles such as Siberian throat singing, Amazonian *icaros,* or other medicine songs, may use the voice along with or instead of drumming or rattling.

Chapter 12

Play

I'm astounded by people who want to "know" the universe when it's hard enough to find your way around Chinatown.

—Woody Allen

The Boruca Indians are one of the few remaining indigenous tribes of Costa Rica. Their major ceremony was named the "Devils' Festival" by the Spanish, but according to a Boruca leader, Alancay Morales, it could more accurately be called the "Spirits' Festival." This pre-Columbian ritual, still held from December 31 to January 2 each year, has play at its core while addressing the mythic theme of "good and evil." After visiting Morales and his family on the Boruca reservation, I followed up by e-mail regarding the festival. Morales explained:

> During the festival, everyone drinks *chicha*, the traditional fermented, but low alcohol, beverage made from masticated corn pulp. The people are euphoric but not drunk. Food is shared widely. The men especially bring playfulness to the festival; they wear brightly colored masks with horns and run around yelling and teasing everyone else in the community. One of the masked men pretends to be a dog on a leash, while another holds the leash to keep the "dog" from harassing bystanders. Since it's hard to recognize who is behind the masks, there is a unique freedom for everyone to step out of the ordinary bounds of behavior, and have a lot of fun.[1]

The Borucans, like most indigenous peoples, consider playfulness to be an extremely spiritual quality. Morales's father, José Carlos, thinks that before the Spanish conquest, there was no distinction between play and spirituality. Although on the outer level, during the Spirits' Festival, a battle is being waged between the Borucans and Spanish domination, there is also an inner struggle being revealed between being playful and taking life too seriously. José Carlos said:

> Play does not really do battle but wins by making everyone laugh and feel good. By encouraging playfulness, along with its other aspects, the Festival strengthens and unifies the community and builds native pride.[2]

I have witnessed similar playful ceremonies among the Hopi and Taos peoples. The sacred clowns dance out of step, sing one beat behind, and taunt the other costumed performers as well as the bystanders. They engage in satire, jokes, and contrary behavior, and even make obscene gestures to shake everybody out of normality and self-importance.

This type of playful behavior is in short supply in mainstream modern society. It is not that we moderns don't play; it is that we just squeeze it into our busy schedules after we are finished with the serious business of survival. After all, haven't most of us been taught that the world is a rather grim place, full of struggle and bound by fixed laws? This perspective is reinforced daily by the mass media, which constantly focuses on violence, disaster, and turmoil, to the exclusion of joy and delight. While many of us live in relatively safe environs with room for enjoying life, we absorb the implication that we must be vigilant, hard working, good consumers—otherwise, something awful will happen.

Although many forms of play occur in the dominant culture, the subconscious assumption is that carefree, wonder-filled play is really the domain of the child. After all, how can we "get ahead in life" if we are playing?

Fortunately, most of us have experienced fun and lightheartedness as adults, and we long for more. There is nothing quite like that rare moment when we find ourselves running around aimlessly with a bunch of friends on a hot summer day, laughing at some inane silliness until our bellies ache.

Playfulness brings more energy to our lives and teaches us renewed flexibility and possibility. It is also disarming and creates a sense of safety. However, daring to "cut loose" directly challenges our fearful conditioning, which says that too much play will somehow endanger our ability to survive. But if we don't reorient ourselves and make authentic play a regular part of daily life, won't we humans unconsciously resent our lives and continue to take this resentment out on each other and the natural world?

What Is Play?

There are many definitions and forms of play. The first major text in play studies, written in the 1930s, is *Homo Ludens* (*The Playful Human*) by Johan Huizinga. Arguing against the anthropological certainty of the times, he suggests that play — not the struggle for survival — was the formative element in cultural development. Huizinga defines play using the arduous prose of his contemporaries:

> Summing up the formal characteristic of play, we might call it a free activity standing quite consciously outside "ordinary" life as being "not serious" but at the same time absorbing the player intensely and utterly. It is an activity connected with no material interest, and no profit can be gained by it. It proceeds within its own proper

boundaries of time and space according to [its own] fixed rules and in an orderly manner.[3]

Since then, Western academic literature has become filled with similar definitions. And although completely sensible, the overall discourse is so complex and cumbersome that one would think that play is anything but fun! Incredibly, there are thirty-four definitions for *play* in the *Oxford English Dictionary*.

However, rising above this verbal mire, play advocate and scholar Gwen Gordon describes play quite well:

> We certainly know positive forms of playfulness when we see them—a lightness of heart, a glint in the eye, alertness, enthusiasm, and readiness for surprise. There is a sense of involvement *and* detachment, self-expression *and* self-transcendence, individuality *and* cooperation. Boundaries become fluid, defenses dissolve, and physical, emotional, or mental movements become spontaneous, expanded, and well-coordinated.[4]

Gordon's insight is equaled by that of psychiatrist and researcher Stuart Brown, author of the book *Play*, who asserts that "play is essential to our social skills, adaptability, intelligence, creativity, ability to problem solve, and more. Play is hardwired into our brains—it is the mechanism by which we become resilient, smart, and adaptable people."[5]

Play Among Our Cousins

Did humans invent play? Hardly—just take some time to observe the animals! As I write this, two chipmunks outside my window are chasing each other. They dodge, starting and stopping, and the joy emanating from their beings seems obvious. And even if they are not playing (how will we ever really know?), observing them in this way draws out the playfulness in us.

Numerous books have been written on the play behavior of animals. For example, Tom Brown Jr., in his books *The Search* and *The Tracker,* writes about his extraordinary observations of wild animals at play, and ethologists Marc Bekoff and John Byers, in their book *Animal Play: Evolutionary, Comparative, and Ecological Perspectives,* document play in a wide range of animals, both wild and domesticated. That impressive compilation includes studies of play in dozens of animals, among them kangaroos, ravens, and even turtles! And, of course, an abundance of movies over the decades have brought us delightful footage of otters, dolphins, horses, and diverse other creatures doing what looks precisely like enjoyable, creative play.

Although playfulness appears to be an inherent feature of many living creatures, most adult humans, for now, need to *decide* to play. Otherwise, the solemnity of the prevailing worldview just weighs us down. How many times have we debated with ourselves, when given the opportunity to engage in some playful activity, whether or not we had enough time? Or even noticed that the more we worked, the less we played?

Play: Universal and Healing

Play is also physically and psychologically healing. Gwen Gordon makes the case again:

> Just look at the work of Norman Cousins who healed himself from cancer by watching Marx Brothers films and laughing all day. When we play, all the pleasure centers in our brains light up and we get a good dose of endorphins, which are great for our immune systems. Our circulation also increases. There are many other great health benefits of play. But most importantly, play makes us *want* to live and there's nothing more important to healing than that![6]

Brian Swimme thinks that play is not only a province of humans and animals, but is woven into the fabric of universe. He writes:

> The universe created our sense of adventurous play as the latest extravagance in a long history of advancing play. By enhancing it, we work with the grain of cosmic dynamics.
>
> Life showed surprise from the beginning. The earliest organisms advanced by a random appearance of novelty. We call this genetic mutation totally random, by which we mean that there is no controlling machine. The genes show a fundamental freedom of activity. Nothing could predict the outcome before the appearance of the new form of life.
>
> This presence of free activity was enhanced with sexual recombination. Now entire complexes of possibilities could be played with, rather than only individual units. The adventurous play of the life forms burst into the bewildering and sublime diversity of the past five hundred million years. All of this profusion of being and beauty is the outcome of play, of risk, of surprise. The creation of new life forms is not determined, but is the outcome of life's intrinsic freedom.[7]

If that is the case, it is not farfetched to say that when a truly sustainable culture takes hold, play will be a natural and central activity.

Play in a Wild Earth Intensive

We play during a Wild Earth Intensive (WEI) for all the reasons explained above, but most of all so that the guides and participants alike can access the wonderful feeling of pure joy.

The games vary in energy, style, physicality, challenge, silliness, and so forth.

In witnessing people at play during a WEI, I am often reminded of Christ's injunction, "Blessed are the meek: for they shall inherit the earth."[8] Why? The word *meek* is the English translation of the Greek term *praus*. *Praus* does not imply weakness, but rather denotes a gentle humility. This quality emerges gloriously through play. How can you be arrogant when you're rolling around on the ground like a dying ant (see Dead Ant Tag below)?

The games played at a WEI enable the group to experience a type of freedom and spontaneity that isn't found through other means. As an added benefit, they also subtly develop trust and cooperation. Exploring the euphoria of sheer play is another way to become more familiar with the present moment—the only place where life is really lived—yet we usually avoid it. Playing at a WEI is done to embrace the now with pleasure and passion.

In a WEI, we make a distinction between the competitive aspect and the wondrous aspect of play. Wondrous play can be active, physical, and, at times, challenging, but it is not competitive. There are no winners and losers. Most competitive games provide a healthy outlet for the human need for challenge, adventure, and dynamic tension, but often the desire to win can overshadow their purpose: fun. This is why competitive games are not part of the WEI schedule. There is such an overemphasis on them—almost to the point of obsession—in modern culture.

One WEI participant described her experience during various play activities this way: "I felt alive and free with no pressure to do something or make anything happen. Some of the games seemed to have purpose, but I was not boxed in or felt like I needed to compete."[9]

Often, some form of competitive game, such as volleyball or a card game, spontaneously arises at a WEI, but this happens by group agreement outside of the curriculum and is optional (as with all the other activities, there is no coercion to participate, only invitation).

In general, a playful attitude is evoked throughout a WEI, although it's through the short, organized games that play is made most explicit. The ability of the guides to model a lighthearted approach, and even silliness, while leading these games is key to the participants feeling safe enough to do the same.

The following "no props" games are among those that have been interspersed throughout the schedule. They serve to enliven transitions between more "serious" activities, helping participants to stay loose and at ease. There are thousands of similar games that could be included in an Intensive, but it's important to choose ones that are appropriate for each group, keeping in mind the setting, the weather, and the physical condition of the participants. It's also a good idea to keep Frisbees and Hula Hoops around for impromptu fun.

Mark Collard's book *No Props: Great Games with No Equipment* is a bible in this field and a wonderful resource. Two of the games described below, Dead Ant Tag and Lean Walk, are adapted from Collard's book or website.[10] Except for the first game, keep the rest brief so people don't tire of them.

Two Mirrors
Duration: 15 minutes
This exercise is used to introduce the concept of play and increase intimacy among the group. It is best done outside and in silence.

Instruct the players to form pairs. If there is an odd number of participants, one of the workshop facilitators joins in. Ask each pair to decide which person will act as the "leader" first. Then ask the partners to face each other at a distance where they can touch palms. The "leader" will move their body in whatever way feels right, while their partner tries to be the precise mirror image. For instance, if the leader moves their right arm in a wavy motion, their partner does the same with their own left arm. Explain to the players that by paying extremely close attention to whoever is leading and by "following the energy," they will maximize the fun and benefit of the game. Advise them that relatively slow movements will be easier to follow, so starting slowly tends to be best.

After about five minutes, ask the partners to trade roles. After another five minutes, invite them to continue playing with neither person designated as leader, allowing the movement of each person to be spontaneous, subject only to the condition that the two keep mirroring each other. Ask them to see if they can get in sync with each other's rhythms, not trying to dance in any formal sense, but simply following the spontaneous movements of the other and doing their best to harmonize with one another. You can suggest they touch palms if they are having any difficulty flowing together. Remind them to be aware of the subtle cues that their "mirror" gives them, as well as to be aware of their own body and energy fields.

At the end of the game, ask the group to share a few impressions. These may be quite insightful. For example, one participant reported "a new kind of union born of cooperation."[11]

Dead Ant Tag

Duration: 5–10 minutes

This is a tagging game done in a flat, open space, indoors or out, where boundaries can be indicated. Having at least ten players works best. During the game, there will be "ants" moving quickly inside an established area.

Explain how the game works before you get underway. Point out the boundaries of the space, and one or two designated "ant farm" areas (explained below) just within those boundaries. By way of introduction, you may choose to make up a story about what has befallen the ants, such as: "Someone has just kicked off the top of an ant nest, and all of the ants are now frantically searching for a new home!"

To play, the ants position themselves throughout the space, and a volunteer serves as the first "it." When you say "go," that person runs about in the space, trying to tag everybody else. Instead of becoming the next "it," a tagged ant must drop to the ground on their back and wiggle their arms and legs in the air, exclaiming: "Dead ant! Dead ant!" This is an emergency signal to other ants that are still on their feet to rescue their fallen comrade. Up to four such "paramedic ants" then grab an arm or leg and *gently* lift and transport the dead ant to the nearest ant farm. A paramedic ant cannot be tagged while in contact with the dead ant. Upon being gently deposited at the ant farm, the dead ant will experience a miraculous recovery and leap back into the game after slowly counting to ten. The game continues until most participants have experienced being a dead ant or most are in the ant farm. In fact, there have been times when everyone is lying on the ground wriggling about, with one "it" looking at the scene incredulously.

Dead Ant Tag can elicit a playful mood long after the game is over, when one of the participants spontaneously calls out, "Dead ants!" and some people drop to the floor and enjoy being wriggling ants again.

Zork

Duration: 10–15 minutes

Divide the group into two teams roughly equal in size (it's OK if one team has an extra person). Team A and Team B form two parallel lines facing each other about four feet apart. Designate one end of the line as the starting point. To begin the game, a person from Team A steps forward within a couple of feet of the person in front of them (on Team B) and says "zork" (no need to repeat afterwards). The person from Team B has ten seconds, using words, sounds, or body language—but without touching—to make the person from Team A laugh or break a smile. (Dying confessions of love are quite effective.) Keep time silently and say "ten seconds" when the time has elapsed. If the person from Team A laughs within the ten-second interval, that person joins the other team and goes to the end of their line. (Yes, it's slightly competitive, but it's for a good cause!) If not, they continue to the next person down the line. If no one from Team B makes the person laugh by the end of the line, the person returns to Team A. Next, someone from Team B walks over to Team A and repeats the process. The game goes back and forth, each team sending over the next person in line. This continues until all the people are on one team (laughing, of course) or there seems to be a stalemate; then just call it quits.

Back to Back

Duration: 3–5 minutes

Begin by asking two people to volunteer. They will sit back to back on flat ground (or a floor), gently link elbows with each other, and then gradually attempt to stand up together while simultaneously pressing their backs against each other. Next, add another person and do it again, this time with three trying to stand together. Continue to add another person whenever the group succeeds. (Our record is eight people!) Break into smaller groups, so everyone can take part.

Lean Walk

Duration: 5 minutes or less

Invite each person in your group to find a partner. Ask for a volunteer to step forward so that you can demonstrate what the activity looks like. Ask them to stand at your side and lean in on your shoulder, as you do the same to them. Looking from the front or back, the two of you should look a bit like an upside-down *V*. Then, your objective is to walk together toward some point, leaning together all the way. A quick three-second demonstration and your group will be ready to move.

Encourage partners to test how far they can lean (i.e., move their feet further away from the center) as they walk, while still retaining a solid, comfortable stance. Naturally, warn about the dangers of pushing past reasonable boundaries.

This exercise is also a fun way to "move" people from one activity to another in a unique manner.

Variation: Invite participants to form groups of three, where one person walks upright in the center of two others, who lean toward that person.

Serpent Tag

Duration: 3 minutes

Four or five players hold hands, forming a chain; these people are the serpent. The serpent runs around and tries to catch as many other players—"the food"—as it can, by forming a circle around them. As soon as one or more of the players are encircled, they must link hands with the others and become part of the serpent. They then help capture the remaining players. The key to the game working is to create a small enough playing field so that the people who are not initially part of the serpent can't run very far.

Human Knot

Duration: 3 minutes

Have the group make a large circle. If there is an odd number of participants, one of the facilitators steps in and becomes part of the group. Then ask everyone to turn sideways (to the left) and move toward the center of the circle, so that they are all close together. Each person then puts out their left hand toward the center, closes their eyes, and grabs the left hand of someone in the circle who is not directly next to them. Once all the left hands have partners, each person reaches over with their right hand

and grabs the right hand of someone not directly next to them. They then open their eyes. Then the group must use teamwork to untangle themselves, without ever becoming disconnected from the others, and form a circle again. At the end, some people may be facing in and some facing out. If, on the rare occasion, there does not seem to be a way for the group to accomplish this, they are allowed one "undo," where two people can unlock arms, and then reunite in a different position.

Speedy Rabbit

Duration: 5 minutes

Gather the group together in a circle, and stand in the center of it. You will be teaching the group the various poses of the game, which are done in groups of three people. After demonstrating the first pose with the help of two other people, point to someone in the circle. That person and the people directly on either side of them will make the pose. Have several groups of people enact the first pose, and then go on to teach the second one.

After all the poses have been taught, call upon various groups to recreate the poses. Point to a person and say "Speedy Rabbit" or "Dung Beetle," for example. That group of three stays in the pose until you point to another person and call out another pose, provided the first group strikes the correct pose. When someone messes up—and someone always does—by making the wrong pose, they become the new leader. As the group becomes more comfortable with the poses, the pace can be quickened.

Here are a few suggested poses; you can also make up some on your own:

Speedy Rabbit

The two side people make their outside legs run in place while the middle person puts their hands in front of them like paws.

Cow

The middle person locks their fingers and turn their palms out so that the thumbs point down, forming udders. The side people then milk the udders.

Elephant

The middle person forms an elephant trunk by putting their arms straight in front of them, crossed at the wrists. The people on each side form the ears of the elephant by bending toward the middle person with their arms outstretched, making the shape of big ears.

Screaming Viking

The two side people make rowing motions on the outer sides of the pose, and the middle person bangs their fists on their chest yelling. (No offense to anyone of Norse descent.)

Dung Beetle

This is a good variation because the two side people *get behind* the middle person (in a line), and all three people extend their arms to the sides and wriggle them.

True or False

Duration: 15 minutes

Either in one circle or in small groups (depending on the full group size), each person in turn tells three personal details about themselves, two of which are false but believable. One by one, the other people guess which statement is true. When they are finished guessing, the "teller" announces the true one.

This game is great to introduce about midway through the Intensive, as people will have become familiar with each other's deeper ecological selves but less so with their personal identities and histories.

Shake the Dessert

Duration: 5–10 minutes

Form two lines facing each other with arms bent at the elbows, and elbows held close to the waist. The lines stand close together with all arms and hands forming a "conveyor belt." People should position themselves so that their arms can bear weight (e.g., with feet in a wider stance than normal). Carefully place one person at a time onto the conveyor belt so that the load is evenly distributed. This is done by having the volunteer *slowly* lean back onto the arms of the awaiting group—the first four to six people—who pick them up. That person is then *gently* shaken down the line by the group members, who are moving their arms up and down a few inches. The person being sent down the line chants the name of their favorite dessert. This exercise requires physical strength of those who are standing and trust on the part of the person who is being conveyed.

Wind in the Willows

Duration: 15 minutes

The group stands shoulder to shoulder in a circle with their hands up, palms facing the center at about chest height. One person volunteers to go first and steps into the center of the circle. That person folds their arms against their chest, closes their eyes, and slowly leans back, at which point they are caught by the nearest hands. Those hands slowly and gently push them in another direction, where they are caught by other hands, which send them in another direction, and so on. The person in the center should be reminded to relax and allow themselves to be guided by the group. With some people, the motion will stay gentle and slow, while with others, it can be speeded up. The motion can last several minutes until the person in the center says "stop" or the facilitator calls "time." The person in the center will then be guided to an upright position. One nice way to end is to have people place their hands supportively on different areas of that person's body, such as the heart, head, belly, and lower back. Each person who chooses to do the exercise can say ahead of time whether they want to go slow or fast and if they want gentle touch at the end. This game is fun and builds trust.

Chapter 13

Stillness

*I am going to venture that the man who sat on the ground
in his tipi meditating on life and its meaning, accepting
the kinship of all creatures, and acknowledging unity
with the universe of things was infusing into his being
the true essence of civilization.*

—Luther Standing Bear

There's a place inside each of us that is very still and peaceful.
This place is more than a feeling. It is a state of pure awareness.
Ordinarily, we are not very familiar with this place and need
practice accessing it. At a Wild Earth Intensive (WEI), we
cultivate stillness in several ways. One way is to spend a lot
of time outdoors, honing our awareness of nature. Another is
meditation.

The type of meditation we practice at a WEI, *vipassana* or
insight meditation, was taught by Gautama Buddha almost
two-thousand, six-hundred years ago. *Vipassana* means to see
things as they really are, and the practice of meditation can help
us do just that.

Much has been written about meditation, and although
in essence it is quite simple, the kind that is described here
is also a vast science that leads to the antidote for worldly
suffering: wisdom and compassion. A person with a good
measure of wisdom and compassion sees a world of unity and
interconnection—and that perspective is at the center of an
ecstatic culture.

This chapter is a brief overview of meditation practice with
an emphasis on "sitting practice." A few books that delve into
this subject with great expertise are located in the bibliography.

Practicing Meditation in a Wild Earth Intensive

How often do we give ourselves the chance just to *be*? Not striving, not achieving, but instead simply listening to the universe as it is—not how we want it to be. In a WEI, we start the day this way, just sitting together in silence. Before relating to others, it can be very supportive to observe—with as much gentleness and focus as we can muster—our thoughts and feelings and the pleasant and unpleasant sensations of our bodies. This kind of observation can also be seen as an inner listening. We are simply curious to discover what will present itself, without trying to push away the "bad" and grasp onto the "good."

Each day right after breakfast, one of the guides leads a sitting meditation lasting roughly twenty minutes. They start out by asking everyone to close their eyes and feel the sensations of their bodies, interspersing silence with soft verbal reminders to be aware of their direct experience. We then simply sit and breathe—although this isn't as easy as it sounds!

As anybody who has tried this practice knows, the mind tends to wander, and the body wants to squirm. To settle down, we start by focusing on the full experience of breathing: noticing each complete in-breath and out-breath, returning our awareness to the breath over and over, drawing our attention back to the present moment. When any other sensations, sounds, or emotions come into our consciousness, as they will, we acknowledge them and let them go, and return our focus to the breath. Gradually, a steadier, more concentrated mind develops.

Sometimes, there will be pain or discomfort in the body, so it is helpful to suggest beforehand that the group try a novel approach to relating to it: turn *toward* the pain—consciously feeling it—before considering whether to move or change positions. This is not to make the practice an endurance test, but instead to investigate our ingrained habit of pushing away any kind of discomfort. By turning toward it, we can discover whether we are simply afraid of the pain and automatically reacting to it or whether we are genuinely in need of making an adjustment. This is the beginning of learning the power of *conscious awareness.* When we begin to bring awareness not only to painful sensations but to all the other passing content that appears "on the screen" of the mind/body, we get a taste of freedom. Freedom from what? Freedom from the incessant pull of every thought, every emotion, and every sensation. This freedom brings peace.

Let's take a closer look at this process. When we first become aware of something, there is a fleeting instant of just being present with it before conceptualization kicks in, before the thinking mind leaps in and says, for example, "Oh, that's a rose." That instant of awareness has a pure, spacious quality. For that moment, we can hold the rose in our gaze without separating it from the rest of existence through abstraction. Sitting practice helps us to prolong these moments of awareness.

In a WEI, the first few sitting periods are spent paying attention solely to the breath, to develop a base level of concentration. Thereafter, suggest that the participants be aware of whatever arises in the present moment. Encourage everyone to gently witness and accept all sensations, emotions, thoughts, and sounds as they arise and pass away.

As we practice this repeatedly, we get more moments of observing our thoughts and feelings—"Oh, thinking is like this," or "There's that sensation in the body again"—and then gradually those moments grow longer. In other words, the awareness of the contents of our mind *as contents* becomes stronger. This is the prolongation of awareness mentioned above. As we learn to do this in a gentle, nonjudgmental way, we begin to develop a natural friendliness toward the experience of being alive. This friendliness is the basis for peace and freedom.

Jennifer Welwood puts it this way in her poem "Unconditional," which WEI guides have read to the group:

Willing to experience aloneness,
I discover connection everywhere;
Turning to face my fear,
I meet the warrior who lives within;
Opening to my loss,
I gain the embrace of the universe;
Surrendering into emptiness,
I find fullness without end.
Each condition I flee from pursues me,
Each condition I welcome transforms me
And becomes itself transformed
Into its radiant jewel-like essence.
I bow to the one who has made it so,
Who has crafted this Master Game.
To play it is purest delight;
To honor its form — true devotion.[1]

Although the full depth of this poem may not be apparent to everyone, a precious seed of perennial wisdom will have been planted or watered within each person, and the practice of cultivating stillness through meditation will further nurture it.

Although there is a relatively small amount of formal vipassana practice offered at a WEI, it can be quite powerful for the group to experience this on a daily basis. It can also lead to a greater receptivity to the natural world.

Space around the Compulsive Mind

One of the reasons slowing down through meditation can be so powerful is that we are taking a break from the chronic tendency to continually think about and analyze our experience. Somewhere in the past few thousand years, especially in the dominant cultures, our brains became hardwired with a constant need to think, in order to help us survive. Surely, the ability to think comes with tremendous benefits, but do we really want to spend so much time being buffeted about by a mind that is constantly jumping from one thing to the next, ad infinitum?

The deeper problem, however, is not discursive thinking but *identification* with thinking—when the stories the mind weaves are equated with who we are. This identification with thinking was eloquently, but erroneously, stated by Descartes in his famous dictum "I think, therefore I am."[2] This confusion causes suffering.

Despite its difficulties, training our awareness through meditation reveals the complete falsehood of this view and gradually breaks the stranglehold that the discursive mind has on our larger intelligence (of which thinking is only a small part). For both experienced and inexperienced practitioners, there are wonderful insights to be gleaned along the way, as we free ourselves from old, unworkable conditioning. One participant in a WEI exclaimed, "Oh, I see! Thoughts are kind of like tiny electrical impulses passing across the monitor of my mind. I don't have to give them meaning unless I want to. It's now easier for me to see that my painful childhood was in the past and not the present."[3]

The essence of this practice is not confined to vipassana practitioners or even to Buddhists. The late Navajo elder Leon Secatero would say, "Get out of your head! Your body is loaded with information and truth. You got to listen to your gut if you want to make a good decision, but you can't do that unless you are paying attention."[4]

So true. The intention to really pay attention increases the periods of awareness—the "wake-up" moments—and we begin to understand something fundamentally important: There is a phenomenal world in which everything is constantly changing, whether we like it or not. The reality of impermanence is transformed from a source of suffering to a source of joy. How absolutely boring and strange it would be if everything stayed the same! There would be no world as we know it.

Again, this level of wisdom may not be revealed during the relatively short time spent meditating in a WEI, even if this practice is coupled with many other transformative activities, but it can give the participants a glimpse of what's possible. Many past WEI participants have expressed gratitude for the periods of inner peace they experienced in silent sitting. The time spent together in this way squarely contradicted the incessant need for busyness that modern life often demands.

And we don't need to be in a "sitting" session to gently, patiently, remind ourselves to come back to the present moment during our daily activities, and to witness them with nonjudgmental awareness. Eckhart Tolle believes this process of awakening is vital to the evolution of human consciousness, and that by participating in it, we are "rising above thought."[5] Rising above thought means we no longer get lost in—identify with—the thinking process. How wonderful is that?

Many environmentalists are prejudiced against meditation. They complain that it is too removed and distant from "real life." They are afraid it leads to passivity and a lack of caring about the destruction of the natural world—and, consequently, a lack of action required to stop that destruction. But this misses the point. Meditation is about the whole body, not just the individual body. Meditation is another way to see that nothing stands in isolation. We are one with the larger body of the Earth and the cosmos, linked both physically and spiritually. With the increased sensitivity learned in meditation, we naturally want to protect the beings within our larger body and can do so more wisely. We also learn a greater level of self-awareness that helps harmonize our human relationships. There is more peace in our lives. These are the reasons that sitting meditation is included in a WEI.

Exercises

A sample guided meditation follows. Draw upon your own creativity, intuition, and experience to modify the following.

Sitting Meditation

Purpose: To relax, slow down, and eventually see things more clearly by strengthening our awareness "muscle"

Duration: 20 minutes

Begin by describing to the participants the basics of why and how to meditate. Then ask them to find a place in the room where they can sit comfortably for about twenty minutes. Finding back support is important for some people, but lying down is not conducive to this practice. Talk them through the beginning of the meditation, using words like those below, with plenty of pauses between your statements so they have time to apply your suggestions. The following suggestions combine the practice of concentrating solely on the breath and the practice of opening to the full range of experience:

> *Close your eyes and shift your attention to your body. What surfaces is it touching? How does your body feel? Become aware of its activities, even as you sit still. Relax any areas of tension. Can you feel your body's aliveness, its subtle energy, and the wide variety of pulsations occurring throughout it? Now gently turn your focus to that activity of the body known as breathing — the taking in of the life-giving air that is freely given to you as a member of the planet. Notice the sensations of inhalation and exhalation, even that space at the end of the out-breath where it seems like nothing is going on. What is the texture of the breath? Is it smooth or rough? How does it feel passing through your nose or mouth? Notice the feelings in your lungs, your ribs, as they take this air in and out. Whatever you notice, it's okay. Just be aware of it.*

If thoughts arise, just let them be. Witness them as if they were clouds passing across the sky, and then gently come back to the breath. When sounds become pronounced, can you hear them as vibrations without naming them? Again, return to the breath—in and out, rising and falling. This is the primordial rhythm of the universe. Relax and allow yourself to "be breathed." Continue to simply observe your experience with an interested curiosity, using the breath as an anchor.

To conclude the session, gently strike a bell or chime and ask people to listen to the sound until it fades away.

Note: Sitting practice may seem less proactive than other activities in a WEI, but it is worth the relatively short time the group invests in it. Some groups may want even more time, and you may want to ring a "bell of mindfulness" every once in awhile to remind people to wake up and be present.

Meditating Anytime, Anywhere

Purpose: To train ourselves to be consistently more aware
Duration: 5 minutes or longer

Whenever we are not sleeping, we can be aware. We don't have to sit down to practice awareness. While guiding the participants through this process, speak slowly and give them time to incorporate each suggestion.

Begin by noticing what you are doing. Now, move your attention to one of your hands. Feel its vitality—the tingling, the temperature, and any pressure if it's touching something. Allow the muscles, tendons, and skin of that hand to relax. Next, change the focus of your attention to your breathing. Allow the breath to rise and fall, and notice if it's rapid or slow or somewhere in between. Experience the anchoring effect of your breathing. Now, widen your awareness to encompass your entire body. Feel the simplicity of just being alive. Feel the subtle energy that animates a body made of flesh and bones.

Next, pay attention to your vision, looking first at whatever is in front of you. Really drink it in visually — notice the colors and shapes, and even the space between things. Try the same thing with the sense of smell, and then hearing. You may find that thoughts and emotions are very distracting. If that happens, simply notice, without judgment, and refocus on the present moment. You can continue this process for as long you like, even after we conclude this session.

Chapter 14

Elders and Mentors

The great object of education ... is to teach self-trust.
—Ralph Waldo Emerson

Including elders and mentors as guest facilitators adds an important dimension to the Wild Earth Intensive (WEI). It is virtually impossible for one group leader—even if highly skilled and joined by very able assistants—to adequately cover all the material contained in the curriculum. Adding elders and mentors into the mix increases diversity* and greatly enriches the group culture that is being created. It also lightens the load on the main facilitators.

Although guest facilitators serve in that capacity for only a short period, their contributions are invaluable. When carefully selected, these individuals can fulfill the role of elders, the keepers of essential knowledge and wisdom in traditional indigenous societies. During a ten-day Intensive, we invite three or four skilled and respected people to each spend a separate day sharing their unique gifts. Before discussing this in more detail, I'd like to mention the historical and social context surrounding their inclusion.

The role of elders worldwide diminished as the industrial worldview gained dominance and societies all over the globe shifted their focus to the rapid production of goods. Worshipping the vigor of youth became a priority and elders came to be seen as useless, even as obstacles to progress. This ongoing devaluation of the elders' wisdom has also contributed to the lack of meaning experienced by so many young people in modern society.

In contrast, Danil Mamyev recently had this to say about the elders of his Altai people:

> Except for the knowledge that has been transmitted directly to us by Mother Earth and the Ancestors, the elders passed to us everything important from generation to generation. For this reason, during their lives, the elders made it a point to remember every detail [of the culture] so they could relate it at a later time. They were and are the storytellers and image carriers, making cultural and spiritual values come alive. Without them, we would cease to exist as a people.[1]

This is a testimonial to the fact that there still exist cultures in which age is seen as an asset and elders play a vital role in the health of the community. In a functional aboriginal society, age tends to be associated with spiritual power, and elders usually hold the most elevated positions. However, the number of years a person has lived is not the only factor that makes them an elder. More important is the recognition, by their community and the larger tribe, of their contributions: a record of dedicated service, a demonstrated ability to impart wisdom and mediate disputes, and a life of exemplary behavior. By serving as teachers and role models, elders—each of whom possess unique skills that have been honed over many years—act to unify and harmonize their community.

Respecting the key role of elders is an integral aspect of a healthy culture. We can learn to once again esteem those with vast life experience, and they, in turn, can gain an increased sense of usefulness as they impart meaning to "the ones coming up behind them." In a WEI, elders and mentors provide "complementary medicine," adding their insights and life skills to those presented by the regular facilitators and thereby enriching the group experience.

For the sake of clarity, and although this may be somewhat arbitrary, let's define the difference between a mentor and an elder in the context of the WEI. Elders can always be mentors, but mentors are not necessarily elders. Mentors are on the sacred path of cultural and ecological restoration but have not necessarily reached the same level of community recognition as elders. They are also usually younger than elders.†

True elders who have learned from life's many experiences, some of which may have been quite difficult, and who can convey their acquired wisdom within a nature-based context are rare. However, we need to start somewhere in identifying elders for the Earth-honoring culture modeled in the WEI. Those of you who serve as WEI facilitators and organizers can greatly enhance participants' experience by looking out for people who closely fit this description. You may be surprised to learn who is humbly but powerfully living within fifty miles of the site of your Intensive. If you are unable to find any elder facilitators in your area, you can invite them from afar. And remember, this entire effort at cultural repair is hampered by our collective amnesia of what it means to live in a healthy, thriving culture — so refrain from setting overly high standards.

The areas in which guest facilitators have greatly contributed in past WEIs include: psychological healing and integration, the sweat lodge ceremony, expressive arts, storytelling, and nature immersion. How these particular areas are incorporated into the program is discussed in the remainder of this chapter, and why they are incorporated is given detailed attention in other parts of the book.

The long-term vision for the WEI is that each of the key cultural ingredients (e.g., play, stillness, listening, and the other subjects focused on in individual chapters in this book) will be expertly modeled by an elder or mentor. To achieve this will ultimately require that the WEI last longer than ten days. Optimally, WEI organizers and facilitators will consider going beyond the workshop format into "real life" situations where they—along with other former participants—work with their local communities to help them learn these skills on an ongoing basis.

When planning an Intensive, the facilitation team will decide whom to invite as guest facilitators and which activities they will be asked to lead. Ideally, the invitation process should focus on elders and mentors within the bioregion where the WEI will be held, so that participants and/or organizers can follow up with them after the close of the WEI. Keep in mind that inviting guests who possess skills that differ from those of the facilitators will provide the most comprehensive learning experience for the participants.

Healing and Integration

A deep psychological wounding born out of a fear-based worldview has taken place in modern culture. Many people simply don't feel good about themselves and the experience of being alive. They may be remarkably functional on the surface, but trauma festers in their cells. Even without a large dose of trauma, the rest of us carry some measure of personal and collective pain. Although the purpose of the WEI is much broader than that of a typical personal therapy workshop, we have found that by about the third or fourth day, the participants need to reflect upon and integrate all their new experiences in a more focused manner.

A nurturing and skilled guest facilitator with psychotherapeutic expertise can therefore be very helpful, even if the lead guide of the WEI also possesses skills in this area. This elder or mentor acts as a compassionate, impartial "outsider," who increases the sense of safety by improving communication between group members. This person helps the participants remember that each of them matters and belongs, and by clarifying for them where they might be projecting their internal lack of ease onto others. The most important way this is done is through the expression of the core perception that people are whole to begin with, and that whatever shame or trauma a person may carry in no way detracts from their basic goodness, completeness, and adequacy. This kind of guest facilitator can also provide other valuable contributions, such as resolving any conflicts that may have arisen and validating the courage of the participants for their willingness to face their own pain and the pain perpetrated by humans on one another and the Earth.

Miriam Dror, a psychotherapist who has worked extensively on the Navajo Reservation and has served as a guest WEI elder/ facilitator, had the following to say about her role within the Intensive:

> The challenge, of course, is bringing individuals, within the supportive context of the group, to a kind of edge where transformation is possible. Over the many years that I've done this work, I've invented many ways of helping people develop a strong inner witness that not only has the courage to observe what exists in one's inner landscape but also the courage to project a vision of what is becoming. In the WEI program specifically, I draw strongly on teachings that have come to me from nature-based cultures, primarily Native American.
>
> A "Medicine Wheel," based on the cardinal directions, is used by many indigenous peoples to describe the powers and features of the natural world—both physical and non-physical. The Lakota Indians of the Great Plains speak of the Wheel as being a mirror of the world or, depending on how it is used, a mirror of ourselves. Using the Medicine Wheel in a very particular way helps people begin to "remember" and embrace a sense of who they are beyond acculturation and beyond adjustments and contractions that may have served as a protection in

4

childhood. It is no surprise that people actually long to make this kind of connection.

Furthermore, I don't see a separation between our work in the world and our personal work. As we endeavor to bring ourselves fully into our work in the world, we will inevitably be brought face to face with our internal walls that no longer serve us. Inner tracking, the process of compassionately witnessing our inner workings, including old beliefs and defenses, can lead to significant personal transformation, making our unique gifts more available to the world.

Community was meant to be the safe holding place for such internal work. It is here, within community, that we learn to witness both ourselves and others in this transformative process and to experience its alchemy. It is here that our gifts may be honestly mirrored, perhaps for the first time, giving each person a greater confidence to offer them to the world.[2]

Sweat Lodge Ceremony

The sweat lodge ceremony is only one of many nature-based ceremonies that could be led by an elder or mentor during a WEI. Each of them provides valuable teachings that can help us deepen our connection to Earth and Spirit. However, we prioritize the sweat lodge during the Intensive because it is so powerful.

As discussed in Chapter 10, it is important to find an elder or mentor who is trained to run a safe sweat lodge and holds deep respect for this ancient tradition. It can be beneficial to invite a Native sweat leader from the local area, but if this is not possible, invite another person with the requisite training. We feel that the competence and respectful attitude of the leader are most important, whatever their ethnic or cultural background.

Most of the sweat lodge ceremonies I have attended were "poured" by men. Ironically, the one that most spoke to my heart was led by a small, blonde woman of Italian descent. Her name is Cathy Pedevillano, and she exemplifies what all the traditional Native leaders I have met have said: "The Spirit knows no color. We are all equal." She has conducted the sweat lodge ceremony as a guest facilitator at three WEIs. She offered the following observations:

The sweat lodge is one of the most powerful ceremonies that I have had the honor to participate in and lead. It is a deep purification of body, mind, spirit, and soul. We enter the moist, warm womb of Mother Earth and we sweat, we pray, we give thanks, we release, we receive, we align with the prayers of our brothers and sisters. All the Elements are present in this ceremony: Earth that we sit upon, Air in the steam, Fire in the glowing stones, Water dripping from our bodies. We are humbled by the heat and the power of the ancient stone beings who release their wisdom in the lodge. The heat, the songs, the prayers, all help us to get out of our everyday minds and into non-ordinary reality where we can feel the presence of Spirit, have visions, cry the pain of being human, and expand into higher consciousness.

Many different Earth cultures created purification rituals using heat. Perhaps the Ancient Ones noticed the effects of Fire, how it burns away the old, transmutes matter from one form to another, and allows for new growth. We give thanks to the Native peoples all over the world who have remembered these ceremonies and passed them on through the generations. I give special thanks to those who have shared them with others outside of their tribes.

My first sweat lodge was in the early 1990s with Grandfather Wallace Black Elk, a Lakota elder who has since passed into Spirit. Several years later, I did a series of weekly lodges with a Lakota-trained man. Over the years, I have participated in lodges led by Natives and non-Natives, and all have had their own unique power. Although the format of lodges may be similar, the content is dependent upon who is leading the ceremony.

The structure of the sweat lodges I lead today are based upon the Lakota ceremonies I have participated in, but the content comes from my connection to Spirit and Earth and from fifteen years' experience of leading them. I like to say I co-lead them with Spirit since, in the lodges, I channel wisdom that comes directly from Spirit and is often exactly what those in the lodge need to hear. As I evolve in consciousness, the ceremonies I lead have greater healing power and relevance to today's world — although it is difficult to capture the essence of a lodge in words.[3]

Expressive Arts

The expressive arts allow us to meet our basic human need to demonstrate to others what is meaningful to us. Under this broad umbrella are the visual arts, song, dance, crafts, and poetry. These activities occur throughout a WEI, and are another part of the healing brew. One WEI participant commented: "Whenever I take part in the expressive arts, especially in a concentrated way like in a WEI, I feel at home within my being and ever so present. I notice that life is beauty and that I live in grace."[4]

Another participant wrote:

All those activities are so much more precious and beautiful than in my "normal" life. Why? I believe it is primarily because I'm not thinking about my day-to-day responsibilities, tasks, and worries. In their absence blossoms an incredible attention to the detail of the moment as well as an increased ability to surrender to the spontaneous and creative fun of these things—things I did when I was a child.[5]

A guest mentor or elder with expertise in this area can draw out the spontaneity and creativity in each person. Musician, artist, and composer Jason Cohen has this expertise. For many years, he has been leading five- to seven-day ceremonial "fire circles" called Forestdance. Before, during, and after the actual time spent communing with the fire, Jason—with the help of many able assistants—guides the participants through various expressive arts. As a WEI guest facilitator, he was able to compress some of the salient features of Forestdance into one day. He had the following to say about why he is involved in this kind of mentoring:

I don't have a choice at this point. What feeds me is music and connection in relation to nature. Singing the songs, playing the drums, dancing the dances, honoring the fire and all life, creating sacred spaces with Earth art ... where we can honor each other and become more subtle ... where we can accept the idea that while we are in this place we have what we need instead of the worried refrain of: "Will I be able to pay the bills? Will I be able to survive? Will I get what I need?" Where there is no one telling us that we can't dance, we can't drum, and we can't sing. Where we create a space where we can truly be ourselves. Of course, we have the old voices from our past that say otherwise, but let's just start the dance. Let's just listen. Let's just sing.

Then the shedding of what is unreal occurs. Then the Divine shows up big time. The most beautiful experiences I have had are when I'm doing this.

I've seen the people who are not familiar with this new culture, and in the beginning their fear is saying what I used to say: "I'm not going to get into that fire circle with these religious freaks." They are holding their bodies bent and crooked. They are upset and confused. Their father or mother is clearly a chip on their shoulder. But after a few days, their hips are loose and they have big smiles on their faces. They're connected to life, they're dancing their animal spirits, and they feel empowered. No one, including themselves, is standing in the way of that. They go back to their communities with that empowerment. They start that group they were thinking of starting or leave the job that is no good for them or create an innovative business. Or they bring together their own circles.[6]

Storytelling

Language is magic. A clearly told story, rich in imagery, enables us to share a vibrant consensual reality. In a nature-based culture, we tell stories not only to make sense of the world but as part of connecting to the Source of Life. In the Internet age, we are in the habit of getting our stories through virtual reality, but this can prevent us from experiencing the full effect of the storyteller's cadence, rhythm, and body language—especially when the teller is outdoors, in relationship with nature, which is simultaneously expressing itself as they speak.

Some people elevate storytelling to an art form and, in the process, pass on the essential knowledge needed for cultural survival. Storyteller and ceremonialist Jim Beard is such a person. Although a non-Native, he is fluent in Ojibwe and has studied extensively with tribal elders, and thus is sought after among Algonquin tribes to help them in cultural restoration.

After mentoring through story at a WEI, Jim reflected on what led him to storytelling and why he continues:

When I was in my late thirties, I began to question the values of the society I was brought up in. I started to seek answers to what I did not understand. As I was a recovering alcoholic, total honesty became extremely important, because I did not get a whole lot of that when I was growing up. Later, when I met the Ojibwe elder Larry Matrious, he showed me how to come to my own truth through Native stories. He changed my life. Each story spoke to me in a powerful way as if I had already known it. Larry did not come to me right away, however. First, during my years of searching, my oldest daughter gave me the book *Bury My Heart at Wounded Knee*. When I finished it, I did not feel sorry for the Native Americans, I felt sorry for humanity. What was done to the Indians was done to the Europeans a thousand years before. And the same thing happened to all the other peoples of the Earth. It's a history of bloodshed and domination.

But the Native Americans survived and they are still fighting for their right to exist. I wanted to know how they did that. While absorbing Larry's teachings, I realized they had something very, very valuable that needed to be passed on. They had a unique perception about life, one that says the Earth is sacred and they don't really die. What is really important just goes on and on. There is no beginning and no end. It's all circles within circles and we are all made of Spirit.

This understanding is in all Native stories, but they don't come right out and say it that way. No one would take the teachings to heart. This is why retelling stories orally is a critical part of helping people to understand who they are and to understand their history. This is the start of cultural repair. There are two dynamics involved; the first is the cultural repair of the Native Americans — and that is essential — but it cannot happen without the cultural repair of the whole society.

The repair starts with remembering the values that really matter, like what you want for your community and what your role is in it. The stories need to be listened to over and over so the universal values are really learned. The stories are so rich. If I were to write down the stories on paper, they would lose eighty percent of their value. There are so many teachings embedded in each one: respect, love, being related to everything around you, and helping others, just to name a few ...

About ten years ago, I told a Lakota story called "The Boy and the Flute" to a black teenager with attention deficit disorder who had been in and out of correction facilities. Amazingly, he managed to hear the story well enough so that he learned to play the flute just by listening to the story. More importantly, over time, he learned to feel good about himself, and I believe that story had a big part in his life turning around.[7]

Nature Immersion

Nature connection through immersion is a vital part of a WEI because it is a key part of reclaiming our power as individuals and re-establishing an Earth-honoring culture. Our disconnection from the natural world is so acute that extra time spent with an elder or mentor who can help us reconnect is always worthwhile. As modern humans, we tend to be overly dependent on other people to reflect back to us our goodness and aliveness. However, a gifted elder or mentor can guide us toward emotional self-reliance, help us experience the wonder of having nature as a constant companion, and teach us to mentor the next generation in the same way. Conscious immersion in our greater body, the Earth, reveals to us the power and strength that were always there, although we may not have been paying attention to them before. Furthermore, the more we pay attention to the Earth, the more we notice the resiliency inherent in natural systems, and, as indigenous cultures have done for millennia, we can then model our communities after these systems.

For example, following a strong disturbance in a natural system—e.g., a hurricane or a forest fire—regeneration occurs among a wide variety of animal and plant communities. "Repair" work gets underway immediately. Likewise, when difficulties beset human communities, we can learn to respond as nature does. The most effective way to accomplish this is by designing our communities, the cultural containers in which we are immersed, in such a way as to honor our differences and engage them as a source of strength.

A resilient system is comprised of distinct parts that benefit the whole. Each of these parts is engaged in short feedback loops that help maintain balance in the system. A human body is an astonishing example of a resilient system (the regulation of body temperature is only one of hundreds of feedback loops). Among humans, encouraging feedback from all individuals and building connection between them supports the greater vision and healthy values of the community.

Mark Morey (see Chapter 15) has spent considerable time using nature connection as the foundation for cultural repair. He shared the following story about one of the times he was a guest facilitator at a WEI:

After doing a whole set of awareness exercises before lunch, I could see that certain people were challenged by certain activities. Some were more present than others, and my goal was to provoke learning edges for each one of them, whether they knew it or not.

Right after lunch was served, I heard someone say, "Hey, Mark, there's something really cool over here." They were pointing to a frog that was sitting on a railing but were not exactly sure what type of frog it was.

Now, that frog had probably been there all week. It was doing something really particular in its behavior. It was a tree frog, and it was clutching the railing with its little grippy feet. It was a very rare thing to see, as far as frogs go.

My goal as a mentor was not to spoon-feed the people information about nature. I wanted to give them a skill set for long-term learning. Earlier in the morning, I had shown them field guides and taught them how, after observing a plant or animal, they could find answers for themselves. Strengthening their basic curiosity is a powerful part of this process.

Then someone else said, "Hey, look at this thing!" A small group gathered and a couple of people asked, "What is it?" As a mentor, I was thinking, "Even though I just spent an hour mentoring them in how to use a field guide so that they can be lifelong learners, the default brain pattern is revealing itself." So, in that moment, instead of giving more information, I asked a few more sensory questions and facilitated nature connection. I said, "Take a closer look at it." Out of habit, they had been turning their attention toward me, the "teacher," and asking, "What is this?" They were not creating a relationship with the creature itself. So, I said, "Let's take a look at this together." I got down close to the frog and asked, "What do you see on the back here? What colors do you see?" Then the attention of the group shifted back to the frog. And suddenly the key moment arrived. One person said, "Take a look at this." And another added: "Take a look at that," and then "Wow! Did you see the eye?" "Look at this color and that color."

You can look up *gray tree frog* in a field guide, but if you don't examine it with your natural curiosity first, you don't develop a living relationship with what you are studying. So I helped this process along by going deeper: "Do you see the stripes? And what about the texture?" Then someone else exclaimed, "Look at the back legs! Oh, wow, what is that?"

It was as if, for the first time, a being actually appeared before their eyes. And what was blowing their minds was not just what they were seeing, but that their eyes could reveal to them new things that had been right in front of them over and over again—and they only saw them because the mentor got them to really look. They saw that at the end of each foot of the frog was a tiny little round thing. It was really quite unusual, and they realized, by the way the frog was sitting, that those little round things were suction cups! Whoa! And then, they were delighted, like joyous children.

One of them asked, "What's the name of this?" I looked at them with a smile and said, "Weren't you the one holding the frogs and reptiles field guide an hour ago, just before lunch?" And they made a sound like "errrr," but they were smiling. They got it. So they went and looked up in the field guide the name of that frog. But the cool thing was that they didn't just shout it out to the whole group. They stayed there and read that field guide for another fifteen minutes.

Mentoring nature connection can be contagious because it feels good to everyone involved. At that point, like an epilogue to the story, I said to the group, "It's really an awesome animal. A lot of times when you get a key nature connection, it informs you about the world you live in. Some animals like this frog act as extra-sensory scouts that are part of our survival—our resilience. The truth is we are not alone; we actually have these informants out there. So this particular guy here [pointing at the frog] can tell you when the rain is coming. He'll let you know when it's about to rain, so listen for the sound he makes." They asked, "How will we know which sound?" I said, "It will be the one that you haven't heard before." And I just left it there.

Later that day, we were out in the woods and this very intense, brooding, dark gray-black cloud came drifting in from the west. It was so overshadowing that the group couldn't concentrate on the tracking that we were doing. So we went back to the lodge and debriefed from the day, and someone brought up the art of questioning that had been going on about the frog. Just then, sure enough, the frog started making this sound. I was the only one in the circle who heard it, because people were paying attention to me. I also have a previous relationship with that animal. It was so apparent, like my mother opening up the back door during my childhood and calling, "Ma-ark! Dinner!" But in this case, it was: "Ma-ark! Rain's coming!" from the gray tree frog. It was a beautiful, high-pitched trill that most people would think was a bird. I paused and said, "Shhh. Listen, listen." Smiles grew upon each of the faces, one by one. And, shortly after that, the rain came in.[8]

Inviting and Hosting Guest Facilitators

In planning an Intensive, ascertain the strengths of the team, and then consider what a guest elder or mentor, or several, could add. Keep in mind that having too many guests in a ten-day period will dilute the bonding and coherence of the group. To facilitate the process of inviting guest facilitators, and to make their visits most beneficial for everyone, here are a few suggestions:

1. After determining which cultural ingredients are the ones most important to supplement in order to round out the curriculum, comb the bioregion to find the elders and/or mentors most suited for your WEI. "Combing" would mean: a) getting recommendations for noteworthy individuals by word of mouth; b) participating in gatherings/workshops in the region that feature one or more of the ingredients; and c) researching organizations that specialize in any of those areas.

2. Visit with the elder/mentor first and then observe them "in action," if possible, to ensure they will provide maximum benefit to your group.

3. Explain the purpose of a WEI and why they are being invited.

4. Ensure that financial compensation, including reimbursement for travel expenses, is agreed upon clearly in advance.

5. Provide the best accommodations available if they will be staying overnight.

6. Before the elder/mentor's arrival, brief the participants on the importance of conduct that is not only respectful but also enables the group to draw out the best from this guest facilitator. Examples of this kind of conduct include: a) practicing receptive listening; b) foregoing preconceptions and argumentation; and c) waiting for the elder/mentor to finish their presentation before reaching conclusions.

7. Share with the group at least a day in advance of the guest facilitator's arrival the purpose of their visit.

8. Introduce the guest facilitator warmly to the group.

9. Express your appreciation for their teachings at the end of the day.

---

* Since diversity generates stability and resilience in ecosystems,[9] why not extend that concept to human cultures? We are part of nature, after all.

† The Navajo and Siberian Buryat tribal leaders with whom I spoke said they did not like to be too specific about what constitutes the age of an elder. However, Buryat environmental leader Erjen Khamaganova observed, "Elders have experienced enough of the stages of life that they can look back and reflect on them, and this really can't happen before fifty and maybe not before sixty. Sometimes, though, a younger person surprises everybody with their wisdom and is considered an elder."[10]

Chapter 15

The Magic of Mentoring:
Including an Interview with Mark Morey

We clasp the hands of those that go before us
And the hands of those who come after us.
We enter the little circle of each other's arms
And the larger circle of lovers,
Whose hands are joined in a dance,
And the larger circle of all creatures,
Passing in and out of life,
Who move also in a dance,
To a music so subtle and vast that no ear hears it
Except in fragments.

—"The Healing," by Wendell Berry

The Wild Earth Intensive (WEI) is designed to be comprehensive, but of course there isn't enough time in a ten-day period to add every desirable ingredient to the nature-based culture we are cooking. When a WEI lasts more than ten days, we can include some additional ingredients to our recipe, and the one at the top of my list is mentoring with an intergenerational focus.

Every human passes through different life stages along the path from birth to death. During that journey, not only do we need each other in a general way to provide the basic necessities of food, clothing, shelter, and love, but we also need specific kinds of guidance and support customized to our age and personality. Elders and younger people have mutually beneficial talents and strengths, and with conscious mentoring administered by the elders, both sides can grow in ways they otherwise would not. True elders, whatever their age, are keenly aware of the needs of the young and respond to them with insight and thoughtfulness. This intergenerational mentoring is built into most intact indigenous cultures, past and present. It is designed not only for group survival but for "thrival."

In this chapter, we present an interview with Mark Morey, whose work epitomizes intergenerational mentoring, followed by an outline of a two-day application of these ideas.

Mark is an expert mentor based in Brattleboro, Vermont. He is also a tracker, life coach, and keynote speaker, and has spent considerable time with elders of the Lakota, Odawa, and Mohawk tribes. He is feisty and fun loving, and clearly enjoys life on his own terms. I met Mark in 1995 during an exceptional overnight outdoor adventure. Since then, he has become one of the premier advocates of nature-based culture. In 2007, he introduced me to the Art of Mentoring (AOM), which he co-designed with Jon Young. The AOM is a glorious experiential program, five to seven days long, that embodies intergenerational mentoring. His talks during the AOM inspired me to interview him for this book.

As we were about to begin the interview, Mark pointed to a ten-inch Paleo-Indian grinding stone on the small table between us and asked me about it.

Mark Morey: So, what's the story with the stone?

Bill Pfeiffer: A couple of years ago, I was kayaking off the coast of Maine, in Penobscot territory, and I stopped at a little island. I was sitting on the shore, enjoying the waves and feeling how beautiful it all was. I looked around, and there was this grinding stone, tucked away, half-buried in the sandy soil. You could tell it had been there for a long, long time. I debated whether or not I should do anything with it, and I received an inner message that this was a symbol for the kind of work we are doing, and that at the right time, a Penobscot elder or someone of Penobscot heritage would show up in my life, and I would pass it on to them. But that's in the future. Right now, this beautiful grinding stone represents a way of living on the Earth that really matters and has staying power. And that is the thrust of this interview. I brought it as a kind of beacon. If the stone is a couple of thousand years old, it challenges us to maintain the old ways under new conditions.

Mark: So true. But before we start the interview, can you tell me the mission of the book?

Bill: The book is intended to provide a manual for small groups — fifteen to twenty-five people — to gather for a minimum of ten days and recreate together what it really means to live sustainably. The assumption is that to live this way on a physical level, we also need to do it psychologically, spiritually, and emotionally. That's the challenge. I believe when we change things culturally — which is the outward expression of these levels — things will fall into place. Practicing living in this way provides a lot of my inspiration. What inspires you?

Mark: Magic inspires me — believing in the impossible, and, in terms of my time on the planet, being regenerative. I want to take the word *sustainable* and up the ante a little bit. The way most people think of *sustainable* is sustaining the way it is now. But what would it mean to increase healthy trends and leave things better than we found them, so there is always a surplus? This is what I like to call the regenerative model. I could fish for people and it might be sustainable, or I could teach people to fish and it would be regenerative, right? As a cultural creative, I'm always looking for leverage points to have maximum regenerative impact. I'm totally passionate about that.

The other big area for me is healing — but reluctantly. It's been painful to take a hard look at what we've all been through. And I keep seeing psychological wounding, mine and others', as

233

first and foremost culturally installed. That larger context could be considered historical trauma. So, facilitating a new context for learning, where we can see past the unconscious cultural patterning, has become an immediate goal of mine.

Advertising, government, and religion all came tumbling down on me at a pretty early age. As a young adult, I came up with a couple of sacred questions: What kind of life would I want to create, if my life were an artwork? And what do I want to create for others as a service to future generations? That's been pretty much my lifelong path.

Bill: Can you say more about healing and historical trauma?

Mark: Okay. I need to start out with healing. I interpret the word *healing* as "wholeness," so any work I do that is regenerative or creative considers the following questions: What does it mean to be whole? What does a holistic education look like? What does a holistic family life look like? What does a holistic relationship to nature look like? What's a holistic community? What's a holistic sense of self?

My understanding of healing and wholeness is influenced by anthropologist Bradford Keeney and his book *Ropes to God*. He has spent a lot of time with the Kalahari Bushmen, who talk about ropes—ropes to spirit, ropes to nature, ropes to community, ropes to self. These really can't be separated, but in terms of discussion, I think it's very helpful to do so. The strength of these ropes determines the health of the individual and the culture.

To get through a childhood with very weak ropes, I had to adapt to the difficult conditions that were taking place then. But—and this is very important—as babies, we come in with a certain set of instinctual instructions, an expectation that the surrounding environment is supposed to be nurturing. The Bushmen have not forgotten this!

For my personal healing, I needed to look at the larger context and go all the way back to Europe and see my Irish ancestors, on my mother's father's side, as Native people who were conquered by the Romans and enslaved, imprisoned, and murdered in the town square—and then the English colonized the Irish and used them as slaves. That was my Irish side. But the oppressor is always traumatized in some way by the oppression as well, and I believe this trauma showed up in the mental illness of my English grandmother—my mother's mother—who came to the United States. Then, instead of her getting a holistic treatment, the doctors handled it with compartmentalization and removed part of her brain. This, of course, greatly impacted my mother, who lost her childhood at that moment. She had to grow up at a very early age and lost her joy.

That is the immediate social environment I grew up in, and it's also part of something much larger: the compartmentalization of the landscape; the conquering of the land. In my case, it played out as the development of the suburbs of Buffalo, New York. At the age of ten, I roamed freely for miles, and by the time I was fifteen, there were chain link fences, lawns, roads, and "No Trespassing" signs. And nobody was talking about it. So, the journey leading from the British Isles to this boy is a real story. Then came a moment to make a choice. It was a turning point, because I felt so isolated, I didn't know who I was. So I had to either end my life or transcend all that.

The choice to transcend it led me to break out of the box. I started to analyze the context of dis-ease and study culture, and decided to turn things around. I started to view my wounding as a gift. This was a major revelation and it shifted my perspective considerably. I recognized that my experience of isolation growing up could be turned into my mission for the world. This reframing was magic! A big part of the hero's journey [see Chapter 9] is rising above the old patterns and saying, "I don't need to do that anymore." I'm not in that survival situation. I'm now engaging in a creative act, and I can create my world.

It's really important to know that trauma does not stop with the individual but is historical and gets passed down through time.

Bill: Trauma, and its healing, is bigger and collective?

Mark: This is key if we are to transcend our challenges. When it's historical trauma, you and I have something in common, instead of saying it's "your" issue or "my" issue. There is something ecological about that. To paraphrase Jake Swamp, the Mohawk elder and worldwide peace tree planter, Native people have historical trauma and non-Natives have historic trauma and historic guilt.[1] I would interpret him as saying that what we have in common is that we're the living people on the planet right now, and we get to say how our relationships impact the future generations together, so let's bury the weapons of war; let's move towards peacemaking; let's forgive and release those things. What Jake proposes is, I think, very noble, courageous work for all of us to consider.

Bill: You've alluded to the overemphasis on individual treatment in the healing professions. The analyst says, "You've got these personal problems, you've had some trauma. Let's work it out. If you see me enough times, then eventually you're going to heal." What's different about your approach?

Mark: Well, as I said before, I never signed up for healing, either for myself or for others [laughing]. It wasn't in my plans. I signed up for something much more innocent: nature connection with children. But since I'm looking for leverage points to make the most difference, healing keeps arriving on my desk. In the spring of 2010, six months before he died, I asked Jake Swamp to come down and talk with us about historical trauma, because we had the tenth anniversary of our nature programs coming up. And I said, "It seems to me, Jake, our mission is about connecting, and after ten years, we've also gotten from it all manner of discomfort—the more we connect people, the more they experience a corresponding disconnection."

Jake kept reinforcing the notion that our ills today exist in the context of historic trauma. Again, healing is about wholeness, re-membering the lost parts and bringing them back into our wholeness. This includes how the wholeness became compartmentalized over time. My self, separated from nature, is a perfect example of that.

Now, the more holistic approach we use in the Art of Mentoring is a process of restoring ongoing relationships. Individually and collectively, we look around and say, "I want to reclaim my connection to my people, my history, my land, and my food." This decision makes a big difference for a lot of people.

Bill: Yes! Your team *has* created a beautiful palette of connecting techniques, both human-to-human and with the natural world. When I took part in the Art of Mentoring program, we would come together after spending hours outdoors and sing, and I felt this tremendous sense of community and bonding—the feeling that we're all in this together and we're looking out for each other—and all of those very primal parts of what it means to be human. And then, suddenly, a wave of separation and grief came to the surface. Later, I was relieved to find out that lots of people reported similar experiences.

Mark: Yes, I have this belief that if we return to the original joy, on the way there, we have to meet the original trauma—the original wound. That just seems to be the sequence. First, we feel blessed, then sad, and even angry. All sorts of things come up. When I help individuals reconnect with nature, it's pretty simple. It's just them out there, and the healing can be very straightforward. But when these techniques bring people into connection with one another, there are a lot more complications, because now, for example, you're reminding me of my father [chuckling], and your stuff triggers my stuff and we just don't get along. If we each think it's only about the two of us, we miss the larger healing opportunity.

Culturally, there are some false freedoms we've inherited that prevent us from actually doing the work of healing and reconciliation. For example, we can just leave town. There's no taboo around leaving. There's no ethic or value telling us to stick with the group, or the community. There's a bigger back door than front door. So, we don't have to do the work; we don't have to figure that part out. I've noticed that when we start bringing people together in community settings — beyond programs — and there's conflict, it's because the adults have forgotten the main reason for being there: *better lives for their children.* That kind of conflict has been difficult for me, but when I remember that a child's development depends on healthy, intergenerational relationships, I become re-inspired to work with every life stage. It's essential.

To do something about this, I'm honing two major cultural initiatives. The first one is a cathartic, body-based group experience that the Kalahari Bushmen would call *trance dance.* It has to do with the body releasing the "nails," and the wounds, and the trauma, and all those painful things. But it's not about any single individual. We do this together. You and I can have a conflict in the community, and twenty or thirty people will get together to dance it out, and we'll just keep dancing until, at the end, we're clean and clear. And we'll do that regularly, like a contra dance, weekly. That's village healing by design.

The second cultural initiative is something along the lines of restorative justice, which is another kind of peacemaking. We're building understanding and language around group approaches to resolving conflicts. In a Native sense, *restorative* means that we're assuming, at the beginning of this process, that we're going to restore the ropes between us. The assumption isn't that there's going to be some punishment at the end of it and we're going to find out who's guilty. We need to restore that rope of friendship. All these other people in the circle are really depending on that, because they all have ropes to us as well. So when we have a conflict, we get in a group of perhaps fifteen people, because they all had some part in it. We actually are not just two people, you and I; we are the sum of many relationships. And the acknowledgment of just sitting in that circle shifts my worldview from being alone and isolated to being interrelated and not wearing the burden of what just happened. I share my historical trauma with everyone else and move through it with everyone else.

So I think those two initiatives would be really helpful for the healing. And when I say "healing," I don't really think of it as a permanent healing. It's an ongoing thing.

Bill: The dominant culture believes so strongly in the isolated self: "I'm in here, the world is out there, and I'd better look out for myself because no one else will." We have the cult of the individual. Because of that, the whole thrust of collective healing you are presenting can be a very foreign concept to the mainstream. It's like trying to describe swimming to a person who has never seen the water. How do you explain to that person what that's like? Can you go a little further and talk about healing, not only at a given event with a large group but also through the long thread of time?

Mark: Intergenerationally?

Bill: Yes. And thinking about what that really means brings tears to my eyes. In a sense, it's all represented by that little poster on your door, showing an elder's hand placing an acorn into the palm of a young child—the promise of abundance long into the future. That's the circle of life, and we're talking about restoring that. What does that mean in practice?

Mark: There is a map that I work with, developed by Jon Young and the 8 Shields Institute, that reveals this insight. In the cycles of nature, there are certain archetypes, and these archetypes are within every person. These archetypes correspond to the cardinal and ordinal directions. For example, somebody between the ages of twenty and twenty-seven actually has a classic, archetypal, overarching developmental pattern called the Southwest Life Stage. They hold the archetype of the wanderer, which epitomizes trying to figure out one's direction and priorities in life. And the eight- to ten-year-old is beginning the Southeast Life Stage. This is about curiosity and motivation, and the first level of competency. It is a very sophisticated map that takes years to internalize, and is best experienced at a program like the Art of Mentoring.

To illustrate, let me explain the Rites of Competence, which is an example of cultural repair and a return to wholeness, focusing on the Southeast Life Stage. Between birth and seven years old, children are fully in the protection of their parents. But sometime around seven, they are becoming capable. I believe that children are born with instinctual, original instructions. Children are nature. As a parent, I watched for the natural developments unfolding as my daughter grew up. I still do. And, particularly as parents, we need to put space around those original instructions and just facilitate exactly what is asked for. No more, no less. We need to listen really deeply. My work of developing a quiet mind is essential to conscious parenting.

One day, my daughter said, "You never let me do anything." There was a tone of importance and emotion in her voice that caught my ear. I heard that and started to see her differently. Then, one day, I came home and quietly discovered her standing on the kitchen countertop. She was opening the cabinets and pulling plates out. My cultural conditioning wanted to say, "Get off of that counter!" But I didn't. It was just on the tip of my tongue, but I decided to just watch. She pulled down big, heavy plates—while holding onto the cabinets—putting them on the counter, not knowing I was there. Then she hopped down and began setting the table. I took a deep breath. I had almost ruined that moment. Later, I understood that she wanted to be acknowledged for being competent in the family, and she was letting us know she could help out. Her original instructions were saying, "I want to belong and participate in the family rhythms."

Synchronistically, I met a Dineh [Navajo] man who told me he put his seven-year-old through a ceremonial initiation to acknowledge a life stage transition. And I thought *that makes so much sense*. So I wanted to create an event for my daughter that really acknowledged and fortified this stage of life, and to do it for many other families. I called this initiation into the Southeast Life Stage the Rite of Competence. It is set up so that the extended family members come together and witness the child's transformation. And by extended family members, I don't necessarily mean blood relatives. I am including the practice of adopting people as family if you share the same path and life values. The parents gather stories and reflections ahead of time about the child's competency. Examples might be: "I noticed that when the next-door neighbor boy comes over, you watch him and take care of him while the mothers are talking in the kitchen," and "You put your clothes away; you help us set the table; you know how to use a sharp knife; you can light a match."

All these things are saved up in the memories of the parents, close friends, and relatives, and then, through the ritual, they are reflected back to the child in a conscious way. The child is moving from one life stage to another life stage, from one room into another room, and this is explained to the child. And the new room comes with new conduct and instructions for how to develop oneself for the next chunk of time. All this is in preparation for the adolescent transition.

Bill: So, would you say the stages of development of a human being take place in roughly seven-year cycles? Accounting for each person's differences, these cycles take place right through until death, and it's all mapped out on the medicine wheel, right? And the elders' responsibility is to ensure that these stages of development are nurtured in an optimal way, so that each person feels as healthy, whole, joyous, and connected as possible. That's the ideal.

Mark: Yes. That's their goal.

Bill: And their ongoing focus is not just about any particular individual, but about strengthening the web of the entire community.

Mark: Yes. Ideally, before the Rite of Competence, the parents of the child are able to choose at least one representative from each of the life stages as extended family, blood or not, to participate. For example, in consultation with community facilitators, they may invite a three-year-old, a thirteen-year-old, a twenty-five-year-old, some forty-year-olds who are the same age as the parents, someone in their sixties, and maybe someone in their seventies. By the time the seven-year-old stands in the middle of the Rite of Competence circle, the parents have built long-term relationships with everyone present. The parents have asked each of them: "Will you be in my child's life? We recognize you as a relative and would like to encourage you to act that way with our child for the rest of your life."

The parents know that each of these people has a certain gift for their child. The thirteen-year-old can be a model for the seven-year-old because recently he's been through a rite of passage: he's got that energy in his bones, and it will create an attractive pull for the younger child. The mother of the three-year-old will invite the seven-year-old to come over to help out around the house. And an elder will spend time with the seven-year-old when the parents are not around, interacting with him or her with wise love and storytelling. When we add nature connection as a primary activity, we have the makings of a regenerative cultural model.

Bill: This model seems to be very much at the core of what I hoped you would talk about. It seems to be the foundation for the kind of long-term healing and reconciliation we've been discussing.

Mark: If we take the long view of human beings as animals on the planet, we know—even with our limited anthropological lenses—that the culture our ancestors created was an imitation of the natural world they inhabited. The amount of nature-based arts that Native cultures have is outstanding—music, storytelling, dance, regalia, crafts; it goes on and on. And you know what? There's no school in sight. The school I grew up with was designed to feed a machine, and I think it kills children's creativity. Sir Ken Robinson and John Taylor Gatto have spent their lives explaining how this happens. Instead, I'm championing a life of intergenerational community mentoring designed around nature's instructions. Nature becomes the school, and that's been *very* successful and resilient over the long haul.

I think facilitating regenerative culture is like a holistic Chinese Five Element acupuncture treatment. Mentors who have spent a lot of time connecting with nature and applying that to people are like a combination of the acupuncture practitioner and the needles. They stimulate the meridians and multiple places throughout the entire body called *culture*, through core routines of nature connection and cultural mentoring.

Bill: Where do we start this cultural change?

Mark: Probably, the easiest place to start is with the extended family. That's why the ritual I just mentioned is particularly doable. It wasn't that long ago that extended family was far more vital, so it's not too hard to actually bring it back. The questions I ask to get people to think along these lines are: How long ago was it that the grandparents still lived with their families? What was life like before the nursing home? And what are the cultures around the world that are still that way? How many of you long to be in a village? How many of you wish to be seen by someone who can see your gift? How many people have adopted you as part of their extended family? The answers to these questions are richer and more meaningful when the extended family becomes familiar with transition ceremonies around death, rites of passage, rites of competence, festivals, and other things like that. This is the beginning of intergenerational healing.

Bill: Again, the emphasis is on the community acting in concert?

Mark: Yes. During that Rite of Competence ceremony with that seven-year-old standing there, and everybody being fully there for them, the adults are also renewing their relationships to their own inner seven-year-olds, because at that age, they were never seen. They are profoundly moved because it's something they never got. And it's not only the child's wholeness that's shining through; everyone is experiencing a healing together. This is why it's important to consider that healing is actually a two-way street. You know, I think, on one level, it's separating to have only a therapist and a client, where you don't know what's going on for the therapist in terms of the reciprocal healing effect, or for the whole community, for that matter. It goes both ways.

Bill: That's been my experience whenever I've been in either role. To wrap up, could you touch on the "how" of mentoring?

Mark: A mentor who really knows about cultural repair knows how to reconnect people to nature, and that always includes respect for the other person's learning process. A person who does not understand mentoring in this way could punish children into connecting to the natural world and ruin the whole thing. This unfortunately happens a lot. Mentoring through nature connection is not really education. It's not even information. It's facilitating relationship. And I think respect is the bottom line. If I'm truly mentoring your relationship to nature, then it's about facilitating the actual connection of your senses to the other beings around you. And you get to add the meaning.

Mentoring is an act of service. I'm not going to give you a direct answer if you come and ask me a question out there. I'll probably tell you a story instead. And then I'm going to ask you a question. The point of this indirect form of guidance is to draw out a person's strengths and resources instead of just feeding them more information.

If I mentor somebody well, and they become profoundly nature connected, they will become a good mentor themselves. The quality of their mentoring will be inseparable from their experience in nature. If I respectfully facilitate a spacious, attractive, curiosity- and passion-based nature connection early on, the young person will become a master naturalist with a profound understanding of the planets and the stars, of the animals and the plants, and of medicines and survival skills, tracking, and more. The way they have been mentored becomes embodied, and it kicks in when they come across someone else to mentor.

I've seen a ten-year-old do this. He had been mentored for three years in a holistic, nature-based, intergenerational community here in Brattleboro. I saw him notice a younger child who was playing with something and say, "Hey, what is it that you've got there?" He sees that it's a dandelion leaf and knows exactly what it is but does not just blurt it out. He knows that it's good to eat. He knows that it's got medicine in it, and he's already made things from the roots, but he asks the child questions like: "What is this? What do you think this is?" And the child says, "I don't know; it's just green." And he says, "Take a look at the edges." He plucks it, and then says, "Hold it up to the sky. Look at the teeth on that thing." And then he smushes it up and says, "It smells so good, doesn't it?" Then the child picks up the leaf and smushes it and says, "Ummmm, it smells so good," and then the ten-year-old balls it up and pops it into his mouth. And then suddenly all the little kids are running around balling up little dandelion leaves and popping them into their mouths.

What is happening there? Literally, the natural nutrition of the dandelion—the minerals, the vitamins, the protein (fresh and raw)—is going into the bodies of these developing children, with joy. It's a complex example of regenerative— beyond sustainable—mentoring that leaves a surplus, an increase in abundance, as it moves through time. It's the opposite of historical trauma. It's healing. When I observed that ten-year-old mentoring the younger child in dandelions as edible food, I asked him, "Where did you learn to do that, mentoring him like that?" I actually imposed on him consciousness of this. And he said, "What do you mean?" I realized that he had already become unconsciously competent in reproducing what he had been taught. And I thought, oh my God, that is amazing. I witnessed cultural repair at its finest, and I felt so hopeful.

So, imagine a community of people—I don't mean living on the same land, but let's just say a density of a hundred people in your town—that embodies the mentoring wisdom that I'm expressing, so that no matter what life stage you're interacting with or what gender or which peer, everybody is pulling you into your highest self through curiosity and passion and love. How phenomenal would that be?

Bill: Phenomenal ... and magical! Thank you, Mark. And it seems we get there with a lot of *Medicine*, the way indigenous people use that word, with a big *M*. Medicine people create magic. And living that way is ecstatic, and the ropes connecting us with everyone and with everything are the ropes of love.

An Extended Program on Intergenerational Mentoring at a Wild Earth Intensive

In a WEI lasting longer than the core ten days, the following hands-on application can be used to explore the principles contained in this interview. During this optional but highly recommended two-day extension, the focus is on developing an experiential sense of conscious intergenerational mentoring, and exploring its role in strengthening one's extended family. It is this extended family, whether blood or not, that can provide the love and support necessary to keep the fire of Earth-honoring culture burning through hard times.

In an atmosphere of gratitude and celebration, the emphasis for the group's time together is what successful, Earth-honoring cultures have as a regular part of everyday life: conscious relationships between those with more life experience and those with less life experience, guided ultimately by the patterns and cycles of nature.

With this purpose in mind, the invitation of two additional groups of people to enter the mix is what distinguishes this from previous WEI activities. The first group is referred to as "elders" and the second is referred to as "mentors," although some of these will be different individuals than those who held the elder and mentor positions during the ten-day Intensive (see Chapter 14).

The elders consist of three to six people of whom at least one — for the purpose of continuity — has been a guest facilitator during the previous ten days. The mentors are people who have shown individual participants some form of significant support during their lives, be it emotional or practical (e.g., the uncle who spent a lot of time with them outdoors, the teacher who opened their eyes to math and science, or the musician who taught them guitar.) The elders are invited by the WEI organizers, and the mentors are invited by the participants. In the latter case, each participant chooses a person (in advance of the ten-day WEI) whom they believe will most likely see the value of participating in the two-day extension and be willing to deepen their commitment to its principles. However, facilitators need to ensure that each participant has a mentor in the case of a no-show. They should also contact all the mentors in advance, asking them to start holding space from afar and sending their "mentees" well wishes.

The method for selecting the elders is the same as finding the WEI guest facilitators: choosing people who have high standing in their communities and are excited about sharing their gifts, whether or not they are elderly in the generic sense of the term. The selection of these elders is a key part of the success of this two-day period because, in addition to the criteria mentioned above, they are chosen for their understanding of intergenerational relationships and for their deep commitment to strengthening and enhancing those relationships.

Exploring this style of mentoring with the intent of putting it into practice means, first of all, recognizing that the art of conscious mentoring has been all but lost in modern society, and that it will take time, patience, and sensitivity to restore it. Elders and facilitators who make this point clear at the beginning of the two-day extension create a more relaxed, lighter atmosphere.

Just as important is the understanding that the participants have been through a powerful and potentially life-altering journey. They may be extremely open and can greatly benefit from an "embrace by the village" as they make their transition from the world of the WEI to the world at large. But in order for this embrace to be absorbed fully by all the participants, the whole group needs to know that openness can sometimes be experienced as rawness or vulnerability. The participants need to be given adequate space to integrate what they have learned.

The first day of this extended program focuses on learning about and practicing conscious mentoring, while the second day focuses on support for the participants. This includes helping them further integrate what they have experienced in the previous eleven days and supporting the birthing of the visions they articulated on Day 9 of the Intensive. It is also an opportunity for everybody present to commit to continuing to walk in this beautiful way.

The caring tone, the attentiveness to both group and individual, and the thoughtful transitions that define the style of facilitation in a ten-day WEI remain the same for this two-day extension. This means plenty of play, music, singing, meal blessings, and silent pauses for present moment awareness.

Sample Outline for a WEI Extended Program on Mentoring

First Day

8:30	Elders and mentors arrival
9:00	Invocation of gratitude
9:15	Introductions and overview
10:15	Panel of elders
12:30	Lunch and solo time
2:00	Small-group activities
4:30	Whole group sharing
6:30	Dinner
8:00	Campfire (music, storytelling, poetry, singing) or similar activities held indoors

Second Day

8:00	Breakfast
9:30	Talking circle, mirroring, commitments, closing
12:30	Lunch

Day 1

Begin the first day with an invocation of gratitude by one or more of the elders. Ask the remaining elders to welcome the group. Then set the context and intention for the next couple of days, perhaps using words similar to these:

> *Our primary reason for being together is to take part in mending the sacred hoop, so that the four races of humans, and the animals and plants, can live together in balance. In order to do that, we need to put our minds and hearts together and remember how to support each other in ways that many of us have forgotten. This kind of conscious support has been around for quite awhile. There is a design to it. Some call it "intergenerational mentoring." We are focusing on this because, during the past ten days, many of us have*

been on an intense journey of living ecstatic culture. As you venture forward, we want to give those of you who have been participants in that journey the best possible help. In helping you, we help ourselves.

After outlining the activities to be conducted over the next two days, ask the mentors to introduce themselves and briefly describe their relationship to the WEI participant who invited them. When they are done, thank them for demonstrating the first tier of support in the mentoring process: showing up! It is also important to convey this message to the participants:

The elders and mentors are here for you. They have known about your journey since it began almost two weeks ago, and they have been holding the light daily for you.

Reminding the participants of this fact is critical because they need to feel as comfortable as possible in a new container with new people. It is all part of providing them with a rare, powerful, and formative experience to help them go forth into their lives.

Then you or someone else with expertise in this area will want to explain a model of human development based on the cycles of nature. A good example is found in the book *Nature and the Human Soul: Cultivating Wholeness and Community in a Fragmented World*, by depth psychologist and wilderness guide Bill Plotkin. In whatever way such a model is presented, the idea is to help people grasp more fully the value of and natural movement toward intergenerational relationships. It is intrinsic to being human to have these relationships, and a conceptual foundation can help people to reclaim them.

Panel of Elders
Next invite the elders to participate in an informal panel discussion on mentoring, to be held in front of the group. As

moderator of the discussion, introduce the subject matter by starting with the basics. Ask the elders to respond to a couple of questions:

You've lived a lot of life and you've been through certain things that we have not. What can you tell us about your own personal experience that would help us in our lives?

Would you say a few words on what mentoring means to you?

What have a few of the different life stages been like for you?

Also, make sure everyone can see the following questions, written on a large piece of paper or something similar: "What is mentoring? What does mentoring look like? What kind did you get? How did you experience it?" These are meant for everybody to consider over the course of the two-day extension.

Ask each of the elders to address this topic for ten minutes and let them know they will have the opportunity to say more throughout the rest of the program. Next, invite the audience to ask the elders questions. During this period, which on the surface seems like a simple Q&A session, the kindness and insight that are at the heart of mentoring starts to shine through.

Small-Group Activities
The panel discussion sets the stage for the small-group activities that will follow after the lunch break (which includes a half hour of solo time outdoors for all who wish to take part). The focus shifts into a more engaged, full-body experience of mentoring as the participants and elders gather in small groups, or even one-on-one, based on connections between them or shared areas of

interest/expertise. The look and feel of these small groups will flow organically from the ideas of both the participants and the elders. The specific content of the activities, mini-workshops, or conversations matters less than the quality of the time spent together.

Here are some examples of small-group activities:

- Mini-workshops that allow participants and elders to delve deeply into common areas of interest (e.g., primitive living skills, holotropic breathwork, nature connection, sexuality, yoga or meditation, parenting, alternative dwellings)
- A nature walk with an elder who is a wild-edible plant expert, with a focus on collecting plants to be contributed to the community meal
- Creation of a ceremony or performance to be held in the evening, such as storytelling, an opening ritual for the evening events, a musical piece, or a poem

Ultimately, the kind of activities will depend on the expertise of the elders and the particular interests of the people involved. It is essential that the mentors join in, too, asking questions and learning what brings the most joy to their mentee and how that came about.

After a break, have the entire group gather again. Ask a representative from each small group to summarize the time just spent together, highlighting what they most appreciated about the interaction.

Dinner
Set up a special table for the elders and mentors to meet and discuss what they have observed about each participant and how best to support them.

Campfire

This festive time is an opportunity for people to share songs, stories, humor, and poetry. Before the activities begin, ask for two kinds of volunteers: one or more fire keepers who can take turns throughout the evening tending the fire physically as well as spiritually, and a couple of musicians who will be willing to help get the energy moving. Welcome everyone warmly and then honor the sacred fire with a brief prayer. Acknowledgement of the sacred invites in a roaring flame of unbounded creativity. Then ask each musician to share a couple of songs. If an opening ritual has been created by one of the small groups, now is the time for it. If not, invite the original participants to sing a few of the songs that moved them during the first ten days. After that, magic is afoot!

Day 2

Morning Talking Circle

After breakfast, facilitate a two-part talking circle. In part one, the elders and mentors will act as attentive listeners as each participant relates their key understanding of what has taken place during the whole WEI. In part two, the elders and mentors will supportively reflect back or "mirror" to the participants what they heard them say. The details that are conveyed will, of course, vary for each elder and mentor, but the overall message is one of heartfelt support and encouragement. In fact, an effective way to transition between parts one and two of the talking circle is to say words such as these to the participants:

We thank you for going deep! Your words are inspiring. We hear you and are with you.

When this is complete, invite the participants to publicly voice their commitments clearly and concisely. These commitments may have sprung forth directly from the visioning exercises they did on Day 9 or may have simply been revealed to them over the course of the Intensive. Here are two examples:

"I realized that I am no good to others unless I take better care of my body and soul. Having been so physical and relaxed for the past twelve days, I commit to eating healthy food, getting enough rest, spending at least an hour a day outside, and reading much more poetry. I will work with my mentors to make this commitment a reality. In other words, I will do it!"

"I've been working on a documentary about medicinal plants in the rainforests of New Guinea and the indigenous people who work with them. In order to finish the film, I need to ask the help of a dozen people I have been anxious about approaching. That means I commit to approaching them with the help of my mentors."

Now is the time for two to three elders to briefly wrap up the program, stating their commitment to this whole process, and giving thanks and blessings to Earth, Spirit, and the Ancestors, as they do. End with a song like "Stand by Me" by Ben E. King. This is a graduation for everyone involved! It's time to celebrate with a feast.

Note: The WEI participant age ranges from young adult to older adult. The focus is the development of a certain level of competency with the various cultural ingredients discussed throughout this book. Specifically, as the participants learn about mentoring, they are asked to consider whom they are going to mentor in the future. This lends itself to the potential of evolving the WEI into new, longer forms that include children and teenagers, a process that will help to restore the lost art of intergenerational mentoring. Then the stage will be set for the WEI to extend beyond a powerful alternative educational program into a living embodiment of Earth-honoring culture.

Conclusion

This practice of conscious intergenerational mentoring is about rediscovering how to learn and teach. Since 2005, Miki Dedijer has participated in numerous mentoring programs with Mark Morey and culture-repair visionary Jon Young, cofounders of the 8 Shields Institute, along with Jon's wife, Nicole. Miki sums up the power of mentoring as follows:

My understanding of mentoring, and how it affects a person's belief system and brings out one's dormant gifts, is experiential. It is based both on one-on-one mentoring and on cultural mentoring through the Art of Mentoring program and other workshops and venues. It has been a bit like tumbling willfully into the unknown, driven by desire and curiosity, rather than by effort and strain.

I'm learning to learn in an entirely new, exploratory way, and it feels like coming home. My mentors have become sounding boards, teachers, friends, guides, and a parenting presence that honors my passion and my searching heart. It's fun and wildly exciting, but when it's done well, I've also found it to be terrifying. A good mentor does not judge but focuses only on guiding the individual in their quest to rediscover their birthright: their magnificence, their gifts and power. Being in a learning relationship with no judgment has brought up grief, paranoia, fear, and awkwardness as I rediscover my inner light and true compass rather than seek the approval or affirmation of another. Also, a mentor's task is to constantly guide the mentee beyond their comfort zone, shining a light just beyond the edge, where the mentee catches a glimpse of something truly exciting or wildly bewildering. I've found myself, time and again, having to choose between holding on to my well-known comforts, habits, and routines and the pressing need to explore a larger, ever-more beautiful world that I can perceive faintly in the distance.[2]

Chapter 16

Art and Music

*As humans we are born of the Earth, nourished by the
Earth, healed by the Earth. The natural world tells us:
I will feed you, I will clothe you, I will shelter you, I
will heal you. Only do not so devour me or use me that
you destroy my capacity to mediate the divine and the
human. For I offer you a communion with the divine. I
offer you gifts that you can exchange with each other.
I offer you flowers whereby you may express your
reverence for the divine and your love for each other. In
the vastness of the sea, in the snow-covered mountains,
in the rivers flowing through the valleys, in the serenity
of the landscape, and in the foreboding of the great
storms that sweep over the land, in all these experiences
I offer you inspiration for your music, for your art, your
dance.*

—Thomas Berry

Humans have been making art and music for a very long time.
It could be argued these two signature features of humanity are
the backbone of culture. When they are fully expressed and not
confined by self-importance and commercialism, they are like
shooting stars brightening the night sky. Those brave artists
and musicians who have tapped into the rich, wild, and mythic
realms contained within nature add light and wonder to the
paths of their fellow humans. At times, their creations are so
stunning that they inspire us to make beauty a way of life.

Perhaps to live in beauty is why we were created. Some
cultures embody this concept more than others and place music
and art at the center of their lives. The artists who painted

elaborate, colorful animals seventeen thousand years ago inside the cave at Lascaux, France, did just that, and the Kalahari Bushmen, the oldest living culture on Earth, continue to do so. In a fascinating example of how shamanic and visionary information transcends the boundaries of time and space, the rock art of these two peoples is very similar. Although their cultures are separated by thousands of miles and years, they share an original wisdom that prioritizes beauty. Jointly, they point to the remarkable continuity of an Earth-honoring worldview that has survived despite a concerted attempt to obliterate it.[1]

Bradford Keeney, Ph.D., who has been characterized by the editors of *Utne Reader* as an "anthropologist of the spirit," lived with the Kalahari Bushmen for many years and has authored two books about them. These insightful and sensitively written works put a telescopic lens on our human past as it has survived into the present day. Keeney describes the Bushmen songs as "older than words," and says their art "arguably depicts the original form of healing and spirituality for human beings." He adds that the Bushmen "have not harmed the Earth and have never declared war on other people."[2]

These powerful statements have tremendous implications for anyone seeking a culture built for the long haul. The modern world could benefit greatly from taking to heart the lessons inherent in Bushman culture and the music and art integral to it. The Bushmen, like the few other remaining indigenous tribes living a traditional lifestyle, represent an extremely rare opportunity to see our ancient ancestry in living color.

Primordial Vibration

For our ancient ancestors, exploring art and music must have been akin to discovering a second fire: a spiritual fire that was a new form of expression on Earth. We can never know with certainty, but we can speculate that, with their keen senses and highly developed intuition, they aligned themselves with what was, for them, a previously inaccessible primordial vibration permeating the universe. Pregnant with rhythm and light, this vibration already existed in the land and cosmos. Laden with the essence of music and art, the vibration was given expression by some animals, including birds, whales, dolphins, and elephants, long before the new "radio receivers" — our early human ancestors — arrived on the scene to unleash another explosion of creativity.

In the present day, Danil Mamyev speaks about the importance of this fundamental vibration to his Altai people: "The vibration at the heart of traditional Altai music and art is infinite and eternal. It expresses the sacred knowledge of the subtle world and human nature."[3]

Halfway around the globe, a similar perspective is described by Joseph Rael, of the Ute and Picuris Pueblo peoples. One of the great living Native American visionaries, and author (with Mary Elizabeth Marlow) of *Being and Vibration*, he writes: "The focus of my whole life became to understand all physical forms as sound and vibration of the infinite Self and to be a working listener to those forms."[4] Rael recalls his grandmother's wisdom:

Once we were busy eating soup with special gourds which we used for spoons. She would tell us: "These gourds are made of music, and so all the food you eat comes from beautiful music. You are eating music so your bodies will make beautiful, sacred sounds, sounds that will make your personal songs. The house that we live in is made of sound and life is a house made of sound and the people are made of that sound."[5]

Sophisticated scientific technology is today providing evidence for the origins of that sound.* However, as we have seen, aboriginal peoples have long known about it, experienced it, and designed their cultures around it. Not only have they accessed and utilized this vibration to express beauty through music and art, but they have used it to enhance their relationship with the unseen spirit world.

One of my dearest and most profound teachers was the late Leon Secatero, the headman of the Canoncito Band of Navajos in the 1990s and spiritual mentor to thousands of Native and non-Native people. He was fond of saying, "Without the spirits, we have nothing. They don't have to help us, but they do. We have to communicate with them and make it an ongoing conversation. Showing them beauty with music and art gets them to notice. It's another way of thanking the Creator."[6]

Writer, musician, and artist Martin Prechtel, who was initiated by the Tzutujil Maya in the 1970s, is more specific:

All human beings come from the other world, but we forget it a few months after we're born. This amnesia occurs because we are dazzled by the beauty and physicality of this world. We spend the rest of our lives putting back together our memories of the other world, enough to serve the greater good and to teach the new amnesiacs—the children—how to remember. Often, this lesson is taught during the initiation into adulthood.[7]

He explains:

If this world were a tree, then the other world would be the roots—the part of the plant we can't see, but that puts the sap into the tree's veins. The other world feeds this tangible world—the world that can feel pain, that can eat and drink, that can fail; the world that goes around in cycles; the world where we die. The other world is what makes this world work. And the way we help the other world continue is by feeding it with our beauty.[8]

If remembering to feed the spirit world with beauty is a primary part of cultures that intentionally seek balance with nature, then music and art are two of the main "foods." One of the customary ways that this feeding happens is through ceremony, where there is usually a creative fusion of music and art. Anishinaabe elder Elizabeth Rose Babin says, "Through ceremony, we really create a beautiful foundation for life. When we put together our voices, instruments, costumes, and dance in harmony, we are the best that we can be."[9]

Another American Indian elder I consulted about this chapter shared the following words but said he could not take credit for them because they "were given to me by my elders and are just the way we think about things." These words could certainly be echoed by thousands of other Native people worldwide:

Have you ever wondered why people are moved when they hear an Indian drum? The drum is the heartbeat of Mother Earth. The beat makes our bodies, minds, and spirits join together in harmony. It continues even when you can't hear it anymore. Every Indian work of art and every one of our songs has a purpose and a reason. They help us to remember where we came from. This is beautiful! This way we can connect to Mother Earth and to each other. It's all part of our ceremonies.[10]

Indigenous cultures have also used music and art to effect physical, mental, and spiritual healing. The *icaros* sung by ayahuasca shamans in the Amazon; the sand paintings and chants used in Navajo ceremonials; the playing of the *khomus* (Jew's harp) by shamans of the Altai mountains, and of the *yidaki* (didjeridu) by the Australian Aborigines; and the mandalas of Tibetan Buddhism are a few examples among thousands of how music and art can keep individuals, communities, and the Earth herself in balance.

There is yet another critical reason for the centrality of music and art in indigenous cultures. Mamyev says, "Our [Altai] music and art are one of the most important ways we preserve our history and traditions. We pass them on as carefully as possible through each generation."[11]

The Archaic Revival

Although traditional indigenous peoples have kept alive the flame of music and art that is grounded in the Earth, these gifts are, of course, universal and belong to all of humanity. In the simplest terms, music and art are the languages of the heart. They are the ways we communicate to one another what is difficult or impossible to put into ordinary language. And while the emphasis of this chapter so far has been on the origins of music and art and their inseparability from a nature-based culture, incredible creativity and beauty have been expressed in modern times. In fact, it could be argued that a huge branch of modern music and art is a dynamic response to the lifelessness of industrialism.

As we touched on in Chapter 4, without a huge social and ecological correcting force, industrialism is a recipe for extinction.† Musicians and artists can be a significant part of that correction. They are known for their ability to sense what is obvious but is suppressed and remains hidden within the subconscious mind. Terence McKenna pulled no punches in this observation made during the 1990s:

> History is ending, because the dominator culture has led the human species into a blind alley ... Every time a culture gets into trouble, it casts itself back into the past looking for the last sane moment it ever knew. And the last sane moment we ever knew was on the plains of Africa, 15,000 years ago ... before standing armies, before slavery and property, before warfare and phonetic alphabets and

monotheism ... And this is where the future is taking us. Because the secret faith of the twentieth century is not modernism. The secret faith of the twentieth century is nostalgia for the archaic, nostalgia for the Paleolithic, and that gives us body piercing, abstract expressionism, surrealism, jazz, rock and roll ...[12]

Feeling the pulse of the times, visionary artists and musicians transcend the rigid structures of the dominant cultures and see things in new ways. The works of Van Gogh and Picasso, the Beatles and the Rolling Stones, and countless other outstanding musicians and artists past and present express a survival instinct that persists in the collective psyche. They exhort us to get back into our hearts and bodies and feel the life force flowing through us—now!

Just as our ancestors tapped into the primordial vibration and created the first human music and art, we can do so today. No matter our level of artistic and musical expression, we all have the innate ability to perceive and respond to the rhythms and patterns in the natural world. By giving them form through art and music, we can realize profound gifts: joy, healing, and connection to self and nature.

Art and Music in a Wild Earth Intensive

Aligning ourselves with the primordial vibration that constantly emanates from the natural world, and then making music and art, is another of the prime ingredients of a Wild Earth Intensive (WEI). This is what Mark Morey, a guest facilitator at three Intensives, has been exploring for years. He says:

One of the keys to healthy culture is the creation of music, art, and story that reflect our values, dreams, and visions. Sometimes, I have looked to other cultures to get a clue about what is authentic. In particular, I've looked for songs written from the land, songs with power. Until recently, this was a pattern ... borrowing songs from other cultures to express the intangible connection to nature that we value so much. Recently in Vermont, at the Art of Mentoring program [similar to a WEI], we put out the high vision that we will become visionaries and artists again. We will write our own songs, from our direct experience with nature, held by our authentic community. I want to see the artists, musicians, and visionaries celebrated and in the center of culture again.[13]

Therefore, the intent of having plenty of music and art at a WEI is to:

- express joy and aliveness
- assist the healing process
- increase sensitivity to energy and vibration
- honor the Earth
- unify the group

One WEI participant put it this way: "Music and art are such great nonverbal communicators. The music and singing really soothed me when I was experiencing some difficult emotions. They were more comforting than any words could be."[14] Soothing music and art can also lead to freer self-expression. Part of the healing that can take place during a WEI is that the participants start to see a way beyond self-condemnation. Some of them — perhaps most — will claim not to be very good at playing music, singing, dancing, or making art. As a facilitator, you need not excel in any of these fields. In fact, participants may even feel more comfortable to explore their creativity if you aren't superb.

What you do need to do is create a nonjudgmental space. You may wish to tell the group directly that no expression will be judged as "bad." An African proverb nicely gets this point across: "If you can walk, you can dance. If you can talk, you can sing."[15]

There is an endless variety of music and art that can be inserted at different times into a WEI. The specific forms chosen will depend a lot on the skills and preferences of the facilitators and the spontaneous offerings of the participants. Some examples follow, divided into the broad categories of music and art, within which we include dancing and poetry. It is deeply satisfying to see how all these forms of expression can weave together, fill us with ecstasy, and chip away at our conditioned sense of self.

Note: All of the suggested exercises are an invitation to express our primal nature, not restrict us from exploring more complex and/or contemporary forms.

Art in a Wild Earth Intensive

To stimulate artistic expression, have present within the interior space some examples of primal art and illustrations of the fundamental patterning in nature. At a minimum, have a few books available that focus on types of art such as Huichol yarn painting, fractal design, Algonquin beadwork, petroglyphs and pictographs worldwide, Mayan weaving, Celtic art, Navajo sand painting, and Australian aboriginal art. If possible, have some actual examples on hand.

A key opportunity for inspiring the participants to create their own art presents itself when they come back from shamanic journeys (see Chapter 11). One WEI participant said of such an art-making period:

I remember vividly the process of drawing our shamanic journeys right after experiencing them. It was an important part of the process, because right after the journey, you are looking for a way to integrate it, remember it, express it, share it ... and my body was excited to draw out my journey, because it was like telling a story, a very powerful, expressive story without having to use words.[16]

Once the artistic doors have been opened in the psyche through shamanic journeys and many of the other activities of the Intensive, making "primitive" art becomes accessible and extremely satisfying. There are numerous possibilities such as:

- Fabricating totem figures out of natural materials
- Making masks inspired by beings who may have appeared either in physical reality or in the shamanic realm
- Creating a collective sand painting on black cloth. (Participants can make a beautiful mosaic, just by pouring colored sands or small seeds into basic shapes like spirals, stars, and waves.)
- Fashioning art on the land, using whatever materials are available. (The art of Andrew Goldsworthy is a prime example.)

The exercises below provide further opportunities for this type of expression. During Intensives that last more than ten days, these primal "seeds" can germinate into more complex arts and crafts, such as pottery, sculpture, and oil painting.

Body Painting

Duration: 2 hours

For thousands of years, body painting among indigenous cultures has infused artistic expression with spiritual meaning. The use of earth pigments to color the body is a method of expressing the intricate relationship between human beings and their surroundings. It's also another way to transcend our customary social identities and explore our deeper ecological selves.

Body painting can range from the basic to the complex. It can be as simple as smearing clay, charcoal, or natural ochres found locally onto the skin in a rudimentary way, or it can be as elaborate as painting detailed geometric motifs on the torso, face, and limbs, using vivid, perhaps commercially purchased colors. For this exercise, try out the simpler method and, if it's popular, explore complex designs further in a longer Intensive.

Begin by locating the earth and plant pigments native to your area (if you don't know how to do this, ask a local herbalist). Divide the group into pairs and ask the partners to take a few minutes to explain to each other what kind of "look" they want. Then, each of the partners will take a turn painting the other. Have a mirror handy for making adjustments.

Once everybody is painted, ask the group if there is a dance or a song that wants to emerge. Being painted can remove inhibitions and provide newfound access to the primordial vibration. This may also set the stage for a ceremony.

Making a Rattle
Duration: 1½ hours

Along with the drum, the rattle is the other primary instrument found in most indigenous cultures throughout the world. It is used for both musical and healing purposes. Rattles tend to be on the high end of the dynamic scale, and their consistent beat — like that of the drum and bass guitar in contemporary music — is often the foundation for musical accompaniment. In rituals, the regular and unchanging sound of the rattle (and drum) can help people to enter into an altered state of consciousness.

Making a rattle is a very tactile, enjoyable activity that combines both artistic and musical elements. A basic rattle consists of three parts: the head, the handle, and the small sound-making pieces.

In advance of this exercise, collect dried gourds (for the heads) and separate groups of seeds, beans, and small pebbles (for the various sound-making pieces). The gourds can be grown in a home garden and dried or bought from a local farmer or online from any of a variety of vendors. You can either collect downed branches for use as handles or, after the group has gathered, instruct participants to go out into the forest and find their own. You will also need to have sufficient tools and materials for the group to use, including small handsaws, drills and bits, knives, glue, masking tape, paint, sawdust, and small pieces of leather or cloth.

When all the materials are at hand and the participants are gathered, take the time to first enter the stillness of the moment and then offer a dedication to this sacred activity. You might say something like:

> *May the rattle that is being born be filled with inspiration, may it be filled with light. May this sacred instrument be used to awaken the dance of life and manifest only good in this world.*

When the dedication is complete, light a candle and/or put on some soothing background music. Ask the participants to reflect on the purpose the rattle will serve in their lives. Then invite each of them to select a gourd that attracts them.

While looking over their gourd, they need to consider the size of hole they will need to make to accommodate their handle. They will be cutting the stem off the gourd with a small handsaw. Let them know it will be easier for them to trim more wood off the handle with a knife to make it fit than to enlarge the hole (with a drill and bit) cleanly once the stem has been cut.

Before fitting the handle into the hole, they will need to scrape the old seeds and pithy membrane from the gourd, and then pour in new seeds, beans, or pebbles. They will be experimenting with different amounts of these elements until they get the sound they want (while their hand covers the hole!). Each element has its own unique sound and energy signature.

Have them make the stick just slightly smaller than the hole using a knife. Of course, they need to cut away from themselves. Then they will be ready to put the stick into the gourd. One method is to put a touch of white or yellow glue on the tip of the stick and insert it all the way into the gourd so that it touches the inside of the top.

Once the stick is in place, they should use some masking tape to temporarily hold it there. Then they will mix a small amount of sawdust and glue paste to make a preliminary collar (where the handle joins the gourd). After the paste dries for ten to fifteen minutes, they will need to reapply the masking tape to make sure the handle does not slip.

After they lightly sand the gourd (not holding the handle just yet), they can begin to paint it. Although complex multicolored patterns are possible, for this exercise, keep it simple. When most of the painting is complete, have them peel off the masking tape. For a nice finishing touch, have them sand the glue/paste collar and glue on a leather or fabric collar. This helps maintain the strength and integrity of the rattle.

Note: Once you have made a rattle on your own a few times, it's easy to teach others.

Music in a Wild Earth Intensive

For inspiration and connection to other nature-based cultures, we occasionally listen to their music. Siberian and Mongolian throat singing, African Pygmy and Bushman rhythms, Amazonian *icaros*, Navajo chants, and songs from the Maori of New Zealand have enchanted us. These, of course, are only a few of the many possibilities.

As Morey mentioned, we also make our own songs or sing ones that have been created in a similar setting.‡ As recently as a hundred years ago, people regularly sang together. This rarely happens in modern society, other than during a religious service or a gathering where a lot of liquor is present. In a WEI, we take lots of opportunities to sing, especially during transitions between activities. We sing songs of gratitude, and songs about the beauty of nature, about community, about funny things, and about other topics that inspire and unite us. We recommend that you have at least a dozen songs at your disposal and that you invite the participants to bring forth songs that they know or make new ones up during the Intensive. If you do not know enough songs, you can invite a guest facilitator to teach the group. The power of song is unparalleled in its ability to harmonize and unify a group.

Sometimes, we bring in the sounds of various instruments to enhance the singing. At other times, we play different kinds of drums and rattles without using our voices. Musical expression often works best if it is spontaneous, but setting aside specific times for it is a good idea. The amount of musical expression that arises during a WEI depends largely on the leanings of the group and the preferences of the guides. If there are several talented musicians, you can devote more time to it, while being careful not to slip into a performance mode in which some participants are the players and others the audience.

Dancing is a glorious expression of how our bodies can move to the flow of music. We can dance slow or fast, in a variety of styles—from simple rhythmic steps, keeping time to drumming, rattling, or singing, to creative free-style dancing. Dances with complex steps can be taught to the group by facilitators or elders trained in these. Crow Indian Sun Dance chief and medicine man Thomas Yellowtail said, "Inside every human being is a need to dance. The dance aligns our minds to think spiritual thoughts. Dancing to the drum is healthy."[17]

Bodies, Hands, Voices

Duration: 45 minutes–1 hour

Invite the group to sit in a circle, close to one another. Cultivate a safe space by explaining that most people have experienced shyness and embarrassment around singing and dancing (use yourself as an example, if that is true for you), and that part of reclaiming these basic "birthrights" is to focus on how human sound and movement are born in the primordial vibration and come through the body and heart.

In the first part of this exercise, ask the group to make an agreement to support one another in creating harmonies. Begin with a minute of silence as people attune to one another. Then, without the use of words, make the first sound and keep it going. Have each person add their sound to it, building a "soundscape." As the members of the group listen to one other, they will intuit what sound will add most effectively to the growing chorus of sounds. Some people may sound or tone continuously, while others will add their voices intermittently. In order to strengthen awareness and concentration, ask the participants to try hearing all the other voices while doing the exercise. Eventually, invite them to contribute unifying phrases or statements (e.g., "We are the dance of the moon and the sun" or "We are alive, as the Earth is alive") that can add to the sense of harmony and connection.

In the second part, have the group stand up and incorporate movement into the exercise. Demonstrating your enthusiasm, encourage them to feel how their bodies can enter into a vibrational exchange with the environment. Show how the feet and hands can make great percussion that provides a foundation for the vocalization. After everyone has joined in, let go of the lead position for a while, to see where the group energy goes. Invite participants to experiment with keeping their eyes open and then with closing them. Mix it up so that half the group is silent, and the other part is "sounding." Keep the group going— with bodies, hands, and voices all in motion—until the energy subsides. A surprising amount of beauty can be created with just the basics!

Toning

Duration: 5–10 minutes

This exercise is similar to the beginning of Bodies, Hands, Voices but is more meditative and introspective.

Ask everyone to sit comfortably in a circle with their eyes closed. Guide them to turn their attention inward, focusing on their breath and simply noting whatever feelings are there. After a while, invite them to begin to sing simple sounds based on vowels (such as *Om*), whenever it feels right for each of them. At first, they are to notice the sounds of others and respond to them, as they feel moved, with sounds of their own. As first one person makes sounds and then others join in, a period of group sounding ensues that will ebb and flow, sometimes involving only a few people, sometimes a full chorus. You will usually not need to bring this process to a close, because it inevitably evolves organically into a crescendo that finds a natural ending.

Doing this with eyes closed is important. It does more than shut out distractions; it plunges the toners into an altered space, an acoustic world that is both anonymous and intimate. This activity also increases sensitivity and attentiveness toward others and facilitates working together harmoniously.

Dance Up

Duration: 15 minutes

This high-energy exercise allows people to express themselves through movement, both individually and within a group. It is meant to be lively, fun, and playful. It can be used as a break between more sedentary processes, such as talking circles, and to energize the group as a prelude to deep inner work like shamanic journeying.

This exercise can be done with live or recorded music. With either, a mix of tempos is desirable, perhaps starting slowly, increasing to a crescendo, and then slowing down again. If you plan on using recorded music, create a mix of songs ahead of time and make sure you will have appropriate sound equipment on which to play it.

Make sure you have enough space for participants to move around freely without being in physical contact with others. Ideally, this exercise is done outdoors where people can relate to the natural world. Otherwise, use a large, spacious room with windows, if possible. Begin by having people spread out in the space and close their eyes. Before the music begins, you may want to lead a meditation to have them relax and connect to their bodies. Then start the music and encourage people to feel the rhythms and let their bodies respond in whatever ways feel authentic, perhaps keeping their eyes closed at first to avoid feeling self-conscious.

At some point, you might also encourage people to dance with others, or that might spontaneously happen. By joining in the dance, you and any co-facilitators can also influence the group just by initiating new kinds of movement. As the dancing winds down, participants can lie down and feel the energy moving inside them, and the Earth beneath them.

Trance Dance
Duration: an hour or more
As everyone becomes more at ease with free, spontaneous expression, the stage is set for trance dance, or ecstatic dance. There are many different versions of this ancient way of combining movement and rhythm, from the primal, exemplified by the San Bushmen and many other aboriginal tribes, to the traditional, practiced by the Sufis, and to the contemporary, performed by Gabrielle Roth. Trance dance is a little like the sweat lodge ceremony in that it is an invitation to have a direct encounter with the unseen forces of nature and the world of spirits. Very simple and very profound, it requires an experienced guide to explain it properly. The best description

I know is in Karen Berggren's *Circle of Shaman*. One particular passage stands out:

> There is an important guideline to cultivating ecstasy through dance: you must enter into *who you are in the moment*. Who you really are beneath the persona you show to the outside world. The dance allows you to connect with these places in yourself. The way to is through, not around. You cannot vault over challenges or bad moods to reach ecstasy. It's actually found by going within, embracing them, and moving through. The rhythms and dance of your body will guide you.[18]

Trance dance is included here because I believe this form of dance is an essential part of an ecstatic culture. In a WEI, we sometimes invite guest facilitators to lead this powerful activity. It can be expanded into an entire ceremony and last through the night. If so, you will need to plan accordingly (not included in the sample WEI schedule).

The Wild Within
Duration: 1½ hours, but allow extra time
This exercise is shared with the group toward the end of the ten days, when a large degree of trust and bonding has developed. The emphasis is on spontaneity and going beyond rigid concepts of what constitutes art and music. It can be done inside, but outdoors is preferable.

Your passion and enthusiasm can help catalyze a unique and powerful experience for the group. You might use the following words in explaining the process:

> *Look and listen. We are swimming in a sea of light and sound. Our ancient wildness — still intact — was born here. It's a place that is unfettered and uncensored. It's preverbal and*

extraordinarily creative, and it wants to express itself through you! Once we begin, try not to think about anything, but, instead, feel your way through the next hour or so. Follow your instincts to the best of your ability. This is an invitation to be your wild selves and express whatever artistic and musical impulses move you. It may not look like anything you have ever seen. Feel free to run, dance, crawl, or just lie down and look at the clouds (or the ceiling!). There is nothing to achieve.

Start out in silence, but if you feel called to make sounds or sing, do so. If you feel drawn to a particular person or persons, see what you can create together with whatever part of nature (or the room) is in front of you. Maybe you want to dance together for awhile, or draw spirals in the dirt, or tap on rocks — whatever moves you. Just keep feeling the energy flowing through you, from one moment to the next. On the other hand, you may need to be alone, and that is totally fine. The only rule is to come back here when you hear the bell [or conch, or other instrument whose sound carries] so the rest of the group can enjoy your presence.

Before the participants return, set up a place that can act as a portal. It might be a pair of trees, a pair of boulders, or just two facilitators facing one another with their hands joined above their heads, forming an archway. Then call them back.

As they come through the portal, say something like:

Welcome back! You are now coming back stronger and wilder than before. Can you feel the deeper resonance? How would you like to share this musically and artistically with the group?

Have a nice collection of art supplies and musical instruments available when they return, in case any of the participants want to use them. Also, if possible, have a small fire or candle burning in the center of the space. This symbolizes the overall WEI theme of returning to the Source.

Poetry in a Wild Earth Intensive

As language became more complex, poetry was born. Possessing a lyrical sound that can resonate beyond the limitations of the spoken or written word, poetry may use rhyme, intensity of feeling, rhythm, abbreviated phrasing, and techniques such as the refrain, in what may have originally been an attempt to fit words to musical forms. Poetry is yet another astonishing expression of the primordial vibration manifesting itself through the human "instrument."

Ask the participants in advance to bring a favorite nature-oriented poem to the Intensive. At meal time, let the group know that anyone who wishes to may read or recite a poem as part of the blessing. After that, poetry just seems to "happen" as another expression of living in beauty. One book that is handy to have is *Earth Prayers*, edited by Elizabeth Roberts and Elias Amidon. *Earth Prayers* is a treasure trove of poems singing praises to the divine in nature. Here are two lesser-known favorites:

Do not stifle me with the strange scent
Of low growing mountain lilies—
Do not confuse me
With salubrious odor of honeysuckle!

I cannot separate in my mind
Sweetness from sweetness—
Mimosa from wild white violets;
Magnolia from Cape Jasmine!

I am from the north tide country,
I can understand only the scent of seaweed;
Salt marsh and scrub pine

Riding on the breath of an amorous fog!

O do not confuse me
With sweetness upon sweetness;
Let me escape safely from this gentle madness—
Let me go back to the salt of sanity
In the scent of the sea...![19]
—Donald Jeffrey Hayes

Soil for legs
Axe for hands
Flower for eyes
Bird for ears
Mushroom for nose
Smile for mouth
Songs for lungs
Sweat for skin
Wind for mind
Just enough[20]
—Nanao Sakaki

---

* A group of cosmologists, including researchers from l'Observatoire de Paris, have developed a model to learn about the vibrations of the early universe. The cosmologists hope to "hear the shape of space," as they put it, by analyzing in detail the temperature fluctuations in the cosmic microwave background radiation (CMBR).[21] Paul Preuss of NASA, goes so far as to say, "The universe may be flat but it is nevertheless musical."[22] Phrases like "vibrations of the cosmic drumhead" and "when the universe sang," are used by Preuss and other scientists to describe this fundamental process.

† Europe and North America may no longer be covered with smokestacks, but they have outsourced much of the dirty business of making stuff to China and other "developing" nations.

‡ To learn many of the songs we sing at a Wild Earth Intensive, see: http://www.billpfeiffer.org/book/songs/

Chapter 17

Vision and Manifestation

In a gentle way you can shake the world.
— Ghandi

When a person really desires something, all the universe
conspires to help that person realize his dream.
— Paulo Coehlo (The Alchemist)

When you picked up this book, likely you were attracted
to the vision of a human culture in an ecstatic relationship
with the Earth. Perhaps you imagined hundreds of
thousands of diverse bioregional communities, filled with
contented people, living self-sufficiently with the land and
communicating and trading with one another for the benefit
of all. This is not just another good idea. In the words of
Thomas Berry, it is the overarching "dream of the Earth,"
the big dream born out of the higher intelligence of planet
Earth, whom the ancient Greeks called Gaia. Gaia invites us
humans at every moment to join in the Dance of Life, instead
of ravaging her.

But this is no easy task. The very nature of the modern era,
with its directives of "just do your job" and "live to consume,"
suppresses our natural creativity. As the consumer culture
spreads to every corner of the globe, we are all susceptible to
its seductive message: happiness is found in acquiring things
and achieving a certain kind of commercially oriented success.
The visions this culture peddles are always about "me" and not
"us." They tempt us, as individuals, to avoid finding personal
fulfillment through pursuing dreams aligned with the greater

good. But, as the great Persian poet Rumi said, "You were born with wings. Why prefer to crawl through life?"[1]

Many of us know all too well that it will take a great deal of work to transform the dominant culture into one that supports that truth. Yet we can choose to join in the dance, to act as if a sustainable culture has already arrived. Sometimes, this means responding to a compelling vision that wells up, geyser like, inside us.

That happened to the great naturalist and preservationist John Muir at the age of twenty-nine. After being confined for six weeks in a darkened room due to almost losing his eyesight in a sawmill accident, he emerged and "saw the world—and his purpose—in a new light."[2] From that point on, he was determined to be true to himself and follow his dream of exploring wilderness and studying plants. Several years later, he surrendered to Gaia's prompting and spearheaded the drive to save Yosemite Valley in California. This became one of the greatest conservation triumphs of the modern era and led the way to saving millions more acres of wild land.

John Muir had his dream. Each of us has ours. Dreams of a better world are like rivers flowing into the ocean of Gaia's dream. Each of us has a unique and valuable contribution to make, no matter how humble. But what is usually missing is the means for doing so, and the support of our community. Sometimes, it can even be difficult to articulate what our contribution is or to believe that what we really want matters.

Fortunately, there is a large body of knowledge, both experiential and conceptual, to assist us in realizing our dreams. The "laws of manifestation" have long been understood by indigenous peoples and the Western mystery tradition.* Emphasizing introspection and spiritual development, these cultures have described the mechanics of an innate part of the human experience, one that usually occurs as an unconscious process. In short, envisioning something in one's mind has the power to create a tangible outcome in the physical realm. For much of history, this knowledge has generally been transmitted orally.

In the past one hundred years, these laws have been extensively written about in the West, and they are now taught in workshops and seminars throughout the modern world. However, the application of these laws has had mixed success, and the whole subject has been controversial. Why? I believe this is largely because people are trying to control the process from the vantage point of the separate self. But before clarifying this concept, let's further explore the process of how vision leads to manifestation.

When Einstein said, "Imagination is more important than knowledge,"[3] he was pointing to this extraordinary ability. Before we create anything, we see an image in our minds. Before there was a canoe, there was an idea of a canoe. Whether it be a house or a telephone, a book or an organization, each started as an idea that preceded form.

In the 1980s, Shakti Gawain, one of the early popularizers of "creative visualization," clearly defined this process and explained how to make it conscious. She wrote:

The idea is like a blueprint; it creates an image of the form, which then magnetizes and guides the physical energy to flow into that form, and eventually manifests it on the physical plane.

The same principle holds true even if we do not take direct physical action to manifest our ideas. Simply having an idea or thought, *holding it in your mind*, is an energy that will tend to attract and create that form on the material plane.[4]

The late Wallace Black Elk, a revered Lakota elder, was unequivocal about how manifestation works, and how it does not:

> In the Spiritual World there is a spiritual Law. The Law says: like attracts like. This means whatever mental picture we hold inside our minds we will attract from the Universe. To make this Law work we must *maintain a constant picture*. If we picture or vision something, and along with this picture we have doubting thoughts, our vision will not happen ... The Law always works. A doubting vision will not materialize what we want. A vision without doubt will always happen.[5]

To not doubt our vision requires determination and trust. In the process, a potent force is generated. One could say that thought and imagination, coupled with intention, is the engine of creation. In service to the separate self, the engine can wreak havoc, leading to global deforestation, nuclear proliferation, and other nightmares. In service to a higher truth, it can create miracles.

Lynne McTaggart, throughout her brilliant book *The Field: The Quest for the Secret Force of the Universe*, documents a series of scientifically rigorous studies that demonstrate how this "engine" shapes reality. She writes: "The consciousness of human beings has incredible powers, to heal ourselves, to heal the world in a sense, to make it as we wish it to be."[6]

Many other contemporary authors researching the relationship between mind and matter have come to the same conclusion: deep down at the quantum level, thought is the cause, and our experience in the world is the effect. If this is the case, then naturally we want to pay attention to what we are thinking. This is why Carl Jung, the great Swiss psychologist, said: "When an inner situation is not made conscious, it appears outside as fate."[7]

Manifesting Our Visions

By applying the following guidelines and making the creative process conscious, we can manifest our visions:

- Surrender to a higher truth.
- Fuel the vision with inspiration and enthusiasm.
- Focus on the vision (not on its opposite).
- Realign with a feeling of well-being.
- Let go of attachment to outcome (live in the Now).
- Believe that the vision is possible.
- Act collaboratively and with ease.

Let's look at each of these. Practicing them in the context of a Wild Earth Intensive (WEI) is described later in the chapter.

Guideline #1: Surrender to a higher truth.
In Eckhart Tolle's words, surrender is "the simple but profound wisdom of yielding to, rather than opposing, the flow of life."[8] In no way does surrender mean submission. It means not believing in the machinations of one's fearful egoic mind and, instead, connecting with the Great Mystery. Surrender takes determination and some grace because we are accustomed to believing that the isolated self (ego) is in charge (and, indeed, egos are currently running the planet). But the ego is a phantom residing in the human psyche, seeming so real and all important. It must be seen for what it is so we may birth our visions unobstructed by its restricted worldview—a worldview that got us into this unsustainable mess in the first place. As Einstein said, "You can never solve a problem on the level on which it was created."[9]

Some people practice the "Law of Attraction"—the concept that like attracts like—with a focus on getting material things: money, cars, a nice house, a better job. While that application may be satisfying, it is not what will transform our species. That's where the phrase *higher truth* comes in. In our visioning process, we surrender to the wisdom of a higher source: the loving intelligence flowing through the universe.

This intelligence is ever present in the natural world and is freely available to us if we give ourselves the chance to access it. The more we access it, the more it reflects our own beauty back to us—and the more we sense that we are "enough" without driving ourselves to overwork, overproduce, and overconsume. This sense of sufficiency is the natural byproduct of surrendering to a higher truth and the platform for manifesting anything of value. The biblical phrase "Seek ye first the Kingdom of Heaven ... and all these things shall be added unto you"[10] has been pointing to this truth for two-thousand years. As nature lovers and protectors, let us reclaim it and bring it down to Earth.

Guideline #2: Fuel the vision with inspiration and enthusiasm.
The roots of the words *inspiration* and *enthusiasm* mean to be full of the Divine. To be full of the Divine is to be full of love, and love is the most powerful of motivators. When we are feeling inspired and enthusiastic about implementing a vision, we are nearly indomitable. The pure enjoyment of what we are doing, born from our inspiration, is extremely magnetic. When we are able to enthusiastically share our talents and gifts, the universe has a way of lining up events and circumstances to support us. This assertion is wonderfully supported by the chapter "When You Have the Right Vibe, It's Not a Coincidence," in Amy Lansky's book *Active Consciousness: Awakening the Power Within*:

Things with the same vibration naturally resonate and reinforce one another—just as two violin strings at the same pitch resonate with one another ... Similarity in vibration has also been used to explain the phenomenon of *synchronicity*—"coincidences" of seemingly unrelated events that share a common meaning.[11]

Guideline #3: Focus on the vision (not on its opposite).
What we focus on becomes amplified, so we want to be careful not to spend a lot of energy reacting against a negative situation that may have inspired the vision in the first place. For example, we may have a vision of healthy coral reefs, but if we start to focus predominantly on all the ways they are being destroyed, we are likely to give up.

In the twenty-first century, there have already been innumerable losses to the biological fabric of the planet, as well as many threats to social integrity. There is always something else that demands our attention, and it is very easy to lose track of where we are going. If we are not resolute that we will fulfill our vision and leave others to fulfill theirs, we endanger our ability to be effective.

Thomas Merton, a twentieth-century writer and Trappist monk, articulates this powerfully:

To allow oneself to be carried away by a multitude of conflicting concerns, to surrender to too many demands, to commit oneself to too many projects, to want to help everyone in everything, is to succumb to violence. More than that, it is cooperation in violence. The frenzy of the activist neutralizes his work for peace. It destroys his own inner capacity for peace. It destroys the fruitfulness of his own work, because it kills the root of inner wisdom which makes work fruitful.[12]

The frenzy of activism that Merton warns us about is rooted in fear. We are understandably afraid of ecological collapse and societal breakdown, but if we stay stuck in reactive fear, we will get more of the same. We become part of the problem and not part of the solution, because we are feeding the negative scenario with our focus and energy.

That is why it's so important to pay attention to the essence of our vision, and to regularly imagine what we *want*, not simply bemoan what we *don't want*. Focusing on "a community of people making choices for a healthy environment" is in alignment with the creative impulse of the universe. Furthermore, spending time focused on a wondrous vision as though it were here already is an extremely enjoyable process. Focusing on "the elimination of a society that trashes the environment" directs the energy back toward the existing problem: a society ignorant of ecosystem health. This does not mean that we should stuff our feelings, however. On the contrary, if we don't unblock our grief, fear, and rage, we will not be able to genuinely imagine what we want to create.

Guideline #4: Align with the feeling of well-being.
Everything, including our thoughts, is vibrating at different energy frequencies. Loving thoughts have a higher vibrational frequency than fearful thoughts.[13] When we become lost in fear, we don't *feel* the miraculous nature of the universe, and we emanate a lower frequency. That, in turn, lessens our ability to attract the resources and circumstances we need to fulfill our vision.

Consciously taking time to experience gratitude is a wonderful way to "raise our vibration." Giving thanks for the infinite blessings of being alive—for breathing, for our senses, for plants, stars, animals, water, and friendship—brings us back to a deeper, fuller perspective. The "bad things" that might be happening in our lives, things that may be fueling our fears, are tiny in comparison with the balance and beauty that is all around us — and just by being alive, we are part of that beauty. How can we be sure those "bad things" are not blessings in disguise? Consider the Taoist parable of the peasant whose son falls off a horse and breaks his leg, but when the war comes, the son doesn't have to fight.[14]

To be clear, realigning with a vibration of well-being does not imply denying the plethora of social and ecological maladies. Rather, it is an invitation to use the penetrating power of *awareness* and *focused thought* in the visioning process, in order to create the highest, most glorious vision we can imagine. In fact, every moment of each day is a chance to affirm that a fundamental well-being permeates the universe. Doing so helps us lighten up and have fun on this earthly journey!

Guideline #5: Let go of attachment to outcome (live in the Now).
As the Buddha affirmed, nonattachment is the cornerstone for a peaceful life. If we anxiously expect our vision to materialize, we imbue our visioning process with struggle and stress. If we passionately desire to realize our vision, yet we let anxiety and agitation run us, we are sending out mixed messages to the universe. With one step, we go forward; with the next, backward. The net gain is zero.

How can we, in a culture that values striving for swift achievement, relax into nonattachment? Cultivating peace, presence, and gratitude is key. These make up the foundation for a strong feeling of abundance, which dispels attachment. When these qualities fill us up — when "our cup runneth over"[15] — we don't get lost in thoughts of scarcity that make us chase a future that never quite arrives. Believing that "I already have plenty" actually allows more of the good to come into our lives.

The challenge is that we can't force this state of contentment. It is a process based on learning from our experiences. We need to be gentle, friendly, and patient with ourselves as we learn. Difficult mind states will arise, but when we are kindly toward them, as if we were tending to a small child, they will recede naturally on their own. The peace and love that were there all along will become our dominant vibration, and our actions to fulfill our vision can bear fruit.

Guideline #6: Believe that the vision is possible.
No matter how well we heed the preceding guidelines, if we do not believe in our hearts that we can manifest our vision, we will sabotage ourselves. To believe in our hearts is to believe with our whole being. This does not mean we do not experience doubt, but the doubt is subordinate to our resolute decision to fulfill our unique role in planetary evolution, no matter how humble.

One of our deepest needs is to know we can make a difference in this world. Bouts of hopelessness and powerlessness can make it difficult to know this truth. Beliefs such as "I can't"; "I'm not worthy"; "I'll be hurt if I do..." can serve as insurmountable obstacles if not observed and changed. These are learned beliefs. They are thoughts we repeat to ourselves, usually because somebody taught them to us when were young and easily impressionable or because we decided they were the only way to make sense of an impossible situation. But these patterns of thought *can* be changed. (See Chapter 9 for more on this.)

Guideline #7: Act collaboratively and with ease.
Action is an essential component of realizing our vision, but only to the degree that we can align the means with the ends. All too often, our actions are fraught with anxiety and struggle. As A.J. Muste, one of the most courageous nonviolent revolutionaries of the twentieth century, said, "There is no way to peace; peace is the way."[16]

As we let go of our attachment to the outcome, I believe, we become more peaceful and feel the dynamic aliveness inherent in the action. In writing this book, I found that when I finally let go of when it would be done and how it would be received, I was far more productive. And at the same time, the momentum of keeping with it—writing at least a little on most days—increased my confidence that this gargantuan task could actually be completed.

And we don't manifest our vision by ourselves. We may be the initiator, but we are co-creating it with other people, guided by Spirit! (This was certainly true with the creation of this book). The perfect antidote to the isolationism and "rugged individualism" so pernicious in modern culture is the feeling of interconnectedness. People who feel connected to others and to nature do not overconsume and outcompete. Instead, they look for ways to cooperate with others, to contribute to the greater good while affirming their own value.

This is collaboration at its best, and it is in stark contrast to an egocentric, controlling approach. Surrounding ourselves with supportive relationships is vital to powerful visioning. Those people who can understand and really listen to our vision help us to relax and *allow* it to manifest. These true friends, who may include unseen spiritual allies, deserve our utmost respect and enduring gratitude. Valuing and thanking them for their assistance is one of the most important factors in realizing our vision.

To sum up: manifesting visions and dreams is a skill like any other, and it takes practice. Understanding the causal level of thought and vibration makes the process more conscious. When we are motivated to sow seeds of balance and happiness, we are leveraged to succeed. Our unique vision, rooted in a deep caring for life, is activating a powerful vibration. It has magnetic power. If we really pay attention to all seven guidelines, it cannot fail.

Visioning in a Wild Earth Intensive

In a WEI, the participants are supported in clarifying, shaping, energizing, and fulfilling their visions. Exercises for doing so are scheduled toward the end of the Intensive, because it is only after we are anchored in our true nature of simply *being* with the Earth and each other that we can look ahead with greater strength and clarity. When we feel good, just being alive and in touch with our unfettered "wildness," *doing*—acting upon our dreams and visions—is spurred by joy. As I understand it, this is the reason various forms of a vision quest have stood out so prominently in indigenous cultures: you don't figure out your vision by yourself; you open up and *allow* Earth and Spirit to show it to you. Without a vision that is rooted in our interdependence with nature, which includes other humans, what we *do* in the world is little more than filling the void of chronic discontent.

Unlike a formal vision quest, a WEI does not emphasize vision seeking from the outset of the workshop. The freedom of *not* thinking ahead seems to relieve some internal pressure valve, and most people are able to receive some insight into their role in creating a life-centered culture.

WEI facilitators support all the participants, allowing time for them to articulate and shape their visions, whatever their level of clarity and whatever the content. There is no expectation that everybody's vision be dramatic, activist, single minded, or "big." Visioning is not competitive! Individuals have different perspectives, different needs and talents, and therefore different visions. We trust that when each person aligns with their greater intelligence, they will know what the right individual path is and act in such a way as to benefit the greater whole. The facilitator can explain this way of thinking, and model respect and encouragement for every person's vision.

The following two exercises, done consecutively on the same morning, are useful both for people who may have only an inkling of their vision and for those who are already pursuing it wholeheartedly. These exercises invigorate and strengthen confidence (especially when done in the order listed). Each accentuates and stimulates one of the two primary ways of human knowing: logical/analytical (Goals and Resources) and intuitive/holistic (Joyful Creation), and they help participants recognize the many resources available to them that are often concealed.

Goals and Resources

(Adapted from the book *Coming Back to Life*, by Joanna Macy, with permission)

Duration: 1–1½ hours

Invite people to work in pairs, taking turns to respond aloud to a series of questions that you will ask. As one person answers, the other serves as a "scribe," recording the speaker's answers on paper. Encourage the speaker to relax—maybe even recline—to give freer rein to the mind. Allow about five minutes to answer each question from the list below, and when a minute remains, gently ask people to wrap up their comments. At the end of the questions, the speaker asks if the scribe would like their hand massaged for a timed minute or two, in thanks for their service, and then they reverse roles.

In a WEI, we frequently pose these questions, in this order (spoken words in italics):

1. *What would you be doing for the healing of our world if you knew you could not fail? Here is our chance to pull out the stops and think big, with no "ifs" or "buts" getting in the way.* (An alternative first question is: *If you were liberated from all fear and open to all the power available to you in the web of life, what would you do for the healing of our world?*)

2. *In pursuing this vision, what particular project do you want to undertake? It can be a new direction in work you're already doing, or something entirely new. Here's your chance to get specific. Think in terms of what could be accomplished, or at least well underway, in a year's time.*

3. *What resources, inner and outer, do you now have that will help you do that? Inner resources include specific strengths of character, relevant experience, knowledge, and skills you've acquired. External resources include relationships, contacts, and networks you can draw upon — not to forget seemingly unlikely sources such as babysitters, rich uncles, computer-savvy friends — as well as your location, employment, goods, and money in the bank.*

4. *What resources, inner and outer, will you need to acquire in order to do what you want to do? What will you need to learn and to obtain? These can run from assertiveness training to grants, and to finding contacts within organizations such as churches, local businesses, and so on, for the support they can give you.*

5. *How might you stop yourself from accomplishing your goals? We all have familiar patterns of self-doubt and sabotage. What obstacles do you foresee that you might throw in the way of fulfilling your goals?*

6. *How will you overcome these obstacles? Draw upon your past experience in dealing with them, and also imagine new ways of moving around them, including getting help from others with expertise in getting past similar roadblocks.*

7. *What can you do in the next twenty-four hours, no matter how small the step, that will move you toward this goal? What can you do in the next week? In the next six months?*

When both partners have scribed the other's responses (and possibly exchanged hand massages), each takes a turn reporting to the other the notes they took as scribe. Instruct each scribe to use the second-person pronoun: "You want to realize ... You already have resources of ... You might stop yourself by ..." and so forth. During this time, the listener hears, perhaps for the first time, their orders from the universe! The notes themselves are then exchanged, so that each person has a record of these powerful, sacred instructions.

For a shorter variation, skip the scribing and have people work alone, writing their own responses to each question, and then share their answers with another person, taking five to ten minutes for each partner.

Joyful Creation
Duration: 2 hours
Usually, a lot of excitement comes bubbling to the surface after Goals and Resources. It is important for you to help focus that excitement in order to fully energize everyone's vision. The following steps are designed to do just that. The purpose of this fun and relaxing exercise is to enable each person to envision themselves succeeding in their vision. A shamanic journey is used midway to invoke larger intelligence for support. Have art supplies handy (oil pastels and paper are ideal) for the final phase of this exercise.

1. Briefly outline the following steps and mention the key principles of visioning explained in this chapter, reminding people that there is incredible power in our thoughts and imagination. Encourage them not to let past disappointment or disbelief dissuade them from expressing their unique gifts and manifesting their vision. Emphasize the lighter touch of this exercise in comparison to the preceding one. Assure the participants that there is no need to "figure anything out" during this process—just allowing oneself to be present with the feeling and tempo of the exercise is enough.

2. Ask the participants to lie down and get comfortable. With soft, gentle music playing in the background (either recorded or live), guide them, using the following words. Note that it's not necessary to follow what is written below to the letter; the main intent is for the participants to feel themselves in inner space, acting out their visions, or some portions thereof, as if they were already happening:

Get comfortable. Relax into the music. Feel your body supported by the floor and the larger Earth. Take some deep breaths, feeling the life-giving force of oxygen entering your lungs and spreading throughout your body. Let your thoughts come and go without following any particular storyline. Feel the breath flow in and out like waves at the beach. Now imagine yourself in an ideal scene from your dream or vision. It could be you simply talking to a friend, expressing yourself with enthusiasm. Or maybe you are performing some action or service. See yourself "plugged in" to the current of life, feeling full of joy, succeeding at whatever you are doing. Keep envisioning this ideal scene. Have fun being the director of your unique and powerful "movie." Replay the movie a few times ...

Now, let your movie go out into the universe. Feel the stars embrace your vision. Relax into knowing that there is a much larger force at work that does the manifesting, and it is your job just to allow it to happen ...

Now, come back into your body. Wiggle your fingers and toes and open your eyes. All is well.

3. Invite people to stand up, stretch, and move for a few minutes in silence, so as not to break up the building energy. Through the shamanic journey that follows (see Chapter 11 for details on leading a journey), they will

call in the power of larger intelligence to propel and energize their visions onto the material plane. The major difference between this shamanic journey and the guided visualization preceding it is that there is no spoken guidance about clarifying one's vision.

Begin by having everyone lie down comfortably and, again, feel supported by the Earth. Let them know that they will be taking the kind of inner journey they should be quite familiar with by now. Beat a frame drum in a slow but steady repetitive rhythm (joined, preferably, by one or two other drummers, later on), while introducing the journey as follows, pausing between sentences.

Now is the time to fully let go and allow the Spirit-That-Moves-Through-All-Things to do the work ... Ask for help from this great mysterious power to contribute your special gifts to the creation of an Earth-honoring culture ... Feel the drum, the heartbeat of Mother Earth, as it massages your soul ... Follow the beat with your whole being ... Reach deeper inside yourself than you ever have, knowing you are far larger and stronger than you may have ever realized. ... You are now ready to go off on your journey!

Next, speed up the drumming rhythm gradually, generating power until you reach a plateau, and maintain the fast rhythm for the next ten minutes. After that time, slow the beat gradually, and finally begin to call the participants back to the present moment, using gentle phrases:

You are on your way back ... Take your time ... Savor what you see and feel.

A minute or so later, call them into full presence:

Now sense your body. Feel the blood moving through your veins as you gradually come fully into this space.

4. Invite participants to draw whatever comes to them, whether or not it specifically involves their vision.
5. Ask each person to write out this sentence on the back of the drawing, completing it however they wish:

I am so happy and grateful now that ...

6. Have everyone take turns sharing their journey experiences and/or drawings, in pairs or small groups.
7. Invite people to share the essence or a nugget of their experiences with the whole group. Depending on what people share, you may want to reinforce and discuss with the group the principles outlined in the first part of this chapter.

---

* *Western mystery tradition* refers to the collected mystical, esoteric knowledge of the Western world. While the Hebrew Kabbalah, Gnosticism, Hermeticism, and the Egyptian and Hellenic mystery schools were not synthesized into one comprehensive system, they are generally considered the foundation for the esoteric traditions that followed (e.g., alchemy and theosophy).

Chapter 18

Final Thoughts

For the Children
The rising hills, the slopes,
of statistics
lie before us.
the steep climb
of everything, going up,
up, as we all
go down.

In the next century
or the one beyond that,
they say,
are valleys, pastures,
we can meet there in peace
if we make it.

To climb these coming crests
one word to you, to
you and your children:

stay together
learn the flowers
go light

—Gary Snyder

There is a certain vista in central Massachusetts where the shape, age, and character of the mountains clearly reveal their essence. As is often the case, it is possible to drive by them without noticing. During those precious moments when I actually *see* what is before me, I am awestruck by how the Earth speaks not only with exuberant brilliance but with such quiet humility. Then I can imagine those forested mountains as ancient sentinels who watched the Algonquin-speaking peoples inhabit the river valleys for a few thousand summers. I believe those mountains smile when they remember the reverence and gratitude showed to them. Later, when the Europeans arrived, both the Indians and the mountains witnessed a strange behavior.

As a reader of this book, you know quite well what that behavior spawned: a dizzying amount of technological change, bringing with it material benefits no human being had hitherto experienced. You also know the cost. Amidst all the goodies of modern life lie ecological devastation and spiritual deprivation. The whole point of the preceding pages is that we can do better!

Richard Heinberg, a prominent American journalist and educator who has written extensively on ecological issues, addressing a class of graduating college students, said: "You will have the opportunity to participate in the redesign of the basic systems that support our society—our energy system, food system, transport system, and financial system."[1]

Redesigning the culture that underpins those systems needs to be added to that list. That, for me, is the most exciting challenge. Do we take the risk, as messy as it may be, to practice a new, Earth-honoring culture for the sheer joy of it—not knowing the outcome? Do we dare form small groups committed to loving one another and the land like never before? Can we allow ourselves to be vulnerable and authentic as we recognize our mutual dependence?

This book and the cultural model it describes are not a recipe for a utopian society. Shakespeare will undoubtedly still be popular in a few hundred years. People will still be mischievous, traverse hardship, and continue to live with uncertainty; but imagine the possibilities if we inhabit a new sense of self, where we are no longer trapped in the illusion of separation!

And it would be shortsighted to suggest that the practices outlined in the preceding chapters, *by themselves*, are sufficient to pass along as guideposts for sustainable living. It is imperative that they are complemented by a "hands in the dirt" understanding of how the Earth's mineral, energy, and water systems work, aimed at ecological restoration and regeneration. In combination, these two approaches can lead us to a natural way of being—a spiritual ecology—in sync with the universe.

Appendix: Wild Earth Intensive
Sample Schedule

The following pages include useful guidelines and a sample schedule to make clearer how various Wild Earth Intensive (WEI) activities fit together. The guidelines cover aspects regarding facilitation and logistics that are not mentioned elsewhere. The overall design of the schedule prioritizes a gradual building of intimacy between the participants, as well as with the land that embraces them.

There are more exercises described in the book than are listed in the schedule. The advantage of this is that a prospective facilitator will be able to make substitutions to create a more vibrant and unique experience, and to allow for variations in group process, weather, site limitations, and a range of unforeseen factors common to experiential group learning. Furthermore, the website associated with this book (http://www.billpfeiffer.org/book/) will be a repository for a multitude of activities that have not been covered in these pages. To support the ongoing work of remembering Earth-honoring culture and applying it to modern circumstances, the website will also serve as a forum for WEI participants to share their experiences and what they have learned from them.

In the schedule, the specific content for days in which guest facilitators mentor the group is left open. However, providing the guest facilitator with a predetermined theme that complements the expertise of the main facilitators will support the overall goals of the WEI. Within that theme, allow the guest facilitators the space to design the day in a way that best suits their gifts and talents. In certain cases, you may want to collaborate more explicitly with them to emphasize certain ongoing topics, e.g., storytelling, listening, and healing.

Many of the outdoor activities can be done in the rain or cold, but if weather compromises safety or makes learning too difficult, substitute any combination of indoor dance, movement, and/or play to keep the energy flowing. At the same time, don't let the elements discourage you from stepping out of your own or the group's comfort zone. Many wonderful surprises, new learning, and laughter have been discovered while playing about in so-called inclement weather, as participants and facilitators shed conventional patterns and assumptions about how important it is to always stay warm, dry, and comfortable.

Consistent mealtimes, occasional breaks from formal activities, and sufficient periods of rest help keep everyone alert. These are part of a reliable container that establishes a sense of safety, which in turn supports wholehearted involvement in the WEI. However, do not be afraid to adjust your plans when the group and the circumstances call for it. "Adjusting plans" can mean changing activities, but, fundamentally, it is about pausing and making sure that the schedule does not deteriorate into "get-it-done" mode. There is no substitute for the joy of being. How much time is recommended for an activity is not fixed. Activities or processes sometimes take longer than planned, although there is value in knowing when to finish up so their effectiveness is not lost—or when not to do them at all.

That's the paradox of guiding this work. At various times during a WEI, it's important to abandon the scaffolding provided by the schedule and step into the unknown. Abundant creativity can be gained by being willing to let go of what has been planned and let your intuition guide you. When you think you have been playing it too safe, that is the time to venture past your internal boundaries and take risks. Experiment with what it feels like to lead "wild and free," while continuing to care sensitively for the energy and needs of the group.

And finally, this can all sound overly serious. It's a great learning adventure. Have fun. Enjoy!

Day 1

9:30	Opening circle: welcome, site logistics, orientation
10:00	Brief introductions, game
10:30	Overview and introductory talk
11:00	Movement, deep breathing
11:15	Longer introductions with focused sharing using stick bundle
12:15	Setting collective intention, dedication
12:30	Lunch (start with poem or song and gratitude prayer)
1:30	Opening ceremony, sacred fire lighting
2:30	"Open Sentences" (with preliminary talk on listening)
2:45	Break and prepare for time outside
3:00	Greeting the landscape, walk
4:30	Solo time on land
5:00	Break
6:00	Dinner
7:30	Fire, storytelling intro, poetry, music

Day 2

7:30	Yoga, qigong, or other similar activity
8:00	Silent breakfast
9:00	Meditation, stretching
9:30	Introduction to feeling and healing
9:45	"Eco-milling"
10:00	"Voices of the Earth"
10:30	"Truth Mandala"
11:30	"Honoring Our Losses"
12:30	Lunch
2:00	Nature connection: geographical overview, "Basic Orientation," "The Embrace of Life," landscape exploration, solo time

4:00   Break
4:30   Shamanic journeying
6:30   Dinner
7:30   "Mythic Landscape Map," storytelling (Jumping Mouse Part 1 or similar)

Day 3

7:30   Yoga, qigong
8:00   Breakfast
9:00   Meditation, stretching
9:30   Guest facilitator: introduction to sweat lodge ceremony
12:30   Lunch
1:30   Lodge preparation
3:30   Making prayer ties, solo time to set intention and prepare for lodge
5:30   Go into lodge
8:00   Light dinner whenever ceremony is complete

Day 4

7:30   Yoga, qigong
8:00   Breakfast
9:00   Meditation, movement awareness,
9:30   Talking circle (integrate time spent so far)
11:00   Dance, nature connection: "Camera Game," "Poet-tree"
12:30   Lunch (Option: after lunch, prepare for twenty-four hours on the land, which will include most of the following activities until lunch on Day 5)
1:30   Water concentration (spend time with/swim in stream, river, pond, lake, ocean)
3:30   Break
4:30   Shamanic journey
5:30   Scientific perspective: Brian Swimme or TED talk video
6:30   Dinner

7:45   Fire, Jumping Mouse Part 2 or similar

Day 5
7:30   Yoga, qigong
8:00   Silent breakfast
9:00   Meditation, play, movement, dance
10:00   Nature connection: "Tracking 101," "Dancing the Landscape"
11:30   Shamanic journeying
12:30   Lunch
2:00   Men's and women's "Medicine Circles"
5:45   Coming-back-together ritual
6:00   Dinner
7:30   Outdoor activities, followed by "Whale Wash" indoors

Day 6
7:30   Yoga, qigong
8:00   Breakfast
9:00   Meditation
9:30   Guest facilitator: integration, conflict resolution
12:30   Lunch
1:30   Guest facilitator led activities, Medicine Wheel teaching, (possibly including "Healing the Stories We Tell Ourselves")
6:00   Dinner
7:30   Body painting, music, fire dance

Day 7
7:30   Yoga, qigong
8:00   Breakfast
9:00   Meditation
9:30   Guest facilitator: expressive arts (possibly including "Imaging Our Gifts" and "Speaking Our Gifts")

12:30   Lunch
1:30   Guest facilitator led activities
6:00   Dinner
7:30   Community celebration (skits, music, poetry, individual performances)

Day 8
7:30   Yoga, qigong
8:00   Breakfast
9:00   Meditation
9:30   Talking circle
11:00   Nature immersion (bring bag lunches). Themes: edge, adventure, confronting and overcoming fears. Include solo time and shamanic journeying.
5:00   Break
6:00   Dinner
7:30   Rattle making

Day 9
7:30   Yoga, qigong
8:00   Breakfast
9:00   Meditation
9:30   Singing, rattle painting/design
11:00   Nature connection or "The Wild Within"
12:30   Lunch
2:00   Shamanic journeying
3:30   Break
4:30   "Goals and Resources"
6:00   Dinner
7:30   "Joyful Creation"

Day 10
8:00   Breakfast
9:00   Meditation

9:30   Sharing circle, solo time, review of mythic landscape map

12:15   Retrospective journey with drum

12:30   Lunch

1:30   Closing ceremony

3:30   Closing prayer and song

6:00   Possible preparation by facilitators for mentoring focus on Day 11 and Day 12

Reference Notes

Introduction

The chapter epigraph is from Rainer Maria Rilke, "Book II" in *Rilke's Book of Hours: Love Poems to God*, trans. Anita Barrows and Joanna Macy (New York: Riverhead Books, 2005), 25.

1. Thomas Berry, *The Dream of the Earth* (San Francisco: Sierra Club Books, 1988), 4.
2. *A Testament of Hope: The Essential Writing and Speeches of Martin Luther King*, ed. James M. Washington (New York: HarperCollins Publishers, 1986), 20. See also M.L. King, Jr., *Stride Toward Freedom: The Montgomery Circle* (New York: Harper & Row, 1958), 56–71.
3. Dana Mrkich, "Writings: Visions for a New Earth," *Evolution Revolution* (blog), 2006, available from: http://www.danamrkich.com/writings/newe/03/wotrainbow.html (accessed 17 March 2012).

Chapter 1: Why a Wild Earth Intensive?

The chapter epigraph is from Joanna Friedlander, personal communication with the author, 18 June 2009.

1. Leon Secatero, personal communication with the author.
2. Ibid.
3. Bradford Keeney, Ph.D., available from: http://www.shakingmedicine.com/shaking-medicine/shaking-medicine.php (Accessed 27 April 2012). See also Keeney, *Shaking Medicine: The Healing Power of Ecstatic Movement* (Rochester, VT: Destiny Books, 2007).
4. Ibid.
5. Derrick Jensen, "Saving the Indigenous Soul: An Interview with Martin Prechtel," *The Sun*, Issue 304, April 2001, available

from: http://thesunmagazine.org/issues/304/saving_the_ indigenous_soul.

6. Mahatma Ghandi, *An Autobiography: The Story of My Experiments with Truth* (Boston: Beacon Press, 1993), xvii.

Chapter 2: How to Use This Book

The chapter epigraph is from Anais Nin, *The Diary of Anais Nin* (Orlando: Harcourt, Inc., 1966), vol. 1.

1. Pierre Teilhard de Chardin, *The Future of Man,* trans. Norman Denny, First Image Books Edition (New York: Random House, 2004).

Chapter 3: A Note to Guides and Facilitators

The chapter epigraph is from Paul Rezendes, *The Wild Within: Adventures in Nature and Animal Teachings* (New York: Berkley Books, 1999).

1. Manitonquat, e-mail communication with the author, April 2010.

Chapter 4: A Spiritual Permaculture

The chapter epigraph is from Lao Tsu, *Tao Te Ching,* Witter Bynner version (New York: Berkley Publishing Group, 1994), vs. 30.

1. Dave Jacke, personal communication with the author.
2. Alice Calaprice, Freeman Dyson, and Albert Einstein, *The New Quotable Einstein* (Princeton, NJ: Princeton University Press, 2005), 206.
3. Alan Watts, *Eastern Wisdom, Modern Life: Collected Talks, 1960–1969* (Novato, CA: New World Library, 1994), 76.
4. Charles Eisenstein, *The Ascent of Humanity: The Age of Separation, The Age of Reunion, and the Convergence of Crises*

That Is Birthing the Transition (Harrisburg, PA: Panenthea Press, 2007), 370.

5. Eckhart Tolle, *A New Earth: Awakening to Your Life's Purpose* (New York: Penguin Group, 2005), 21.

6. Martin Prechtel, from a review of *Stealing Benefacio's Roses: A Mayan Epic* (Berkeley, CA: North Atlantic Books, 2002), available from: http://www.floweringmountain.com/Toe03.html (Accessed September 2009).

7. Ibid.

8. John Seed, Joanna Macy, Pat Fleming, and Arne Naess, *Thinking Like a Mountain: Towards a Council of All Beings* (Gabriola Island, BC, Canada: New Society Publishers, 1988), 36.

9. Carl Sagan, *Cosmos* (New York: The Random House Publishing Group, 1980).

10. David T. Kyle, *Human Robots & Holy Mechanics: Reclaiming Our Souls in a Machine World* (Portland: Swan Raven, 1993), 188.

11. Terence McKenna, *The Archaic Revival: Speculations on Psychedelic Mushrooms, the Amazon, Virtual Reality, UFOs, Evolution, Shamanism, the Rebirth of the Goddess, and the End of History* (San Francisco: HarperSanFrancisco Publishers, 1991), 242.

12. Terence McKenna, "The Final Earthbound Interview," October 1998, available from: http://www.youtube.com/watch?v=NCaK35DQ4uk.

13. Paul Devereux, *Re-Visioning the Earth: A Guide to Opening the Healing Channels Between Mind and Nature* (New York: Simon & Schuster, 1996), 97.

14. The Buddha, *The Dhammapada: Verses on the Way: A New Translation of the Teachings of the Buddha with a Guide to Reading the Text,* trans. Glenn Wallis (New York: Random House, 2004), 3.

15. John Perkins, *Hoodwinked: An Economic Hit Man Reveals Why the World Financial Markets Imploded—and What We Need to Do to Remake Them* (New York: Random House, Inc., 2009).
16. John Perkins, *The World Is As You Dream It: Teachings from the Amazon and Andes* (Rochester, VT: Destiny Books, 1994), xii.
17. Ibid.
18. Thomas Berry, *The Dream of the Earth* (San Francisco: Sierra Club Books, 2006).
19. Daniel Quinn, *Ishmael: An Adventure of the Mind and Spirit* (New York: Bantam Books, 1995).
20. Lori Arviso Alvord, M.D., and Elizabeth Cohen Van Pelt, *The Scalpel and the Silver Bear: The First Navaho Woman Surgeon Combines Western Medicine and Traditional Healing* (New York: Random House, 1999).
21. Lynn Margulis and Dorion Sagan, *Slanted Truths: Essays on Gaia, Symbiosis, and Evolution* (New York: Springer-Verlag, 1999), 34.
22. Malcolm Margolin, *The Ohlone Way: Indian Life in the San Francisco-Monterey Bay Area* (Berkeley, CA: Heyday Books, 1978), 142.
23. Robert Wolff, *Original Wisdom: Stories of an Ancient Way of Knowing* (Rochester, VT: Bear & Company, 2001).
24. Wade Davis, *One River: Explorations and Discoveries in the Amazon Rain Forest* (New York: Touchstone, 1996), 56.
25. Tim Plowman, quoted in Davis, *One River*, 56.
26. Adalberto Villafane, quoted in Davis, *One River*, 56.
27. Altai elder, personal communication with the author.
28. Robinson Jeffers, "The Tower Beyond Tragedy," *The Selected Poetry of Robinson Jeffers* (New York: Random House, 1938).
29. Riane Eisler, *The Chalice and The Blade: Our History, Our Future* (New York: HarperCollins, 1988). See also: http://rianeeisler.com/.

30. Riane Eisler, *Sacred Pleasure: Sex, Myth, and the Politics of the Body—New Paths to Power and Love* (San Francisco: HarperCollins Publications, 1995), as quoted in an online bibliography, available from: www.proutcollege.org/bibliography.htm.

31. Herb Goldberg, Ph.D., *The Hazards of Being Male: Surviving the Myth of Masculine Privilege* (Ojai, CA: Iconoclassics, 2009).

32. Jed Diamond, Ph.D., *The Warrior's Journey Home: Healing Men, Healing the Planet* (Oakland, CA: New Harbinger Publications, 1994).

33. Chogyam Trungpa, *Shambhala: The Sacred Path of the Warrior* (Boston: Shambhala Publications, 1984), 28.

34. Alfred Russell Wallace, *Miracles and Modern Spiritualism* (Charleston, SC: Forgotten Books, 2010), x–xi (Preface to the Third Edition).

35. Joanna Macy and Molly Brown, *Coming Back to Life: Practices to Reconnect Our Lives, Our World* (Gabriola Island, BC, Canada: New Society Publishers, 1998), 21.

36. Duane Elgin, *Promise Ahead: A Vision of Hope and Action for Humanity's Future* (New York: HarperCollins, 2001).

37. Thomas Berry, quoted in Stephen R. Kellert and Timothy J. Farnham, eds., *The Good in Nature and Humanity: Connecting Science, Religion, and Spirituality with the Natural World* (Washington DC: Island Press, 2002), 88.

Chapter 5: Getting Started: Guidelines and Overview

The chapter epigraph is from R. Buckminster Fuller, *Critical Path* (New York: St. Martin's Press, 1981).

1. Joseph Goldstein, e-mail communication with the author.

2. Martin Luther King, Jr., "Nobel Prize Acceptance Speech," available from: http://www.nobelprize.org/nobel_prizes/peace/laureates/1964/king_acceptance.html.

Chapter 6: Listening

The chapter epigraph is from Carl R. Rogers and Richard E. Farson, "Active Listening," in *Communicating in Business Today,* ed. R.G. Newman, M.A. Danzinger, and M. Cohen (Lexington, MA: D.C. Heath & Company, 1987).

1. Danil Mamyev, personal communication with the author.
2. Thich Nhat Hahn, *Interbeing: Fourteen Guidelines for Engaged Buddhism* (Berkeley, CA: Parallax Press, 1987).
3. Christine Longaker, "Listening with Presence, Awareness, and Love," in *The Wisdom of Listening,* ed. Mark Brady (Somerville, MA: Wisdom Publications, 2003).

Chapter 7: Feeling and Healing

The chapter epigraph is from Rainer Maria Rilke, *Rilke's Book of Hours: Love Poems to God, Book II*, trans. Anita Barrows and Joanna Macy (New York: Berkley Publishing, 2005).

1. Steven Soderbergh, *Sex, Lies, and Videotape* (Santa Monica, CA: Miramax Films, 1989).
2. Joanna Macy and Molly Young Brown, *Coming Back to Life: Practices to Reconnect Our Lives, Our World* (Gabriola, BC, Canada: New Society Publishers, 1998), 59.
3. Wild Earth Intensive participant, June 2009, name withheld by mutual agreement.
4. Macy and Brown, *Coming Back to Life*.
5. Ibid.
6. Matt. 5:4 (King James Version).

Chapter 8: Nature Connection and Immersion

The chapter epigraph is from Albert Einstein, quote by Hanna Loewy in A&E Television Einstein Biography, VPI International, 1991, available from: http://www.asl-associates.com/einsteinquotes.htm.

1. Richard Louv, *Last Child in the Woods: Saving Our Children from Nature-Deficit Disorder* (Chapel Hill, NC: Algonquin, 2008).
2. Paul Devereux, *Re-Visioning the Earth: A Guide to Opening the Healing Channels Between Mind and Nature* (New York: Fireside, 1996).
3. Bruce Chatwin, *The Songlines* (New York: Penguin, 1988).
4. Ibid.
5. Devereux, *Re-Visioning the Earth*.
6. Wendell Berry, quoted in Wallace Earle Stegner, *The Sense of Place (Essays)* (New York: Random House, 1992). Available from: http://www.mtbaker.wednet.edu/tlcf/The%20 Sense%20of%20Place.htm.
7. Paul Rezendes, e-mail communication with author, 20 July 2012.
8. Wild Earth Intensive participant, name withheld by mutual agreement.
9. Joseph Bharat Cornell, *Sharing Nature with Children*, 20th *Anniversary Edition* (Nevada City, CA: Dawn Publications, 1998).
10. Eckhart Tolle, *Stillness Speaks* (Novato, CA: New World Library, 2003).

Chapter 9: The Power of Story

The chapter epigraphs are from Muriel Rukeyser, *The Speed of Darkness* (New York: Random House, 1968); and Pauline McLeod, Australian Aborigine, interview with Helen McKay, "Telling Tales: Newsletter of the Storytelling Guild of Australia (NSW)," Feb–Mar, 1998, available from: http://www. australianstorytelling.org.au/txt/mcleod.php.

1. Daniel Quinn, *Ishmael: An Adventure of the Mind and Spirit* (New York: Bantam, 1995).
2. Ibid.

3. Bruce H. Lipton, Ph.D., and Steve Bhaerman, *Spontaneous Evolution: Our Positive Future (and a Way to Get There from Here)* (Carlsbad, CA: Hay House, 2009).

4. Lotte Hughes, *The No-Nonsense Guide to Indigenous Tribes* (Brooklyn, NY: Verso Books, 2003), 20.

5. Joseph Campbell, *The Hero with a Thousand Faces* (Novato, CA: New World Press, 2000).

6. Wild Earth Intensive participant, name withheld by mutual agreement.

7. Bernie S. Siegel, M.D., *Love, Medicine & Miracles: Lessons Learned about Self-Healing from a Surgeon's Experience with Exceptional Patients* (New York: HarperCollins, 1998).

8. Joanna Macy, *World as Lover, World as Self: Courage for Global Justice and Ecological Renewal* (Berkeley, CA: Parallax Press, 1991).

9. Hyemeyohsts Storm, *Seven Arrows* (New York: Ballantine, 1972).

10. Ibid.

11. Susan Bridle, "Comprehensive Compassion: An Interview with Brian Swimme," *What Is Enlightenment?* 19:4, available from: http://www.thegreatstory.org/SwimmeWIE.pdf.

12. Ibid.

13. Robert Lanza and Bob Berman, "The Biocentric Universe Theory: Life Creates Time, Space, and the Cosmos Itself," *Discover Magazine* (Waukesha, WI: Kalmbach Publishing), May 2009, available from: http://discovermagazine.com/2009/may/01-the-biocentric-universe-life-creates-time-space-cosmos/article_view?b_start:int=1&-C.http://www.thegreatstory.org/SwimmeWIE.pdf

14. Wild Earth Intensive participant, name withheld by mutual agreement.

15. This exercise is part of a larger workshop designed and facilitated by Mother Turtle, available from: http://www.healingthestories.com.

16. Ibid.
17. Ibid.
18. Mother Turtle, personal communication with author.
19. Ibid.

Chapter 10: Ceremony

The chapter epigraphs are from Dolores LaChapelle, "Ritual Is Essential," in *In Context: A Quarterly of Humane Sustainable Culture*, no. 5 (Spring 1984): 39; and Leslie Marmon Silko, *Ceremony* (New York: Penguin, 1977).

1. Elizabeth Rose Babin, personal communication with the author.
2. John Neihardt, *Black Elk Speaks: Being the Life Story of a Holy Man of the Oglala Sioux* (Lincoln, NE: University of Nebraska Press, 2000).
3. Ai-Churek Shiizhekovna Oyun (Moonheart), personal communication with the author.
4. John Seed, interviewed by Ram Dass, excerpted from a seven-part series: "Reaching Out," PBS, 1998, available from: http://www.rainforestinfo.org.au/deep-eco/ramdass.htm.
5. LaChapelle, "Ritual Is Essential," in *In Context*, 39.
6. Elizabeth Rose Babin, personal communication with the author.
7. Felipe Ortega, as told to Benjamin Jojola and overheard by the author, 4 October 2012.
8. Frank Fools Crow, quoted in Ed McGaa (Eagle Man), *Mother Earth Spirituality: Native American Paths to Healing Ourselves and Our World* (New York: HarperCollins, 1990).
9. Jamie Sams, *Sacred Path Cards: The Discovery of Self Through Native Teachings* (San Francisco: HarperSanFrancisco, 1990).
10. James "Noodin" Beard, conversation with the author, 6 May 2012.

11. William J. Broad, "The Core of the Earth May Be a Gigantic Crystal Made of Iron," *The New York Times* (4 April 1995), available from: http://www.nytimes.com/1995/04/04/science/the-core-of-the-earth-may-be-a-gigantic-crystal-made-of-iron.html?pagewanted=all&src=pm.

Chapter 11: Altered States of Consciousness

The chapter epigraphs are from Black Elk, quoted in John G. Neihardt, *Black Elk Speaks: Being the Life Story of a Holy Man of the Oglala Sioux* (New York: Washington Square Press, 1972), 43; and William James, *The Varieties of Religious Experience* (New York: Simon & Schuster, 1997).

1. Ralph Metzner, quoted in D. Patrick Miller, "Altered States Revisited," *Yoga Journal* (El Segundo, CA: Cruz Bay Publishing, 1990): 53.
2. Andrew Weil, *The Natural Mind: An Investigation of Drugs and the Higher Consciousness* (New York: Houghton Mifflin Books, 1972).
3. Starhawk, quoted in D. Patrick Miller, "Altered States Revisited," *Yoga Journal* (1990): 52.
4. Thomas Berry, *The Dream of the Earth* (San Francisco: Sierra Club, 1998).
5. Leslie Gray, quoted in D. Patrick Miller, "Altered States Revisited," *Yoga Journal* (1990): 53.
6. D. Patrick Miller, *Yoga Journal* (1990): 97.
7. Mircea Eliade, *Shamanism: Archaic Techniques of Ecstasy*, Bollingen Series LXXVI (Princeton, NJ: Princeton University Press, 1964).

Chapter 12: Play

The chapter epigraph is from Woody Allen, Chapter 4 in *Getting Even* (London: Vintage Books, 1978).

1. Alancay Morales, e-mail communication with the author, June 2010.
2. Jose Carlos Morales, e-mail communication with the author, June 2010.
3. Johan Huizinga, *Homo Ludens: A Study of the Play-Element in Culture* (Boston: Beacon Press, 1955).
4. Gwen Gordon and Sean Esbjörn-Hargens, "Integral Play: An Exploration of the Playground and the Evolution of the Player," *AQAL Journal of Integral Theory and Practice* 2, no. 3 (Fall 2007): 65.
5. Stuart Brown, M.D., *Play: How It Shapes the Brain, Opens the Imagination, and Invigorates the Soul* (New York: Avery, 2009).
6. Gordon, "Integral Play," available from: http://www.gwengordonplay.com/pdf/Gordon_Play_Final.pdf.
7. Brian Swimme, Ph.D., *The Universe Is a Green Dragon: A Cosmic Creation Story* (Rochester, VT: Bear & Company, 1984).
8. Matt. 5: 1–5 (King James Version).
9. Tara Dean, Wild Earth Intensive participant, e-mail communication with the author, September 2009.
10. Mark Collard, *No Props: Great Games with No Equipment* (Beverly, MA: Project Adventure, Inc., 2005).
11. Wild Earth Intensive participant, name withheld by mutual agreement.

Chapter 13: Stillness

The chapter epigraph is from Luther Standing Bear in Howard Zinn, *A People's History of the United States* (New York: HarperCollins Publishers, 2010), 525.

1. Jennifer Welwood, "Unconditional," copyright 1998, reprinted with permission in Bob Stahl and Elisha Goldstein, *A Mindfulness-Based Stress Reduction Workbook* (Oakland, CA: New Harbinger Publications, 2010), 118.

2. Rene Descartes, trans. Donald A. Cress, *Meditations on First Philosophy: In Which the Existence of God and the Distinction of the Soul from the Body Are Demonstrated*, 3rd ed. (Indianapolis: Hackett Publishing Company, Inc., 1993).

3. Wild Earth Intensive participant, name withheld by mutual agreement.

4. Leon Secatero, personal communication with the author, 2003.

5. Eckhart Tolle, *The Power of Now: A Guide to Spiritual Enlightenment* (Novato, CA: New World Library, 2004), 16.

Chapter 14: Elders and Mentors

The chapter epigraph is from Ralph Waldo Emerson, "Emerson on Education," *The Complete Writings of Ralph Waldo Emerson: Containing All of His Inspiring Essays and Miscellaneous Works* (New York: Wm. H. Wise & Co., 1929).

1. Danil Mamyev, personal communication with the author.

2. Miriam Dror, personal communication with the author (5 June 2011), and e-mail follow-up (3 May 2012).

3. Cathy Pedevillano, e-mail communication with the author, April 2011.

4. Nika Fotopulas-Voeikoff, Wild Earth Intensive participant, e-mail communication with the author, May 2012.

5. Michael Iacona, Wild Earth Intensive participant, e-mail communication with the author, May 2012.

6. Jason Cohen, interview with the author, 23 March 2012.

7. Jim Beard, interview with the author, 24 March 2012.

8. Mark Morey, interview with the author, 12 February 2012.

9. Dave Jacke with Eric Toensmeier, *Edible Forest Gardens*, vol. 1, *Ecological Vision and Theory for Temperate Climate Permaculture* (White River Junction, VT: Chelsea Green Publishing, 2005).

10. Erjen Khamaganova, e-mail communication with the author, May 2012.

Chapter 15: The Magic of Mentoring: An Interview with Mark Morey

The chapter epigraph is from Wendell Berry, "Healing," *What Are People For? Essays by Wendell Berry* (New York: Farrar, Straus, and Giroux, 1990).

1. Jake Swamp, paraphrased by Mark Morey in interview with author.
2. Miki Dedijer, e-mail communication with the author.

Chapter 16: Art and Music

The chapter epigraph is from Thomas Berry and Mary Evelyn Tucker, ed., *Evening Thoughts: Reflecting on Earth as Sacred Community* (San Francisco: Sierra Club Books, 2006).

1. Art among the Lascaux cave painters and the Kalahari Bushmen, available from: http://www.antbear.de/bushman-rock-art.htm, http://www.drakensberg-tourism.com/bushman-rock-art.html. See also: http://www.thamesandhudson.com/9780500051696.html.
2. Bradford Keeney, e-mail communication with the author, 1 August 2010.
3. Danil Mamyev, personal communication with the author.
4. Joseph Rael and Mary Elizabeth Marlow, *Being and Vibration* (Tulsa: Council Oak Books, 1993).
5. Ibid.
6. Leon Secatero, personal communication with the author.
7. Martin Prechtel, in Derrick Jensen, "Saving the Indigenous Soul: An Interview with Martin Prechtel," *The Sun Magazine*, April 2001, no. 304, http://www.thesunmagazine.org/archives/742.

8. Ibid.

9. Elizabeth Rose Babin, personal communication with the author.

10. Eastern seaboard American Indian elder, personal communication with the author, name withheld by mutual agreement.

11. Danil Mamyev, personal communication with the author.

12. Terence McKenna, *The Archaic Revival: Speculations on Psychedelic Mushrooms, the Amazon, Virtual Reality, UFOs, Evolution, Shamanism, the Rebirth of the Goddess, and the End of History* (San Francisco: HarperSanFrancisco Publishers, 1991), 242.

13. Mark Morey, an interview with the author.

14. Wild Earth Intensive participant, name withheld by mutual agreement.

15. Zimbabwean proverb, available from: http://www.quotationsbook.com/quote/27685/

16. Wild Earth Intensive participant, name withheld by mutual agreement.

17. Thomas Yellowtail, quoted in Don Coyhis, *Meditations with Native American Elders: The Four Seasons* (Aurora, CO: Coyhis Publishing, 2007).

18. Karen Berggren, "Trance Dance: Healing Through Ecstasy, Rhythm, and Myth," *Circle of Shaman: Healing Through Ecstasy, Rhythm, and Myth* (Rochester, VT: Destiny Books, 1998), 160.

19. Donald Jeffrey Hayes, untitled poem in ed., Elizabeth Roberts and Elias Amidon, *Earth Prayers from Around the World: 365 Prayers, Poems, and Invocations for Honoring the Earth* (New York: HarperCollins, 1991), 155. 20. Nanao Sakaki, untitled poem in Roberts and Amidon, *Earth Prayers*, 133.

21. Jean-Pierre Luminet, "Vibrations of the Cosmic Drumhead," *Innovations Report*, June 1, 2003, available from http://

backend.innovations-report.com/html/reports/physics_
astronomy/report-15549.html.

22. Paul Preuss, Berkeley Labs, June 5, 2001, *Science Beat,*
available from: http://www.lbl.gov/Science-Articles/
Archive/cmb-harmonics.html.

Chapter 17: Vision and Manifestation

The chapter epigraphs are from Mahatma Gandhi, quoted in
David DeFord, *1000 Brilliant Achievement Quotes: Advice from the
World's Wisest* (Omaha, NE: Ordinary People Can Win! 2004),
165; and Paulo Coelho, *The Alchemist*, trans. Alan R. Clarke
(New York: HarperCollins, 2006).

1. Rumi, as quoted in Larry Chang, *Wisdom for the Soul: Five
Millennia of Prescriptions for Spiritual Healing* (Washington,
DC: Gnosophia Publishers, 2006), 26.

2. Amy Leinbach Marquis, "A Mountain Calling," *National
Parks Magazine* (Fall 2007) available from: http://www.
webcitation.org/5yV7qVp6y, (accessed 10/23/2009).

3. Albert Einstein and George Bernard Shaw, *Einstein on
Cosmic Religion: With Other Opinions and Aphorisms* (New
York: Covici-Friede, Inc., 1931), 97.

4. Shakti Gawain, *Creative Visualization: Use the Power of Your
Imagination to Create What You Want in Your Life* (Novato,
CA: New World Library, 2002).

5. Wallace Black Elk, quoted in Don Coyhis, *Meditations with
Native American Elders: The Four Seasons* (Aurora, CO: Coyhis
Publishing, 2007).

6. Lynne McTaggart, *The Field: The Quest for the Secret Force of
the Universe* (New York: HarperCollins, 2008).

7. C.G. Jung and Wolfgang Pauli, *The Interpretation of Nature
and Psyche* (New York: Pantheon Books, 1955).

8. Eckhart Tolle, *A New Earth: Awakening to Your Life's Purpose*
(New York: Penguin, 2008).

9. Albert Einstein, quote is available from several websites, including: http://www.bytesolutions.com/Einstein_Quotes. aspx. For an in-depth discussion of sources for this quote, see: http://en.wikiquote.org/wiki/Talk:Albert_Einstein.
10. Matt. 6:33 (King James Version).
11. Amy L. Lansky, Ph.D., *Active Consciousness: Awakening the Power Within* (Portola Valley, CA: R. L. Ranch Press, 2011).
12 Thomas Merton, *Conjectures of a Guilty Bystander* (New York: Doubleday Religion/Random House, 1966).
13. Eckhart Tolle, *The Power of Now: A Guide to Spiritual Enlightenment* (Novato, CA: New World Library, 1999), 124.
14. Taoist parable, version 2, available from: http://www. noogenesis.com/pineapple/Taoist_Farmer.html.
15. Ps. 23:5 (King James Version).
16. A.J. Muste, quoted in "Debasing Dissent," *The New York Times* (16 November 1967): 46.

Chapter 18: Final Thoughts
The chapter epigraph is from Gary Snyder, "For the Children," *Turtle Island* (New York: New Directions Books, 1974), 86.

1. Richard Heinberg, "Peak Oil: A Chance to Change the World," *Yes! Magazine*, May 14, 2011, available from: http:// www.yesmagazine.org/peak-oil-a-chance-to-change-the-world.

Selected Bibliography

Abram, David. *The Spell of the Sensuous: Perception and Language in a More-Than-Human World*. New York: Vintage Books, 1996.

Bateson, Gregory. *Steps to an Ecology of Mind: Collected Essays in Anthropology, Psychiatry, Evolution, and Epistemology*. New York: Ballantine Books, 1972.

Beck, Don, and Christopher C. Cowan. *Spiral Dynamics: Mastering Values, Leadership and Change*. Malden, MA: Blackwell Publishing, 1996.

Bekoff, Marc, and John A. Byers. *Animal Play: Evolutionary, Comparative and Ecological Perspectives*. Cambridge, UK: Cambridge University Press, 1998.

Berggren, Karen. *Circle of Shaman: Healing Through Ecstasy, Rhythm, and Myth*. Rochester, VT: Destiny Books, 1998.

Berry, Thomas. *The Dream of the Earth*. San Francisco: Sierra Club Books, 1988.

Berry, Thomas. *The Great Work: Our Way into the Future*. NY: Bell Tower, 1999.

Bittman, M.D., Barry, et al. "Composite Effects of Group Drumming, and Neuroendocrine-Immune Parameters," *Alternative Therapies in Health and Medicine 7*, No.1 (January 2001): 38–47.

Brady, Mark, ed. *The Wisdom of Listening*. Somerville, MA: Wisdom Publications, 2003.

Broomfield, John. *Other Ways of Knowing: Recharting Our Future with Ageless Wisdom*. Rochester, VT: Inner Traditions, 1997.

Brown, M.D., Stuart. *Play: How It Shapes the Brain, Opens the Imagination, and Invigorates the Soul*. New York: Avery, 2009.

Cajete, Ph.D., Gregory A. *Igniting the Sparkle: An Indigenous Science Education Model*. Asheville, NC: Kivaki Press, 1999.

Capra, Fritjof. *The Tao of Physics: An Exploration of the Parallels between Modern Physics and Eastern Mysticism.* Boston: Shambhala Publications, 2010.

Chatwin, Bruce. The Songlines. New York: Penguin Books, 1988.

Chopra, M.D., Deepak. *Quantum Healing: Exploring the Frontiers of Mind/Body Medicine.* New York: Bantam, 1990.

Cohen, Ph.D., Michael. Project NatureConnect. Project NatureConnect is an online learning community offering Applied Ecopsychology programs such as Ecotherapy and Integral Ecology. Information is available from: http://www.ecopsych.com.

Collard, Mark. *No Props: Great Games with No Equipment.* Beverly, MA: Project Adventure, Inc., 2005.

Consalvo, Carmine M. *Changing Pace: Outdoor Games for Experiential Learning.* Amherst, MA: HRD, 1996.

Daniels, Jaki. *Heeding the Call: A Personal Journey to the Sacred.* Calgary, Alberta: Hearthlight Publishing, 2007.

Davis, Wade. *One River: Explorations and Discoveries in the Amazon Rain Forest.* New York: Touchstone, 1996.

Devereux, Paul. *Re-Visioning the Earth: A Guide to Opening the Healing Channels Between Mind and Nature.* New York: Fireside, 1996.

Diamond, Jed. *The Warrior's Journey Home: Healing Men, Healing the Planet.* Oakland, CA: New Harbinger Publications, 1994.

Drake, Michael. *The Shamanic Drum: A Guide to Sacred Drumming.* Bend, OR: Talking Drum Publications, 2009.

Eisenstein, Charles. *The Ascent of Humanity: The Age of Separation, The Age of Reunion, and the Convergence of Crises That Is Birthing the Transition.* Harrisburg, PA: Panenthea Press, 2007.

Eisler, Riane. *The Chalice and the Blade: Our History, Our Future.* San Francisco: HarperCollins, 1988. See also: http://www.rianeeisler.com/

Elgin, Duane. *Promise Ahead: A Vision of Hope and Action for Humanity's Future.* New York: HarperCollins, 2001.

Endredy, James. *Ecoshamanism: Sacred Practices of Unity, Power & Earth Healing.* Woodbury, MN: Llewellyn, 2005.

Fisher, Andy. *Radical Ecopsychology: Psychology in the Service of Life.* (SUNY Series on Radical Social and Political Theory) Albany: State University of New York Press, 2002.

Goldberg, Ph.D., Herb. *The Hazards of Being Male: Surviving the Myth of Masculine Privilege.* Ojai, CA: Iconoclassics, 2009.

Goldstein, Joseph, and Jack Kornfield. *Seeking the Heart of Wisdom: The Path of Insight Meditation.* Boston: Shambhala Publications, 2001.

Gordon, Gwen, and Sean Esbjörn-Hargens, "Integral Play: An Exploration of the Playground and the Evolution of the Player," *AQAL Journal of Integral Theory and Practice* 2, no. 3 (Fall 2007): 65.

Hemenway, Toby. *Gaia's Garden: A Guide to Home-Scale Permaculture.* White River Junction, VT: Chelsea Green Publishing, 2001.

Hopkins, Rob. *The Transition Handbook: From Oil Dependency to Local Resilience.* (Transition Guides) White River Junction, VT: Chelsea Green Publishing, 2008.

Ingerman, Sandra. *Medicine for the Earth: How to Transform Personal and Environmental Toxins.* New York: Three Rivers Press, 2001.

Jacke, David, with Eric Toensmeier. *Edible Forest Gardens.* Vol. 1, *Vision and Theory for Temperate Climate Permaculture.* White River Junction, VT: Chelsea Green, 2005.

Jensen, Derrick. *Walking on Water: Reading, Writing, and Revolution.* White River Junction, VT: Chelsea Green Publishing, 2005.

Keeney, Ph.D., Bradford, ed. *Kalahari Bushmen Healers.* Profiles of Healing Series. Stony Creek, CT: Leete's Island Books, 2000.

Keeney, Ph.D., Bradford. *Ropes to God: Experiencing the Bushman Universe.* Profiles of Healing Series. Stony Creek, CT: Leete's Island Books, 2003.

King, Serge Kahili. *Urban Shaman: A Handbook for Personal and Planetary Transformation Based on the Hawaiian Way of the Adventurer*. New York: Fireside, 1990.

Kötke, William H. *Garden Planet: The Present Phase Change of the Human Species*. Bloomington, IN: AuthorHouse, 2005.

Kyle, David. *Human Robots & Holy Mechanics: Reclaiming Our Souls in a Machine World*. Portland: Swan Raven, 1993.

LaChance, Albert. *Greenspirit: Twelve Steps in Ecological Spirituality: An Individual, Cultural and Planetary Therapy*. Rockport, MA: Element Books, 1991.

LaChapelle, Dolores. "Ritual Is Essential," In *Context: A Quarterly of Humane Sustainable Culture* 5 (Spring 1984): 39.

Lanza, M.D., Robert, with Bob Berman. *Biocentrism: How Life and Consciousness Are the Keys to Understanding the True Nature of the Universe*. Dallas: BenBella Books, 2010.

Lawlor, Robert. *Voices of the Dreamtime: Awakening in the Aboriginal Dreamtime*. Rochester, VT: Inner Traditions, 1991.

Lipton, Ph.D., Bruce H., and Steve Bhaerman. *Spontaneous Evolution: Our Positive Future (and a Way to Get There from Here)*. Carlsbad, CA: Hay House, 2009.

Louv, Richard. *Last Child in the Woods: Saving Our Children from Nature-Deficit Disorder*. Chapel Hill, NC: Algonquin, 2008.

Macy, Joanna. *World As Lover, World As Self: Courage for Global Justice and Ecological Renewal*. Berkeley, CA: Parallax Press, 1991.

Macy, Joanna, and Molly Young Brown. *Coming Back to Life: Practices to Reconnect Our Lives, Our World*. Gabriola Island, BC, Canada: New Society Publishers, 1998.

Maitreya, Balangoda Ananda. *The Dhammapada*. Berkeley, CA: Parallax Press, 1995.

Manitonquat (Medicine Story). *Return to Creation*. Spokane, WA: Bear Tribe Publishing, 1991.

Mann, Charles C. *1491: New Revelations of the Americas Before Columbus*. New York: Vintage Books, 2005.

Marty, Martin E. *Reflections on the Nature of God.* Edited by Michael Reagan. Radnor, PA: Templeton Foundation Press, 2004.

Matthiesson, Peter. *The Tree Where Man Was Born.* New York: Penguin, 1995.

McKenna, Terence. *The Archaic Revival: Speculations on Psychedelic Mushrooms, the Amazon, Virtual Reality, UFOs, Evolution, Shamanism, the Rebirth of the Goddess, and the End of History.* San Francisco: HarperSanFrancisco Publishers, 1991.

McTaggart, Lynne. *The Field: The Quest for the Secret Force of the Universe.* New York: HarperCollins, 2008.

Miller, Patrick D. "Altered States Revisited." *Yoga Journal* (1990): 52–53, 96–97.

Montgomery, Pam. *Partner Earth: Restoring Our Sacred Relationship with Nature: A Spiritual Ecology.* Rochester, VT: Destiny, 1997.

Moon, Jennifer A. *A Handbook of Reflective and Experiential Learning: Theory and Practice.* New York: RoutledgeFalmer, 2004.

Neidhardt, John. *Black Elk Speaks: Being the Life Story of a Holy Man of the Oglala Sioux.* Lincoln, NE: University of Nebraska Press, 2000.

Nelson, Melissa K., ed. *Original Instructions: Indigenous Teachings for a Sustainable Future.* Rochester, VT: Bear & Company, 2008.

Orr, David W. *Earth in Mind: On Education, Environment, and the Human Prospect.* Washington, DC: Island Press, 1994.

Perkins, John. *The World Is As You Dream It: Teachings from the Amazon and Andes.* Rochester, VT: Destiny Books, 1994.

Perkins, John, and Shakaim Mariano Shakai Ijisam Chumpi. *Spirit of the Shuar: Wisdom from the Last Unconquered People of the Amazon.* Rochester, VT: Inner Traditions, 2001.

Plotkin, Bill. *Nature and the Human Soul: Cultivating Wholeness and Community in a Fragmented World.* Novato, CA: New World Library, 2007.

Plotkin, Bill. *Soulcraft: Crossing into the Mysteries of Nature and Psyche*. Novato, CA: New World Library, 2003.

Quinn, Daniel. *Beyond Civilization: Humanity's Next Great Adventure*. New York: Broadway books, 2000.

Quinn, Daniel. *Ishmael: An Adventure of the Mind and Spirit*. New York: Bantam Books, 1995.

Rael, Joseph, and Mary Elizabeth Marlow. *Being and Vibration*. Tulsa: Council Oak Books, 1993.

Rezendes, Paul. *The Wild Within: Adventures in Nature and Animal Teachings*. New York: Berkley Books, 1999.

Rilke, Rainer Maria. *Rilke's Book of Hours: Love Poems to God*. Translated by Anita Barrows and Joanna Macy. New York: Riverhead Books, 2005.

Roberts, Elizabeth, and Elias Amidon, ed. *Earth Prayers from around the World: 365 Prayers, Poems, and Invocations for Honoring the Earth*. New York: HarperCollins, 1991.

Rosenberg, Ph.D., Marshall B. *Nonviolent Communication: A Language of Life*. Encinitas, CA: PuddleDancer Press, 2003.

Ruiz, Don Miguel. *The Four Agreements: A Practical Guide to Personal Freedom: A Toltec Wisdom Book*. San Rafael, CA: Amber-Allen Publishing, 1997.

Russell, Peter. *The Global Brain: Speculation on the Evolutionary Leap to Planetary Consciousness*. Los Angeles: J.P. Tarcher, 1983.

Sams, Jamie. *Sacred Path Cards: The Discovery of Self Through Native Teachings*. San Francisco: HarperSanFrancisco, 1990.

Seed, John, Joanna Macy, Pat Fleming, and Arne Naess. *Thinking Like a Mountain: Towards a Council of All Beings*. Gabriola Island, BC, Canada: New Society Publishers, 2007.

Sheldrake, Rupert. *The Rebirth of Nature: The Greening of Science and God*. Rochester, VT: Park Street Press, 1994.

Siegel, M.D., Bernie S. *Love, Medicine & Miracles: Lessons Learned about Self-Healing from a Surgeon's Experience with Exceptional Patients*. New York: HarperCollins, 1998.

Silko, Leslie Marmon. *Ceremony*. New York: Penguin, 1977.

Somé, Malidoma Patrice. *The Healing Wisdom of Africa: Finding Life Purpose Through Nature, Ritual, and Community*. New York: Jeremy P. Tarcher, 1999.

Starhawk. *The Earth Path: Grounding Your Spirit in the Rhythms of Nature*. San Francisco: HarperSanFrancisco, 2004.

Storm, Hyemeyohsts. *Seven Arrows*. New York: Ballantine, 1972.

Suzuki, David, and Peter Knudtson. *Wisdom of the Elders: Sacred Native Stories of Nature*. New York: Bantam, 1993.

Swimme, Ph.D., Brian. *The Universe Is a Green Dragon: A Cosmic Creation Story*. Rochester, VT: Bear & Company, 1984.

Tolle, Eckhart. *A New Earth: Awakening to Your Life's Purpose*. New York: Penguin, 2008.

Tolle, Eckhart. *The Power of Now: A Guide to Spiritual Enlightenment*. Novato, CA: New World Library, 2004.

Tolle, Eckhart. *Stillness Speaks*. Novato, CA: New World Library, 2003.

Trungpa, Chögyam, and Carolyn Rose Gimia. *The Collected Works of Chögyam Trungpa*. 8 vols. Boston: Shambhala, 2004.

Weil, Andrew. *The Natural Mind: A New Way of Looking at Drugs and the Higher Consciousness*. Boston: Houghton Mifflin Company, 1972

Willoya, William, and Vinson Brown. *Warriors of the Rainbow: Strange and Prophetic Dreams of the Indian Peoples*. Happy Camp, CA: Naturegraph Publishers, 1963.

Wolff, Robert. *Original Wisdom: Stories of an Ancient Way of Knowing*. Rochester, VT: Bear & Company, 2001.

Young, Jon, Ellen Haas, and Evan McGown. *Coyote's Guide to Connecting with Nature*. 2nd ed. Owlink Media, 2010. Ordering information available from: http://www.owlinkmedia.com.

Ywahoo, Dhyani. *Voices of Our Ancestors: Cherokee Teachings from the Wisdom Fire*. Boston: Shambhala, 1987.

MOON BOOKS
PAGANISM & SHAMANISM

What is Paganism? A religion, a spirituality, an alternative belief system, nature worship? You can find support for all these definitions (and many more) in dictionaries, encyclopedias, and text books of religion, but subscribe to any one and the truth will evade you. Above all Paganism is a creative pursuit, an encounter with reality, an exploration of meaning and an expression of the soul. Druids, Heathens, Wiccans and others, all contribute their insights and literary riches to the Pagan tradition. Moon Books invites you to begin or to deepen your own encounter, right here, right now.

If you have enjoyed this book, why not tell other readers by posting a review on your preferred book site.

Readers of ebooks can buy or view any of these bestsellers by clicking on the live link in the title. Most titles are published in paperback and as an ebook. Paperbacks are available in traditional bookshops. Both print and ebook formats are available online.

Find more titles and sign up to our readers' newsletter
www.collectiveinkbooks.com/paganism

For video content, author interviews and more, please subscribe to our YouTube channel.

MoonBooksPublishing

Follow us on social media for book news, promotions and more:

Facebook: Moon Books

Instagram: @MoonBooksCI

X: @MoonBooksCI

TikTok: @MoonBooksCI